D1131091

SOUTHERN HOMEFRONT
1861-1865

Other books by John Hammond Moore

Before and After, or The Relations of the Races at the South

Research Materials in South Carolina: A Guide

The Juhl Letters to the *Charleston Courier*: A View of the South,   1865-1871

The American Alliance: Australia, New Zealand, and the United States, 1940-1970

Australians in America, 1876-1976

The Young Errol: Flynn Before Hollywood

Albemarle: Jefferson's County, 1727-1976

The Faustball Tunnel: German POWs in America and Their Great Escape

Over-Sexed, Over-Paid, and Over Here: Americans in Australia,
1941-1945

Wiley: One Hundred and Seventy-Five Years of Publishing

The South Carolina Highway Department, 1917-1987

South Carolina Newspapers

South Carolina in the 1880s: A Gazetteer

Columbia & Richland County, 1740-1990

A Plantation Mistress on the Eve of the Civil War: The Diary of Keziah Goodwyn
Hopkins Brevard, 1860-1861

The Confederate Housewife: Receipts & Remedies, Together with Sundry Suggestions for Garden, Farm & Plantation

The Baileys of Clinton: A South Carolina Family, 1860-1996

SOUTHERN HOMEFRONT
1861-1865

John Hammond Moore

Summerhouse Press
Columbia, South Carolina

Published in Columbia, South Carolina
by Summerhouse Press

Copyright © 1998 by John Hammond Moore

All rights reserved. No part of this publication may be reproduced in any manner
whatsoever, excepting brief excerpts in reviews or promotional materials, without the
written permission of
Summerhouse Press
P.O. Box 1492
Columbia, SC 29205
(803) 779-0870
(803) 779-9336 fax

Library of Congress Cataloging Information

Moore, John Hammond.
    Southern homefront, 1861-1865 / John Hammond Moore.
       p.   cm.
    Includes bibliographical references (p.   ) and index.
    ISBN 1-887714-30-8 (alk. paper)
    1. South Carolina--History--Civil War. 1861-1865. 2. Confederate
Status of America--History. 3. United States--History--Civil War.
1861-1865--Social aspects. I. Title.
E577.M66 1998
973.7'09756--dc21   98-31487
                                 CIP

E
577
.M66
1993

Dedication

To Allen H. Stokes, Jr.,
and the staff
of the South Caroliniana Library.

Their daily labor makes possible an ever-increasing
appreciation of South Carolina's rich past.

KELLY LIBRARY
EMORY & HENRY COLLEGE
EMORY, VA 24327

CHARLESTON

MERCURY

EXTRA:

Passed unanimously at 1.15 o'clock, P. M. December 20th, 1860.

AN ORDINANCE

To dissolve the Union between the State of South Carolina and other States united with her under the compact entitled " The Constitution of the United States of America."

We, the People of the State of South Carolina, in Convention assembled, do declare and ordain, and it is hereby declared and ordained,

That the Ordinance adopted by us in Convention, on the twenty-third day of May, in the year of our Lord one thousand seven hundred and eighty-eight, whereby the Constitution of the United States of America was ratified, and also, all Acts and parts of Acts of the General Assembly of this State, ratifying amendments of the said Constitution, are hereby repealed; and that the union now subsisting between South Carolina and other States, under the name of " The United States of America," is hereby dissolved.

THE

UNION

IS

DISSOLVED!

CONTENTS

TABLES

MAPS

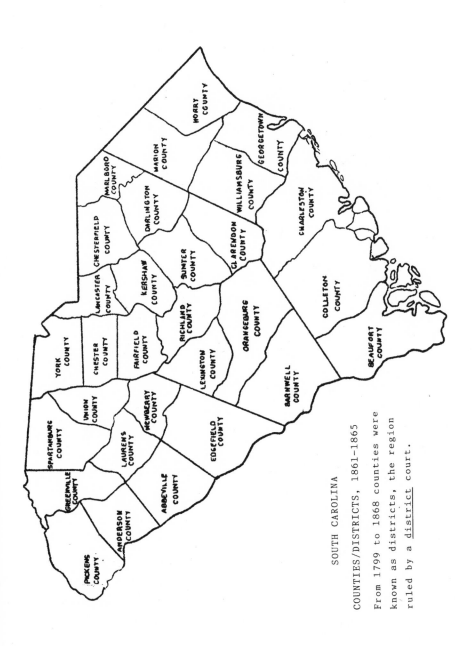

SOUTH CAROLINA

COUNTIES/DISTRICTS, 1861–1865

From 1799 to 1868 counties were
known as districts, the region
ruled by a <u>district court</u>.

INTRODUCTION

The Civil War from the southern perspective is somewhat like a football game in which the offense of the home team sputters throughout the first half while those playing defense perform brilliantly (albeit in their own territory). In the second half, however, after Gettysburg and Vicksburg, the visitors take command and gradually wear down both squads. As a result, spirit wanes, passes are dropped, opportunities missed, fumbles occur, and disillusioned fans begin to drift out of the stadium. But anyone who watches only the men on the field and meticulously diagrams each move they make (as many Civil War buffs and some historians do) misses much of the drama of a truly big contest. What about those long practice sessions, the bonfire and pep rally the night before, behind-the-scenes organization (bands, cheer leaders, pompom girls, concessionaires, etc.), massive traffic jams to be negotiated, crowd reaction during the game itself, all the half-time hoopla, and the Saturday night parties that follow?

There is much more to any big game than just sixty minutes of football, and the same is true of war. Marching, campaigning, and maneuvering for advantage are only part of the story. Nor does victory always fulfill promises made or achieve goals proclaimed under stress such as to make the world "safe" for democracy. We Americans of all people should know that the societal effects of war are difficult to predict—far more so than those of a gridiron classic—and they clearly outweigh in importance any battlefield heroics. Just in the last half century or so, World War II gave us desegregation, substantial internal migration, and a GI Bill that moved millions up the economic ladder. Vietnam produced disarray at home, fostered a drug culture, and sent wave after wave of Asian immigrants to our shores.

As expected, the Civil War freed the slaves, although treatment meted out by their liberators then and in succeeding decades is both troubling and puzzling. Was the struggle as altruistic as our textbooks tell us or perhaps, like most wars, basically just another economic slugfest? In any case, emancipation gave birth to a bitter Reconstruction era during which white Southerners had to have, above all else, unity. Internal divisions of 1861-1865 soon were forgotten, and those who profiteered, shirked their duty, hired substitutes, or even became "Tories" were forgiven...at least, their sins were obscured or muted in the face of greater peril. Regardless of actual war records, all who ever donned a uniform of gray or butternut served brilliantly, fought bravely to the end, and surrendered with "Marse Robert" at Appomattox Courthouse.

And this warm cloak of forgiveness envelopes the Confederate homefront of literature and myth in much the same manner, although a gentle conspiracy to mold the past into a more pleasant image is by no means a unique wrinkle in American history. Under the circumstances the impulse to do so is quite understandable and thus constitutes one of the most important results of the Civil War itself. However, this process of revision has expanded over the decades—abetted by non-Southerners self-conscious about the brutal conflict and racial turmoil in its wake—so as to distort *what* happened and *why* it happened. Rebellion becomes a grand crusade backed with universal enthusiasm by all Southerners, white and black, from the Potomac to the Rio Grande; the cause of this disruption in our national life is portrayed as defense of personal liberty and the rights of individual states, not human bondage or a clash of economic systems; and the Confederacy, stripped of its true raiment, takes on a benign, heroic quality.

We know in our heart of hearts such tales cannot be entirely true: this is not the way people act in real life situations. That is one reason this book opens with words recorded during the conflict itself, not after-the-fact reminiscences that have been cleaned up and rendered politically correct in a postwar setting. Admittedly, the path from ecstasy and bravado to disillusionment and defeat is tortuous, disturbing, and at times even unpleasant. Yet the words of the Elliotts, Straits, Tuckers, Middletons, and scores of other South Carolinians tell us much about four eventful years in the life of this state and our nation...in fact, *both* nations.

The pages that follow, after a cursory look at the war itself, are filled with people of the 1860s—white, black, slave, free, young, old, male, female, rabid rebel, Unionist, and uncommitted—as they dealt with what were probably the most tempestuous times they would ever know. Personal experience, community pressure, age, sex, color, even geography (upcountry, lowcountry, midlands) dictated how each individual reacted. Homefront shortages of various kinds led to bizarre innovation, rampant speculation, and unattractive displays of selfishness. Blacks often appropriated goods abandoned by their masters, only to lose those possessions to "backwoods" folk who pillaged their meager dwellings as the Confederacy began to unravel. Even those in gray were known to rob and plunder, especially if serving in communities to which they had no personal ties.

On the other hand, thousands of South Carolinians, many of them womenfolk, sacrificed much and worked long hours for "the cause," at least during the first two years. However, after July 1863, material shortages and battlefield news tended to circumscribe these efforts. The war opened new doors for a few women who became teachers, nurses, clerks, and relief workers, but those same doors were slammed shut after 1865. Even during the war years, women who initiated various programs to help servicemen and their families often found themselves nudged aside by men thought more experienced in management techniques.

The slave, the individual most frequently encountered on the South Carolina homefront, clearly enjoyed a unique status. His owner was fighting to keep him and his family in bondage, the invader, to set him free. War could not help but loosen those bonds. With masters away, slaves being moved from place to place (either to work on fortifications or keep them out of Yankee hands), and enemy lines often enticingly close, discipline suffered. Also, blacks with produce to sell in a time of shortage possessed special leverage. And, late in 1864 when Richmond began to talk of giving them guns and converting them into soldiers, white South Carolinians were understandably confused. What, after all, were they fighting for?

As one would expect, these various homefront pressures led to erratic mood swings in Confederate households (joy one moment, despair the next), keeping in mind that white South Carolinians bore a special burden throughout this struggle. Having ignited the whole affair by seceding in December 1860, they had to assume substantial responsibility for whatever ensued. Yet those riding this morale roller coaster could relax at times and have fun. Charleston enjoyed an especially gay winter season (1862-1863), and, even as Sherman approached Columbia early in 1865, the state capital, crammed with refugees, was enveloped in a similar orgy of merriment.

There are those, of course, who merely cast a pale shadow on the homefront and about whom we know all too little. These include speculators, upcountry "Tories" who defied conscription and anyone who tried to put them in uniform, prisoners of war, and Northerners who came through the lines to visit relatives. The role of refugees—thanks to letters, diaries, and the work of Mary Elizabeth Massey—is more clearly defined. Nevertheless, battlefield or homefront, America's Civil War will always fascinate millions for very obvious reasons. It touched in some fashion every household of the 1860s, North and South, and contains sufficient drama and unanswered questions to intrigue even those whose ancestors had nothing whatsoever to do with the struggle.

For dedicated Southerners, one query surfaces over and over—"What if...?" Usually it refers to what a general did or did not do at some big engagement where, from their point of view, things could have turned out differently. But one might also ask, *what if* South Carolinians had organized their homefront more effectively? Or, even before a homefront evolved, *what if* they had analyzed their situation with a more critical eye in the fall of 1860? Ann Morris Vanderhorst did just that on 1 July 1865, five years too late.[1]

Unless one launches into the realm of speculation, there are no satisfactory answers to "what if" questions, and even those that emerge are of a hypothetical nature. What follows is not an attempt to pose or answer such queries about life in South Carolina, 1861-1865. Instead, this is, if you will, an exercise in a primitive sort of "oral history"— *insofar as possible using words written or recorded by South Carolinians during those four years to shed light upon what was transpiring on the Palmetto State homefront.*

In the process, a basic theme or thesis of sorts emerges, namely that raw emotion swept thousands of South Carolinians into a military confrontation for which they were woefully unprepared. This tragic miscalculation, in turn, reverberated with disastrous effect throughout the homefront. To add to the turmoil, citizens of the Palmetto State harbored mental quirks destined to cause still more chaos and confusion. They talked much of *defending* the soil of their native state (not that of a new nation) and seldom gave voice to schemes designed to carry the war to the enemy; yet, in time, they were openly critical of Richmond's "defensive" policy. In addition, both soldier and civilian apparently expected front rank in secession to automatically confer key Confederate posts upon their leaders. When this did not happen, they became distressed, resentful, and even bitter.

Unlike the battlefield, lines of allegiance and concern on the homefront often are not clear-cut. Any such community is beset by many pressures, both apparent and subtle, and those living there must tread carefully, all of which complicate daily life greatly. This is especially so during rebellion. Who amongst us, despite what they say, are not truly committed to the "cause"? Why are certain individuals asked to contribute more, sacrifice more? Why are some people hoarding supplies that should go to our men in uniform? All of these questions (and many more) were asked in South Carolina during the Civil War, which only adds to the complexity and fascination of the home scene, a turbulent world that became still more complex as defeat loomed during the final months of that struggle.

[1]See p 42-43. Ann Morris Vanderhorst (1794-1879) was the daughter of Lewis Morris, Jr., of Morrisana, New York, who served on General Nathanael Greene's staff during the Revolution and then settled in South Carolina. Her planter husband, Elias Vanderhorst (1791-1874), owned over 260 slaves in 1860, his major plantations being "Kiawah Island" and "Chickasee Island" on the Ashepoo River. Their Charleston home was located on the northwest corner of Chapel and Alexander streets.

I

A CACOPHONY OF VOICES

These pages contain, in chronological sequence, thoughts and random comments expressed by thirty-seven South Carolinians during wartime and, as such, provide an overview of the ongoing struggle and its impact upon their daily lives. Of those who speak to us from the 1860s, thirteen are women, including the slave Eliza. Of the twenty-four males, one—Francis Pickens—served as governor, a dozen shouldered arms at some juncture, and two of their number died as a result of battle wounds or disease. Half of these thirty-seven individuals, representing various segments of the population, were at least twenty-five years old in 1860—the eldest being Ann Morris Vanderhorst; the youngest, teenage students such as Claudius Fike, Anna Donaldson, and "Babe." Most, admittedly, were relatively well-to-do and well educated, for these are the folks whose letters, diaries, and journals find their way into archival holdings. Of utmost importance is the fact that whatever they say was recorded *at the time*, not years or decades later. Thus these are neither reminiscences nor romantic hindsight but on-the-spot observations reflecting hope, pride, ecstasy, gloom, and despair...whatever came to mind as each one pondered the present and wondered what the future might hold.

※

I have not the slightest doubt but that it will be peaceable as far as the revolution is concerned, for no one can point out to me where the war is to come from. The North certainly will not trouble us, and Uncle Sam *can't*, unless we may be placed in a hostile position to him by some violent and unwise act on the part of some of Carolina's Sons who are anxious to enroll their names on the pages of history. This is all that can, in my humble opinion, bring about a war, and if the matter is only managed properly no one could tell, unless he saw it in the Papers, that we were in the midst of a revolution. At any rate we are getting ready for it and very properly. The State is now pledged to go out of the Union, and

William Elliott (1838-1907)   *Isabella Elliott Barnwell (1841-1867)*

every member of the Legislature who voted to call the convention is just as much pledged to Secession as if he had voted directly for it. Charleston to all appearances is a unit, but I am afraid there may be a reaction; for the hot and hasty men always speak first—the old fogies generally wait until things get quiet.

> William Elliott (1838-1907) to his fiancée, Isabella Elliott Barnwell (1841-1867), of Beaufort, 16 November 1860.[1]

We send you up three cheers for Sumter and our Independent and sovereign State. We greet you as brethren embarked in the same glorious cause, the assertion of Carolina's independence.

Clarendon has over two hundred and forty men who are determined to achieve Carolina's Independence or fall in arms. Tell the young men of Sumter to *'stand to the fire and fall like men.'* Our regiment musters on Saturday when a host of other volunteers will come forward. I know what I assert when I say there will be a draft to keep men enough at home. We have had but few cockades among us until the news that an act of aggression had been committed in our harbor but now they are every where.[2] I have witnessed some scenes in the last few days that deeply touched my feelings. One mother in [the] village has given her only son—and she a widow—to go forth to battle for his country. Four fathers came to me yesterday, and entrusted their sons to my care bidding me to teach them to stand like men to the Palmetto. Our women are worthy of the 'best' days of Rome or of Sparta, they give their best and dearest treasures ungrudgingly to the State. Personal animosities and resentments are laid aside—every man is his neighbour's friend and brother. A better feeling never prevailed....

We send you a hearty God speed and hope to stand near our brethren of Sumter in the smoke of battle.

> John W. Ervin (1823-1902) of Manning to John Smythe Richardson, 3 January 1861.[3]

The war prospect seems to be growing beautifully less, and instead of Tents, drums, and muskets, ploughs 'decree by default' and *Pills* will be the order of the day. So mote it be.... For my part I am ready to bury the Tomyhawk, and 'put clods on its head!'

> Gilbert Lafayette Strait (1834-1863) of Lewisville to Colonel James H. Rion (1820-1886) of Winnsboro, 2 March 1861.[4]

I feel now like I could be more reconciled to camp life, since I've seen you & talked it all over—& I think you are much better satisfied—you can bear our separation better—But if I can get off by any fair or honorable means, I'm going to do it.

> Francis Marion Tucker (1828-1862) from Camp Ruffin near Columbia to his wife in Spartanburg District, 9 May 1861.[5]

...it is the hardest times ever you saw to get things [.] I dont think there is a yd of flannel in Joe Wylies store [.] the store is pretty much empty [.] I believe they are not going to lay any thing more in, people is trying to learn to do without coffee. there is no tea to be got [.] some are using confederate tea ie Sassafras [.] I expect there will be slim eating of meat next year [.] there is going to be hard times [.] get nothing for whats made, be enormously taxed and what is going to become of the honest and honorable, be trampled under foot by the speculators and Villians that is roving among us taking all advantages they can, and looking to the time when poeples property will be sold thinking they will make a fortune [.] God curse such pests. if I had no ties to bind me here I would be with you in a few hours [.] if I could get there no other way I would cut off my hair and put on [a] uniform and make a tolerable tib McFarlin but its no use to talk.

> Isabella Wylie Strait (1819-1881) of Lewisville to her son, Captain Gilbert L. Strait, in Virginia, 29 September 1861.[6]

.⁂.

I suppose you are aware of the success of the federals at port Royal, the result of bombast & selfsufficiency, Rhettism & 'Peaceable Secession'—why did they not have it properly fortified? They certainly had sufficient time—our soldiers run like Hell, Gill Dunovant's Rigement lost all of their tents and clothes of every Kind—I cannot see what they were doing in the position they occupied.... The veritable Julius Mills is trying to organize a company thinking to get an *office* of course— Our District is well nigh drained of men— We are awfully beset about money, it cannot be had. The cloth for the uniforms for your company has been lying in the Depot at Chester for weeks, but we cannot raise the money to pay for the cloth, and they will not let it go without the money—our country is in a deplorable condition [.] the evident tendency both South & North is to military despotism. I fear your grandfathers predictions are all about to be verifyed [.]

> William Wylie (1819-1868) of Lewisville to Gilbert L. Strait in Petersburg, Virginia, 24 November 1861.[7]

.⁂.

I feel sad for my country. I fondly thought a few months ago we were safe, & could form a free & a happy govt. But my heart sickens now at the many signs I see in passing events. We have been a selfish & idolatrous people—vain, & without any large & settled faith, & I feel that the hand of God must be upon such a people. It never was intended by a just God that such vanities & intense selfishness as we have exhibited shall go without punishment. Those who pride themselves because they are rich & because they are not as other people, are sure to fall & suffer, and if a people exhibit these same disgusting vices, why shall they not suffer too? ... It is the arm of God alone that raises up, & puts down a nation— This is a great truth I have ever believed— And I have but little faith now save in this Providence.

> Governor Francis W. Pickens (1805-1869) writing from Edgewood in Edgefield District to his wife Lucy, 24 January 1862.[8]

If Holmes can only manage to make some thing to live on, I will not care for much else. To this end he should put plenty of land in corn, take care of the *Hogs* & raise sweet potatoes in abundance, making cotton a secondary object. I think it would be well for the whole country to stop the production of that staple until England shows more disposition to help us. The Yankees for the present seem to be getting the upper hand, but I hope this is not to last, & if it should have the good effect of impressing upon our people the need of more action and less talking it may prove of benefit to us in the end.

Do not allow the bad news from the west, to distress you more than you can help. We are far from being conquered, even after the capture of every city—or coast or river. Our cause is right & just & must succeed in the end although Providence is now frowning on us for our ingratitude for past mercies.

> John William McLure (1829-1921) writing on 23 February 1862 from Centreville, Virginia, to his wife Jane in Union District.[9]

This was more generally observed (as a day of fasting &c) than last Friday. At the Baptist church, the congregation was about as large as it usually is on Sunday. Mr. [J. L.] Reynolds preached from the same text as on last Friday— He had been requested to repeat the sermon, delivered a week ago, but he could not do this. He recapitulated briefly, and then enlarged on points not mentioned before. An admirable discourse it was. While he was preaching, I wished for the whole Confederacy to hear him. He alluded to the Providences of God as manifested in the recent disasters sustained by our arms.... Perhaps our reverses were designed to humble us &c.— Several evils had increased among us— A tendency to blend church and state had been evinced— it was the source of untold evils—they (C & S) should be separate. Profanity & drunkenness had increased. The speaker rejoiced that measures had been taken to shut down the stills and thus quench the liquid fire.— We had the responsibility of taking care of a peculiar institution—we had not discharged our duty with fidelity—servants should not be sent off to worship by themselves, but should meet at the same time and place as their masters. Notwithstanding the Divine's unqualified reception of the Bible doctrine of the utter depravity of the human breast there were some phases of crime at which he stood aghast. He then alluded to the fall of Fort Donelson in the most pathetic manner—the families of the brave men that fought there deserved sympathy & aid but instead thereof, speculators and extortioners raised the prices of the common necessaries of life, as soon as the wires brought the news that the fort had fallen. If these were specimens of the people of the C[onfederate] S[tates] he should hang his head in despair, and resign himself to any judgment God might send upon us. But he rejoiced that they were not—they were only here and there, colossal statues of human guilt that the law could not reach. Perhaps no law could be made to meet so heinous crime.— It was the duty of all good men to arraign them before the tribunal of public opinion. In conclusion, he exhorted to a more firm reliance on the Providence of God and to a more consistent walk, on the part of all.— Such is an imperfect outline of one of the best discourses it has ever been my fortune to hear.

John B. Patrick Diary, 28 February 1862.[10]

You spoke of the licking that Beauregard give the yankees at Corinth[.] if the paper tells the truth he has lick them [.] the yankees loss was between twenty five and thirty thousand and the papers also say that old Buel is kill [.] I hope it is so but I wish they had killed every one of them [.] if they can whip them at Yorktown I hope they [sic] blamed rascals will be willing to give it up.

I tell you the 19 Regt has acted smart [.] they were ordered to Corinth and they come up to Augusta and nearly all of them run away and come home, all of them but about 300 [.] they went on, and about the time they got home they got orders to go back again [.] if they did

not go with out making they were goin to make them go [.] Old
Quattlebaum Company was in the mess [.]

> Thomas Aiton's sister (Fran) writing from Phoenix to her
> brother in Virginia, 16 April 1862.[11]

What desolation Alas! Proverty seems closing fast upon us [,] the
structure of an ancient family gradually tumbling down & there is nothing to stay the impending injury. 25 of our negroes gone to the yankees
& the rest perhaps waiting their opportunity— The land to be left to
weeds & destruction.... They are fighting this Sunday desperately in
Richmond. Oh! My God— Save my poor child—

I cannot see thru the vista of time one Solitary ray of hope [—] all
is Dark Dark— now 32 of our negroes have left us at Ashepoo [—] the
strongest the best [—] there will be none left to work the land & we must
endure poverty such as we have never known, my poor sons [,] gentle-
manly honorable brought up in the lap of luxury [—] what is to become
of you [?] you have no professions, I think I see your countenances
shaded with sorrow   [—] misfortune does not come on us gradually—it
envelopes us in its folds & seems to crush us down with a heavy ———
[.] my poor patient John & what is to become of you [?] crippled [,]
shattered in constitution [,] dependent upon your father for support—it
may please God to take us all away at once, for perhaps I shall never
smile again— As I rock in the carriage I made up my mind it might be
my last ride— How the heavy Booming Cannon of the yankees is threatening destruction to our fair City & God of Battle & justice look with
pity upon us & save & Defend us from our Enemies—

> Diary of Ann Morris Vanderhorst, 30 May and 1 June
> 1862.[12]

I am of the opinion that there are some very indolent men in high
positions in our army and government. Otherwise, they would be more
active in removing army stores and munitions of war that are in danger
of falling into the hands of the enemy.

> John B. Patrick Diary, 31 May 1862.

The news of the rout of the yankee army in Virginia I presume you have heard.... It is certainly a great victory and blessing, and I hope it is as complete as it is reported to be.— The recognition of our nation is also spoken of. I suppose the victory will have a considerable effect in that quarter. I begin to think that England and France are just going to let us alone, and let us fight it out our own way.— On the reception of the news last Thursday night about 9 o'clk. a salute of 13 guns was fired at this place.

> Claudius L. Fike (1845-1894), a student at Arsenal Academy in Columbia, to his father in Spartanburg, 6 July 1862.[13]

⁂

The telegraph announces officially another great victory at *Manassas*...the enemy were totally defeated & flying to Washington— no particulars given. I have never before felt such a dread of seeing the list of killed and wounded. All that I have heard today contributed to depress me. Mary Boykin came to see us, just from Columbia and says Beauregard's nephew Proctor, who is about nineteen has left the Arsenal.... The Arsenal cadets have been very rebellious breaking all kinds of rules—some have been expelled, & others left and joined the Cadet Rangers to which James [Beauregard] belongs. Then Sallie [Bull] and Lilly [DeSaussure] are going on outrageously—encouraging those cadets who jumped out the window to go to the theatre with them, & one night while there, the boys received a note saying they were discovered & expelled, and had to leave the girls, & go to the Arsenal—the latter would have been in a considerable dilemma, but for James. Then they have taken to *rouging* & Sallie wont submit even to her grandfather's control. I had hoped so much from his firm, but gentle authority, & cousin E[liza DeSaussure] says since Sallie came she cannot manage Lilly—it makes me too sad to see such young girls going to ruin, & Sallie has the elements of such a fine character, but her father's over indulgence has already caused many a heart ache to her friends.

Emma Holmes Diary, 2 September 1862.[14]

⁂

Attended a meeting of the citizens of Columbia this evening, called for the purpose of devising measures to supply the destitution of our army in clothing. From the accounts that have reached us, our army is indeed in a deplorable state of destitution. After some discussion, a committee of thirteen was appointed to devise a plan by which the evil may be remedied and report at a called meeting.

John B. Patrick Diary, 8 October 1862.

Politics has become lean, hungry, and gloomy, and that member of her family—Peasible Secession is in its last gasp— There is almost no men in the district since the reserves have been called into service— The Country presents a dark picture[.] I am doubtful there may be as much danger at home as in the army. I have reference to *'insurrection'*— Our prospects are gloomy in the extreme. There is no prospect of a termination of the damned war. I can see nothing favorable [;] our only chance is to fight, die and be damned—

Our country is suffering from the necessaries of life [.] Salt cannot be had [;] it is all in the hands of speculators, they ask $300.00 for a sack of salt and many other things in proportion, leather $5— per lb. &c, &c.

It is reasonable to suppose our damned old Governor and counselers favor swindling and speculation [.] I dont doubt but they are secretly engaged in it or he would have put a stop to it long ago—

William Wylie of Lewisville to Gilbert L. Strait in Virginia, 23 November 1862.[15]

I have often been walking in Main St. when I've seen our women arrayed in rich & costly dress which swept the pavement, and with showy men of gold lace & brass buttons dashing up & down in their chariots and splendid equipage, when I have tho't if a stranger who did not know our state were to look in on us, he'd never believe we were in a state of war and under the rod. The theatre under another name has been open a good deal thro the summer—drunkenness prevails to a fearful degree and profanity and vulgarity is still common—such being the state of things I am afraid to indulge the hope of a speedy termination of this terrible war.

> John N. Fripp writing from Columbia to Stephen Elliott, Jr., in Charleston, 14 January 1863.[16]

Rumors are rife of an attack on Charleston very soon. They say on the streets that it will take place in 48 hours if the weather is favorable.... I believe that if they make a persistent attack that Charleston will be taken.... I hope that I am taking a gloomy view of matters but I don't know. People here are perfectly apathetic—the citizens I mean. I would not like the troops to be animated by my spirit but it is the sort of spirit for a commander to have because it leads him to leave nothing untried. All of this about Charleston is confidential as I don't want to be considered a croaker.

> Stephen Elliott, Jr. (1830-1866), from Charleston to his wife in Camden, 3 February 1863.[17]

I see by your letter to Osgood that you expect to spend the *month* of may there [Spartanburg], do you think that you will reduce your father to poverty by such an extended stay— I understand he has not been able to afford to buy butter for three months...and yet he told me that in less than a month he more than paid for the house that his family are living in by speculating in the *necessaries* of life (flour &c) and expected to make much more the coming month....[18] I would propose to you that you offer to pay board for the time that you are there, but I am afraid it would cause a row....

And now *my own dear Wife* before closing there is one thing more I have to say about your projected visit. It has come to my Knowledge... that the whole of your fathers family from himself down is completely possessed with the speculating mania and even Dora has become contaminated. Let me beg of you for the sake of humanity, and your own peace of mind afterwards, do not in any way engage in this *terrible vice*. I believe the curse of God will rest upon all who do it—think of the hundreds, aye thousands of starving wretches, brought to this misery,

Joy on the Battery. Frank Leslie's Illustrated Weekly, 27 April 1861.

by the speculating extorsioner in flour, corn, &c, &c who silences his conscience with the remark, 'that if he did not do it, somebody else would, and make money'—because others do wrong to make money, and worship mammon, it is no reason why we should—rather my dear Beckie act your own part, assist the poor to live, than assist in grinding them to starvation,— I have no fear for you, I believe that you think with me that the money made in that way (be it much or little) will be a dreadful curse to the maker—

> Theodore Honour (1831-1913) on duty in Charleston to
> his wife in Newberry, 6 April 1863.[19]

Two years ago today at about this hour in the morning, our City was thrown into a joyous state of excitement by the report that 'Fort Sumter is in flames,' and then there was a hurrying down to the wharves to witness as we all supposed the demolition of the Fort, but the hour for surrender had not yet come, and the now hated but glorious Star Spangled Banner floated in proud defiance from the battlement.

You will remember the subsequent events of the day, and the beaming countenances of every one at the first victory of the Stars and bars over the Stars & stripes, who among the vast crowd that thronged every avenue of our beautiful City would have prophecied the vast amount of misery and anguish that would have resulted from that days work— The desolate hearthstone, the widowed, and the orphaned, the bereaved of every class, the flying from once happy homes, ah my dear wife truly the price of liberty is indeed a heavy one. God grant that the sufferings that our beloved country has passed through in the past two years may be a sufficient sacrifice, and that soon the Angel of Peace may spread her broad wing over our land, and the clarion notes of war may be sounded no more, and we all be permitted to return to our homes and there enjoy all the blessings that peace brings it.

> Theodore Honour from Charleston to his wife in Newberry, 10 April 1863.[20]

I have succeeded in getting some 25 Conscripts—part of which number have already been forwarded to Col [John S.] Preston. The people here are behaving disgracefully—their want of patriotism is amazing. The act of Congress to 'further provide for the public defence' defeats itself by having attached an Exemption Act which exempts all classes of mechanics actually engaged as traders & every owner or overseer of 15 hands. The mechanics have in some instance I think sworn to falsehoods and the owners and overseers—a stout athletic class—have in every instance availed themselves of the possession of a few negroes to keep out of the service. They are a mean Yankee population & I intend the coming week to take away the exemptions of some of them. This is also a great country for dodgers and deserters—and I expect to be engaged as soon as the office records are finished in having them arrested.

> William Elliott, Jr., writing to his mother from Greenville, 12 April 1863.[21]

I wish you could see our fair city now; it is, I know the prittiest place in the world— The trees and flowers seem to bloom in peculiar luxuriance— The General Assembly of the Presbyterian church is to meet here next Thursday— It will be pleasant—these hard times make some difference in the provision line—but 'man was not made to live by bread alone.' We girls have been quite busy lately arranging our wardrobe for the summer, turning things up side down and inside out, making new things out of old— Tell Mary Palmer the only vail I have taken is an old brown one, just as good as new but for the worse of wear— How are you making out for your summer attire?

"Babe" from Columbia to school friend Harriett Palmer in St. Stephen's Parish, 2 May 1863.[22]

You speak of hard times and troublesome times. Just permit me to say that you do not know anything about trouble. Suppose you had to lie night after night and day after day in dread of your life every moment, and perhaps the cannon firing at every point—and you knew not what minute a shell would land you into eternity, while you were so near to marching to death that you could not sit down a moment without going to sleep. Do you call this hard and troublesome times? Do not talk about troubles and hard times while God and your country permits you to stay at home with your family and friends.

David Ballenger (1830-1909) writing from Virginia to his brother, 13 May 1863.[23]

Hire me a substitute [,] make the fellow in jail 50. Col [James L.] Orr thinks the old man C——— will not be received in my place. Arrange it so as to pay when received.... I learned last night at Anderson that the conscript age was raised to 45.... Now Jim help me...go to work before some one gets ahead of me.

S. E. Maxwell of Walhalla to James Hagood (1826-1904), clerk of Pickens District Court, 25 June 1863.[24]

I am afraid we have not men fit for such trying times. For altho Lee is Deified by some people I confess I must want perception in not being able to discover what benefit has accrued to us by his invasion of Pennsylvania at this *late period*. A sacrifice of many brave & valuable lives has been the result [,] but little gained. He did not even burn any towns by making them to feel in some degree what they have inflicted upon us. But it seems to me 'he marched up the hill & then marched down again' & after losing many of our bravest men has to recross the Potomac [,] I supposed to defend Richmond which place our enemies are again threatening to assail. And I am afraid he has betrayed our weakness to our enemies thus convincing them that he could not hold his position but was compelled to retreat & thereby assuring them there will be no necessity for them to enforce the conscription. Which was causing riots in New York....

> Mrs. Robert Smith, writing from Columbia to her daughter-in-law, Mrs. William Mason Smith, in Greenville, 18 July 1863.[25]

You spoke of a good many men deserting from South Carolina and coming home. There has been more deserters from this Army since we started into Pennsylvania, than I ever knew before, and I cannot give but one or two reasons for it, and one is this: there was a great many men who did not want to cross the Potomac River. They also heard of the fall of Vicksburg and I think that discouraged them. And there are a great many low-down fellows, who do no good in the war now, nor never had, and that is not half told, they never will do any good. They will act the coward, and be bucked and gagged before they will go into battle...while there are others who will fight till they die, if their officers tell them to.

> David Ballenger to his wife from Madison Court House, Virginia, 30 July 1863.[26]

I went up in town yesterday for a few hours as the ship had to go up to the city on business.... The house looks very lonesome & made me feel badly to go into it. They have thrown up a heavy embankment just opposite Lightwood Alley as the first parallel; the second is to be built at Broad St, & so on thro' the town. The town is to be burnt in divisions in this way & then fought street by street.

> Augustine Thomas Smythe (1842-1914) from Charleston to his mother in Summerton, 2 September 1863.[27]

I have just received your two letters—and am not surprised at Richard's running away— I am certain that it has been a long settled plan with him which was the reason I begged you to sell him— I fear that you will never see him again— George is in the work house— I shall bring him up with me as I cannot sell him without a bill of sale signed by you— If you get R. sell him as soon as possible— The negroes generally are very much demoralized, which is to be expected when we see so many whites demoralized and scared....

> Henry Hunter Raymond (1822-1876) from Charleston to his mother in Greenville, 3 October 1863.[28]

The fare is good enough. We have bread and beef for breakfast very well seasoned, the same with potatoes, and sometimes cabbage for dinner, and bread and molasses for supper. Mr. Blake sais it is not his fault that we have nothing better to eat, people will not let him have provisions for love nor money. He asks most every one who brings daughters here if they can spare something to eat.

> Anna Donaldson, student at Spartanburg Female Academy, to her parents in lower Greenville District, 10 October 1863.[29]

The Legislature met last night and I judge the session will not last very long from the fact the members receive about one fourth of what it costs them to live here.... I must confess our Legislature is the poorest that has ever assembled since I can remember anything about legislative matters.... I receive ninety dollars per month and my actual expenses for board and lodgings are just one cent more or less $102.00 for the same period. I cannot live at this rate.

> Gustavus Augustus Follin, Jr. (1842-1927), an employee in the State Adjutant and Inspector General's Office in Columbia, to his father in Charleston, 24 November 1863.[30]

...if them Reports be True [that Bragg and Longstreet have been defeated] I count us in a bad condition but not wars than I was Expecting for I have thought that we was Ruined for a long time and now it is a plain case but we coudent Expect nothing better from such treatment as we have met with [.] all the time the big men has no pitty on the Poore soldiers and the Treatment gits wars but I think it will soon stop for this war is coming to a close as fast as it can [.]

> J. O. B. Barkley of Anderson District to his brothers stationed near Charleston, 7 December 1863.[31]

One would hardly recognize town now. To go along the Bay & Broad St. it seems like Sunday. Every store is closed, & no one is to be seen except some stray straggler who may chance to pass along, while up town is the business part entirely. There all is life. All the head quarters of the different departments are up there, around & above the Citadel, & the old city is turned upside down. Nobody is considered safe below Wentworth St. but I reckon they wont hurt me so I shall risk it & stay.

> Augustine Thomas Smythe from Charleston to his sister Sarah Ann, a refugee in Clarendon District, 10 December 1863.[32]

Your son left here on yesterday who will report the affairs relating to the plantation better & more satisfactorily than I could on paper. I had not quite finished thrashing the swamp rice when he left, but did finish late in the afternoon. The yield is 5,500 bushels besides some little dirt & scrapings which will probably amount to 100 bushels more.... The mill worked tolerably. The cow hide lacing soon cuts out and does not answer the purpose so well, but we must submit to many inconveniences and congratulate ourselves that it is as well with us as it is....

The use of Lard for the engine does very well as the warmth melts it easily but for the other portions of the machinery the lard cools as soon as it comes in contact with the iron and does not penetrate into every part of as it should, but as I said before we must make out with being more particular in the application....

I will distribute to the negroes such rations as you have always allowed on Christmas and will endeavour myself to spend as cheerfully as possible the times and trying circumstances will admit of, wishing you all a pleasant time—

> Overseer S. H. Boineau to Edward B. Heyward from
> Combahee Plantation, 24 December 1863.[33]

If Lincoln is reelected, as I suppose he will be—it will take another such series of summers as we had summer before the last to give us any prospect of peace—peace which we prized so little when we had it. Indeed we must look for another four years of war—in which time we may be overrun—I will not say subjugated. We cannot be as long as we can feed our army.... How sad it is that there should be a panic in the up Country. Even the Greenvillians I hear are getting alarmed—starvation too—you must congratulate yourselves on getting 'shut' of it, as the Greenville people say. We feel the want of sugar here and Coffee, but other things are still to be had & we dine on wild ducks, or turkey nearly every day. The man I board with being a good provider and having a farm.

> William Elliott, Jr., from Georgetown to his sister Emmie
> at Oak Lawn in Colleton District, 4 January 1864.[34]

Snow all over the ground and very cold for the season.— I have been concerned for several days to devise a plan for getting my corn here. It is becoming a serious matter to subsist one's family. There is corn in the country, but it is so difficult to get transportation, that we are almost as far to seek as if it were not there.

> John B. Patrick Diary, 22 March 1864.[35]

I think both white and colored people ought to pray for peace, for if we dont it will bring starvation to our land—we can buy nothing in our town to eat but rice. Our money wont buy one pound of sugar for 20.$ We are now looking for another Brig[ade] of soldiers. We understand they did not only take what they wanted to eat but took carpet [,] silver spoons and the castors off the table, and if this crowd does as the others I think they will allmost strip Greenville but they have not bothered us any....

> A slave named Eliza apparently sent this letter (written by "Frank" and dated 9 April 1864) to the daughters of her mistress.[36]

⁂

I have been having a very nice time in a very quiet way for of course I visit no where myself but Columbia is all excitement and even the quietest must share a little in the general bustle. the cause of the excitement of course the soldiers as usual. There are five regiments here now, all cavalry. The first and second just relieved after three years service in Virginia for a little easier duty on the coast [.] they look very proud & their spirit is high. they say just give them some new recruits and a few fresh horses & they are ready and eager for another campaign in Virginia, but I could hardly look at them without tears in my eyes. to think of their full ranks and nice uniforms & bright faces when they first went off and now to see them with only between 200 and 800 men and they miserably clothed, with their poor frames of horses, and skins burnt the color of mahogany, oh! it is pitiful to look up and down the line and miss at least three fourths of the faces, young boyish faces, so full of ardent hope and life, but the spirit is higher than ever and the faces have that look in them that shows they are men to *do* or *die*. God bless them, is my prayer whenever I see them.

Sophia Lovell Cheves Haskell Diary, 21 April 1864.[37]

⁂

We have been attending to the wounded, who come on now in great numbers; we have been at the R. R. every afternoon for some time with coffee and any other refreshments we can get for their benefit. It is a sad pleasure, but one that I have longed to participate in ever since the war began.... Poor fellows, they are so patient, and many of them so mangled. We have some romantic times with them, too. Do you begin to tire of the war, and are you willing to have a cessation of hostilities? ...at one time there were six thousand [soldiers] in & around our city, poor fellows, so many have gone to return no more.... I have been in the treasury department now for nearly a month, and will remain as long as possible.... We have to write so fast...I sign my name 3200 times every day, and are occupied for six hours—from 8 A. M. to 2 P. M. It reminds me very much of school days— There are about two hundred ladies employed, each has her own desk, and I know Bable its self was not more confusion—

> "Babe" from Columbia to school chum Harriett Palmer
> in St. Stephen's Parish, 22 June 1864.[38]

You speak in your letter of selling corn to pay taxes, I do not think we will have any to spare, there is nothing to be had now except in exchange, I have to give Corn for Iron, Salt, Weaving, and indeed *every* thing that I buy, has to be paid in Provision, and the prospect for a crop now is very poor, we have no wheat to spare, and the corn here will make but little, & I think we had best keep all we have, on hand until we see what we shall have, from this year; I do not think it right to take high prices for Bread, and I see the Secretary of the Treasury advises for the People of South Carolina to do as the Noble Virginia Farmers have done (protest against high prices) but of course I am quite willing to submit to your judgment....

> Jane McLure (1829-1921) of Union District to her hus-
> band in Virginia, 18 August 1864.[39]

How quiet our life is here, and yet so much suffering, so much horror around us, and what a terrible uncertainty. We know not what a day may bring forth, or at what time the peaceful town may be spread in ruins and another instance of barbarous spite be added to the long list of outrages committed by the Yankees. Yet our life flows evenly on, we hear of battles, we see friend after friend brought home coffined and ready for the churchyard, and we know of others who sleep on the battle field. The mourning garb is common, the cork leg and one armed men have ceased to attract attention. We've gotten use to it all. War does not break into a quiet breakfast or disturb a night's rest.

Grace Brown Elmore Diary, 8 September 1864.[40]

My visit to Millwood gave me the blues. I always become low-spirited when thrown among croakers, and for days after my visit I would think of nothing but the horrors of a Yankee raid, for we can not blind ourselves to the fact that what happens elsewhere will certainly happen here if the Yankee comes. I have almost determined suicide, in some circumstances, would be justifiable. We are hard pushed on every side, and there is much despondency felt. Not as to the ultimate result, but we fear the iron foot of war is to be planted in our homes, and that our eyes shall witness the burning of homesteads, the desolation and the hideous outrages that have ever accompanied the Yankee army. One is almost tempted to doubt the existence of justice, and the right in heaven as well as on earth when listening to the tales of horror we hear and read every day.

Grace Brown Elmore Diary, 15 September 1864.[41]

...yankees are as near here as they are to charleston [sic] so we are in as much danger in one place as another. We use wheat and rhy [sic] flour togather [sic] to make bread. We have made seven or eight straw hats [,] mother plaits them and alice and myself sew them [,] they pay us in vegetables, we got last night for one hat a bushel of corn meal.... The shells coming up town will make houses more called for and will shut up a great many churches, a great many people think charleston will be taken, whatever they intend to do I hope will be done soon for it must cause a great deal of suffering, people have waited so long for better times they are tired of waiting now.

S. Macdonald writing from Cherokee Ford to Mrs. Mackenzie in Charleston, 18 September 1864.[42]

There is so much wickedness mixed up in this war that I sometimes almost dispair of a blessing coming upon the people— If you could know how the truly noble are sacrificed to those who are making immense fortunes out of the soldiers who are fighting the battles, you would be grieved—while the best people of the land find it hard to feed and clothe their families, the extortioners are revelling in unheard of extravagance. To give you an idea of what is going on—the other day one of the millionaires gave a dinner party to several of the Dignitaries of the place who all came dressed in homespun cloth while the servants were dressed in fine broadcloth—which is selling at $75 a yard! The homespun itself is $20 a yard.

> Annie De Wolf Middleton (Mrs. Nathaniel Russell Middleton) writing from Summerville to her mother, Mrs. Henry De Wolf, in Bristol, Rhode Island, 19 September 1864.[43]

A great many of our men hardly know their right hand from their left, as long as they been in the army; and there are plenty of men that know so little that, if Jeff Davis were to bind them hand and foot to cast them into Hell, they would be keen enough to swear it was all right. They have become so estranged to anything like Liberty and Republicanism that they do not know the difference between principle and 'a piece of plug' as Dow Junior said of President Taylor.[44] I hear a great many say that if General George McClellan is elected President, and will give us our rights in the Union, they do not intend to fight any longer, and that is exactly my notion. If he does offer us our constitutional rights, and our men do not accept, it will show to a demonstration that we are fighting for separation alone, and nothing else; and had I known that was all we were fighting for, I never would have pulled a trigger.

There are a great many of our men so ignorant as to say that Lee has been whipping Grant all this year. Strange way of whipping, when Lee is now seventy-five miles farther south than he was when he commenced fighting last spring! Besides Grant now holds the Petersburg and Weldon Railroad, and, according to my notions, he will ere take Petersburg, and perhaps Richmond as well. But if he gets Petersburg he can take Richmond, for the former place is key to the latter; or at any rate, this is according to my generalship. Our editors along last Spring, said that General Johnston, in Georgia, was prepared for either offensive or defensive movements; but I knew all the time that was a lie, as the Indian said when he scalped the man with the wig on. They also said if Sherman went on as far as Atlanta, that his army would be all torn to pieces, and that he would never get back. But now they see who is all torn up; it is *our* Army that was torn up. But I have known ever since Grant took Missionary Ridge, that Atlanta was gone.

I have gotten so that I do not think it lies in the breeches of an Editor to dupe me. (I believe I understand them as well as any common man.)

David Ballenger to his brother from New Market Heights, Virginia, 25 September 1864.[45]

...you ask if people up here want the war to go on, a great many wish the yankees would come in [,] anything for peace.

S. Macdonald writing from Cherokee Ford to Mrs. Mackenzie in Charleston, 21 October 1864.[46]

I have come to believe that this is one of the most unjust and inglorious Wars that I have ever read about. It is nothing but a War for power and plunder, and has degenerated into murder and cruelty, battles into butchery; and therefore I intend to leave it at the risk of my life, unless you say for me to stay and linger out a painful existence here.

It is lamentable that our Country is ruined to all intents and purposes; and besides all this, the morals of the people, both male and female, are ruined. The whole Country is filled with houses of prostitution. There are numbers of men and women reared by [as] respectable parents as there are in the Country, who are now full of vice and crime, unfit to associate with civil people.

David Ballenger to his mother from Virginia, 12 December 1864.[47]

...it is surely and truly hart rending in the extreme to be obliged to leave our homes, but such I believe is our fate and we must try to submit patiently to the trying reality.... It is thought by nearly every one that the yankee army will move upon Augusta, if so, all our troops will necessarily be taken away from this line of defe[n]ce, and this part of the Country will of course be abandoned [.] in that case we shall be in a sad plight indeed [,] deserters from our ranks, yankee raiders & negroes who have left their owners will be prowling and plundering all over the Country, twenty miles from the sea board [.] I can see no hope whatever for us. Misery and starvation will necessarily be the consequence. It is not despondency that causes me to write thus, truly I am distressed, but not alarmed, with hundreds of others I shall patiently wait the dreadful calamity which I believe in store for us and bow in submission to the will of providence [.]

I have thought & said that if the yankee army was allowed to march through the entire State of Georgia and occupy Savannah they could with greater ease march over South Carolina, we have no men to oppose such a force as will be concentrated upon our soil. the fighting material of our Country is exhausted, or nearly so, when compared with the resources of the north. our soldiers are beginning to become dishartened, their monthly pay will buy one bushel of Corn for their destitute familys & how can men contend with an enemy flushed with so many recent successes....

Overseer S. H. Boineau from Combahee Plantation to
Edward B. Heyward, 29 December 1864.[48]

The alarm in Charleston has not subsided much and I grieve to say many of our citizens are very calmly anticipating the fate of Charleston and openly declaring their intention to take the oath of allegiance to Lincoln's Government. Danl Horlbeck says he has written to his Brothers advising their return to the city, with a view to save their property by a quick and ready adhesion to the approaching new order of things— And he stands only one of hundreds— I mention his name because you know him— For myself I am still unable to realize such extremity of danger and among the 'hopeless hopeful still'....

I suppose you heard the rumors that Lee had been made absolute ruler of our armies and was authorized to call out 300,000 slaves. Public confidence rose with the report—but unfollowed by any thing confirmatory [,] citizens faces soon lengthened as before and people relapsed into their habitual gloom and despondency.

Gentlemen from the neighborhood of Aiken and Barnwell, where Wheelers cavalry are stationed tell terrible stories of these terrible troopers— Some of them seem scarcely to recognize our farmers as even 'neutrals' but prey on them as if they were quartered in Massachusetts. Wheeler it is said boasting that he has no commissary in his whole corps or division, and looking to the country around him for support.

Eleven hundred are in Aiken [.] Mrs Gregg gave a party to all the officers, but these rough western men frightened all the 'Gals' as they termed the young ladies— Mrs G—— hurrying up supper was glad to say good night to her brave but 'unpolished' guests—

One of them addressed a group thus, 'Well Gals I tell you how I treated seven yanks who had just fired an old woman's barn—clothes were scarce so we stripped 'em pretty clean and as it was right smart cold we tied 'em hard and fast and pitched 'em into the Barn to prevent their catching cold'— Is not this a too horrible reality of war for the light talk of a drawing room.

> Thomas P. Lockwood (1826-1877) of Charleston to
> Harriett Palmer in St. Stephen's Parish, 7 January 1865.[49]

Gentlemen from Richmond tell me that the talk there, is to give up Richmond to save Charleston, & such is, I suppose, the case. I hear sad accounts from North Carolina, however.... Georgia, too, is whipped. The only two States who are in it heart & soul, are Virginia & South Carolina. Hurrah for the Palmetto! God grant we may never be brought low! Here we are quiet.... Robbers plentiful as usual, & despite all my efforts, No 36 has suffered severely. As fast as I would put up the fence & nail up the windows, they would break them down. All the lead, &c has been taken out, & worse than that, three of the mirrors.... I have notified the police.... It is useless almost to attempt to stop those fellows. They live all around, & as soon as night comes, they knock down the fence, cut open a window, & go to work. No law down in this part of town now. Assaults every night or so. The other night they robbed a man here just at our door, & another night pulled one Courier off his horse, robbed him & then put him on again & sent him off. It is horrible, the lawless state now of old Charleston formerly so orderly. No shelling tho'.... My! My! but the people do curse Jeff Davis now! And the *Mercury!* is it not savage?

Augustine Thomas Smythe from Charleston to his aunt, Jane Ann Adger, a refugee in Pendleton District, 23 January 1865.[50]

Our Brigade followed on after the yanks within 8 miles of Columbia. And was then ordered back to this point [a camp in the Barnwell-Aiken area]. I do hope the yanks will not go as far as Anderson but they are getting pretty close to you. I hear this morning that they are in Abaville [Abbeville].

We hav now orders to be ready to leav at a moments warning. I have no idie where we will go. But it is rumored in camps that we are going to Alabama. We are drawing 4 days Rations for our selves and 2 for our Horses. Our Horse Rations are very scanty.... As for our selves we are doing pretty well [.] We kill a Hog when we get out of meat. And buy meal. So you see there is no danger of us perishing.... Our comand are all in low spirits and pretty badly whiped yet altho our prospects look gloomy...I cant believe God will ever allow men to prosper that has acted like the yanks hav in Georgia and Carolina. The men say here we are whiped and there is no use in fighting any longer [.] But I say fight them as long as we can get any thing to eat. I get mader and more determined every day.

J.T. Bleckley to his sister, 4 March 1865.[51]

Three weeks since the servants left. What this miserable race is to do, is engaging much of the thoughts of their former owners. We have gone through so much, that this breaking of old ties has excited little feeling, both parties are indifferent, and the most that is felt is a polite and gentle interest in the affairs of each other. In most instances there is I believe a bitter feeling, and a sharp antagonism between the two races. I almost think they are natural enemies and that only their relative positions bound them together in affection, as well as by law. For we see this antagonism just as strong in the Yankee as in the Southerner, and with no reason whatever, they seem in private life to consider the negro worth-less, and to treat him as such. Already they do not hesitate to express utter contempt for the race, and while they insist upon our treating them as equals, they show their scorn and indifference, in every way, to the same race. We cannot tell what the future holds, indeed human wisdom has been so utterly at fault, in all its deductions, with regard to this war and its results, that one dares not draw any conclusion, however plau-sible, from passing events. Our life for four years has been the 'baseless fabric of vision,' and now we can deal with the hard realities of the present. We have truly said goodbye to being ladies of leisure, my time is fully occupied, often not having time to sleep. Rise at 5 o'clock, dress, come down to see after breakfast, then a multitude of small cares; among them reading to Jack his contract, which he ought to know by heart. For every day he makes some demand and when I decline, he says, 'But Miss Grace, aint it in de contract,' whereupon I take him gravely to the library and read the document signed by the parties in the presence of the Yankee Colonel Haughton; and which he told Jack was binding. I sometimes get very impatient and then I reason, he is not a knave, only a poor ignorant negro. So Jack has his contract read and explained ev-ery day before his work is over. For, if he does not make a demand, he is sure to refuse one of mine. I don't like to live among the pots and kettles. I hate being beset by small worries. Oh how different our feelings if we had won our 'Cause.' With what spirit and heart would we have gone to work, how willingly would loss of home and wealth been borne for the sake of being free. But now we are forced to work; without hope of our country,—but that we might obtain bread.

Grace Brown Elmore Diary, 25 June 1865.[52]

A dreadful war has swept over our land— Then on the battle field with the vultures hovering around them lie 150,000 of our bravest men. In the solitary home the bitter tears are coursing down the pale cheeks of the desolate widow—& the poor little orphans are calling for their father & for bread, Impoverished forever—$3,000,000 gone to the winds & Confederate bonds pasting the barbars Shop, with the Bills of the con-federates. Look at our plantations [,] one scene of Desolation [—] Houses Mills Barns levelled to the ground— Villages & cities in mouldering ruins & the heart sickens with the tales of the horrid murders— The Poor ruined planter who ministered to the wants of thousands hangs his head in desolation & weeps where he sees his poor little ones in want of the necessaries of life—the pale vissage & the thread bare attire wringing the heart with misery— We were told by our leaders that the yankees would not fight—Mr [Robert Barnwell] Rhett said they would be driven from the land with a heavy stick, & he would drink the blood that would be shed.... Mr Rhett safely lodged in Alabama—making a fine Crop— then we were 8,000,000 fighting against 22,000,000, we having no navy [,] army or manufactures, the North having all these with an influx of Strangers, & our Negroes— Alas how many a man hid himself from conscription & left our brave ones in the front of the Battle. mean wretches not fit to die. Poor Joe Johnson in his muster roll with 70,000 men [;] only 14,000 remained to fight by the gallant General [.] how did they serve our Gallant R Lee— where were those who ought to have died by his side [—] some enjoying the luxury of home, some meanly extending their furloughs, some straggling, some deserting....

Ann Morris Vanderhorst Diary, 1 July 1865.

NOTES

[1] Elliott Family Papers, South Caroliniana Library. This young man was studying law in Charleston in the fall of 1860.

[2] A reference to Major Robert Anderson's decision on 26 December to move his federal force from Fort Moultrie to Fort Sumter. A cockade was a patriotic rosette worn on a hat or in one's lapel.

[3] John Smythe Richardson Papers, South Caroliniana Library. Ervin and Richardson (1828-1908) knew each other as a result of association with Sumter newspapers in the 1850s. Although three of Ervin's sons served during the war, their father's role was limited to collecting taxes and home defense activities. See Anne King Gregorie, "John Witherspoon Ervin," *South Carolina Historical Magazine* (July 1945), pp. 166-70. Richardson, who became an officer, later served in the General Assembly and U. S. Congress.

[4] Gaston, Strait, Wylie, Baskin Papers, South Caroliniana Library. By *Pills*, Strait perhaps means "bitter pills" will have to be swallowed. "Mote" is an archaic verb form—"so may it be." Some members of these Chester area families were outspoken in their opposition to secession. As for Strait, he clearly favors peace, not war ("bury the Tomyhawk"), and a return to farming ("ploughs 'decree by default'").

[5] Duncan, Kinard, Sanders, Tucker Papers, South Caroliniana Library. Six days later, Tucker rebuffed his wife's inquiry concerning some "big-to-do," cautioning her to shun wartime gossip..."to use a vulgar expression—'Don't run & tell every *fart* you hear let.'" On 25 April 1862, then stationed near Charleston, Tucker remarked to his wife, "The war news is any thing but favorable— We are I believe a ruined people—our destiny is almost fixed— Subjugation with all its hideousness is upon us— or the Cloud is about to burst forth in all its fury— I would that I could believe otherwise—" He died four months later in Virginia. Note: From 1799 to 1868, the most common unit of regional government in South Carolina was known as a "district," not county, the region ruled by a *district* court.

[6] Gaston, Strait, Wylie, Baskin Papers. Strait, who led a rather tempestuous life, was assistant surgeon of the Palmetto Sharpshooters. He died in Chester of dysentery in October 1863.

[7] Ibid. "Rhettism" refers to Robert Barnwell Rhett and his son, both violent proponents of secession. Colonel Richard N. G. Dunovant commanded the 12th South Carolina [Infantry] Volunteers at Port Royal. Julius Mills became a major in December 1861 but resigned from the service six months later.

[8] Francis W. Pickens Papers, South Caroliniana Library.

[9] McLure Family Papers, South Caroliniana Library. McLure frequently advised Jane concerning management of his plantation. Many of these letters can be found in Sarah Porter Carroll (ed.), *Lifeline to Home for John William McLure, CSA—Union County, S.C.* (Greenville, 1990).

[10] South Caroliniana Library. Patrick (1832-1900) was a teacher at the Arsenal Academy in Columbia throughout the war.

[11]Thomas Aiton Papers, South Caroliniana Library. General Don Carlos Buell (1818-1898) obviously was not killed at Corinth. Captain John Quattlebaum (1807-1865) resigned as commander of Company C, 19th Regiment, when his unit was reorganized following this incident. The cause of the trouble was the fact that many men did not believe they were obligated to serve outside of the state.

[12]Vanderhorst Papers, South Carolina Historical Society. These entries were written during a brief visit to Charleston from Aiken where the family sought refuge. Son John became an invalid following amputation of limbs frozen while serving in the army. Subsequent remarks reveal this lady's New York property was being confiscated by the federal government and relations with both her husband (Elias Vanderhorst) and embittered son were strained.

[13]Claudius L. Fike Papers, South Caroliniana Library. This letter refers to the Confederate repulse of the Union campaign to take Richmond.

[14]South Caroliniana Library. Emma Holmes (1838-1910), member of a prominent Charleston family, was living in Camden at this time. This bit of Columbia gossip concerning rebellious youth highlights a phenomenon often evident during wartime. See also, John F. Marszalek (ed.), *The Diary of Miss Emma Holmes, 1861-1866* (Baton Rouge, 1979).

[15]Gaston, Strait, Wylie, Baskin Papers.

[16]Elliott Family Papers.

[17]Ibid. Stephen, brother of William, held various wartime posts throughout South Carolina, including command of Fort Sumter during the severe bombardment in the fall of 1863.

[18]A few weeks earlier, Honour met his father-in-law on the train to Columbia, whereupon the latter urged Honour to sell his Charleston home at auction, even offering to attend and "run up" the price to $10,000. He also boasted his Negroes were worth $60,000 and his store $50,000, vowing he planned to sell everything before the Yankees came. Honour reported all this to his wife in a letter of 29 March, noting he doubted if her father could consummate his various wartime schemes.

[19]Theodore Honour Papers, South Caroliniana Library. His wife, the former Rebecca Caroline Segnious, and two small children moved to the upcountry when Honour enlisted early in 1862.

[20]Ibid.

[21]Elliott-Gonzales Papers, Southern Historical Collection, University of North Carolina.

[22]Palmer Family Papers, South Caroliniana Library. Many of these letters have been published in Louis P. Towles (ed.), *A World Turned Upside Down: The Palmers of Santee, 1818-1881* (Columbia, 1996).

[23]David Ballenger Papers, South Caroliniana Library. Ballenger, a South Carolina native who saw considerable action, then was serving as captain, Company D, 26th Alabama Regiment. His wife and family were living near Tigerville, where Ballenger made his home after the war. In May 1864 he joined Hampton's Legion as fifth sergeant of mounted infantry. Note: There are several versions of the Ballenger

letters. Some original manuscripts are at North Greenville College, and both that institution and the South Caroliniana Library have typed copies made at various times. The latter in no way alter the intent of his words and are merely attempts to make readable rather primitive grammar and spelling.

[24]James Earle Hagood Papers, South Caroliniana Library. On 3 August, still desperate, Maxwell wrote, "Give the man we were talking to $3000 if you can do no better.... Make all arrangements for me as you would for yourself.... if you dont get me a substitute I am obliged to go to the army." Maxwell added, "*P.S. My overseer too has to go.*" Existing records indicate this effort to avoid service probably succeeded.

[25]William Mason Smith Family Letters, South Caroliniana Library.

[26]David Ballenger Papers. "Bucked and gagged" was a common, 19th Century disciplinary practice—mouth gagged, wrists tied together, arms thrust over bent knees, and a stick inserted over arms and under knees.

[27]Augustine Thomas Smythe Letters, South Carolina Historical Society. Smythe, a signalman, was serving aboard the *C. S. S. Palmetto State*. His parents had gone to Summerton the previous month, although a few servants remained in their home at 10 Meeting Street.

[28]Henry Hunter Raymond Papers, South Caroliniana Library. Raymond, a staff officer, noted six weeks later that George still was in the Charleston work house. Despite whippings, his attitude remained the same—"incorrigible."

[29]Anna Donaldson Papers, South Caroliniana Library. William K. Blake (1824-1898) headed up the school, which closed soon after this letter was written.

[30]Gustavus Augustus Follin Papers, South Caroliniana Library.

[31]Barkley Family Papers, Southern Historical Collection, University of North Carolina. J. O. B. Barkley also was in uniform for a time in 1861.

[32]Augustine Thomas Smythe Letters.

[33]Heyward Family Papers, South Caroliniana Library. Boineau obviously was using cow hide and lard to replace leather and oil as he tried to operate the steam engine that provided power for the rice mill.

[34]Elliott-Gonzales Papers. William, who served as an enrolling officer in Greenville and Georgetown, subsequently was transferred to Clarendon District, prompting this outburst to his sister on 23 March 1864—"as if I have not had enough already of Crackerland." "Why oh why," he moaned, "can we not have this war over. You may think me absurd, but unless the republicans can have their candidate defeated by the influence of Southern victories—this war will last four years longer. I dont see the way out of it."

[35]Four days later Patrick arranged an exchange of corn with the government. He would have his corn delivered to the nearest railroad depot, and Confederate authorities in Columbia then would allot him a similar amount.

[36]Anonymous letter, South Caroliniana Library. Eliza notes the town is crowded with soldiers and adds she is eager for the family to return..."ain't had any body to cut wood for me since you have gone."

[37]Cheves Family Papers, South Carolina Historical Society. Sophia (1809-1881), who lived near Lowndesville in Abbeville District, is witnessing the reorganization of Wade Hampton's Legion in the spring of 1864.

[38]Palmer Family Papers. "Babe" is describing a unit of the Confederate Treasury that moved from Richmond to Columbia during the war.

[39]McLure Family Papers. John William McLure—a native of Chester who became a merchant-farmer in Union District—lived near Pacolet Mills.

[40]South Caroliniana Library. Miss Elmore (1839-1911), member of a distinguished South Carolina family, lived in Columbia.

[41]Ibid. Millwood was the home of General Wade Hampton (1818-1902), South Carolina's foremost Civil War leader and later governor and U. S. senator, thus the fact that Miss Elmore thought it a nest of "croakers" takes on special significance.

[42]Mackenzie Family Papers, South Caroliniana Library. Macdonald, a Charlestonian, was a refugee on the Broad River near the King's Mountain Iron Works in western York County.

[43]Nathaniel Russell Middleton Papers, Southern Historical Collection, University of North Carolina. Mrs. Middleton requested an ounce of quinine be sent, noting the army took all that came through the blockade, and added that her son, Nathaniel, Jr. (born in 1851), had written several letters to his grandmother in the North, but they were so argumentative she chose not to send them. Note: Such mail usually went via Nassau.

[44]"Dow Junior" was the pen name of a popular Manhattan journalist, Eldridge G. Page.

[45]David Ballenger Papers.

[46]Mackenzie Family Papers. In this letter, Macdonald talks of rent for a house she owns in Charleston, acquiring a coat with the help of Mrs. Mackenzie, and a trip her father is making to Charleston. She said she would like to go but feared for her safety.

[47]David Ballenger Papers. Ballenger's last wartime letter was written in January 1865. What he did during the next few months is unclear, although someone (perhaps a descendant) has added his name to records at the South Carolina State Archives listing those who surrendered at Appomattox.

[48]Heyward Family Papers. Boineau's grammar is so different from a letter written one year earlier that one cannot help but conclude he is exhausted or shaken by what is transpiring.

[49]Palmer Family Papers. Lockwood, a private, had obtained a commission and was contemplating the wisdom of trying to form a forty-five-man company. Mrs. Gregg probably was the wife of well-known industrialist William Gregg.

[50]Augustine Thomas Smythe Letters. The home of merchant Robert Adger, his uncle, was located at 36 Meeting Street. To some degree, Charlestonians blamed Confederate soldiers from the upcountry and other states for the crime wave engulfing their city. On 30 January 1865, Philip Palmer, writing to his sister Harriett, said of Jeff Davis: "I wish that some one would poison the old bugger. I believe he has brought

all of this trouble on us by his hard headiness [sic] and petty conceits about Genl Johnson" (Palmer Family Papers).

[51]J.T. Beckley Papers, South Caroliniana Library.

[52]This fine diary recently has been published by the University of Georgia Press. See Marli F. Weiner (ed.), *A Heritage of Woe: The Civil War Diary of Grace Brown Elmore, 1861-1868.* (Athens, 1997).

II

THE WAR IN SOUTH CAROLINA

Although the main thrust of this inquiry into life in the 1860s is what civilians were doing (or not doing), it is impossible to ignore the armed conflict that was going on since it created the homefront. No war, no homefront. From the military standpoint, the first big event in South Carolina was the attack upon the beleaguered federal garrison at Fort Sumter in April 1861, which, as every schoolboy (and girl) knows, started the Civil War. The euphoria spawned by this spectacular success and the stunning Confederate victory at Manassas a few months later evaporated in November of that same year when 12,000 Union soldiers and marines came ashore in the southern corner of the state at Port Royal. As federal strategists pondered this invasion of South Carolina soil, they had at least three goals in mind: establish a coaling-repair station to service the U.S. fleet and especially to supply vessels blockading southern ports, force the Confederacy to divert manpower to this region from other parts of the new nation, and mount a drive against Charleston, described by Captain S.F. Du Pont (U. S. Navy) as "that focus of rebellion—the scene of great indignity to our flag."[1] Of course, once the enemy landed and gained a foothold, whatever territory he held no longer can be considered part of the *Confederate* homefront. Civilians who remained certainly were not lending much support to the rebel cause after the Stars and Stripes were unfurled there once more.[2]

Virtually all armed combat occurring within the state to the close of 1864 took place along the coast, largely in and around Charleston Harbor and on various islands stretching south to Port Royal and Beaufort, as federal forces tried to expand and strengthen their sometimes precarious positions. The sole exception would be shoot-outs between Confederate officials and draft dodgers—often called "Tories"—whose numbers increased, especially in upland regions, as the war dragged on. Then, early in 1865, Sherman slashed and burned a northeasterly path through Blackville, Orangeburg, and Columbia en route to Cheraw and North Carolina; and, as the war was winding down, yet another Yankee general (Edward E. Potter) conducted a much smaller but similar raid

49

inland from Georgetown, his goal being destruction of locomotives, rolling rail stock, and supplies in the Camden-Sumter neighborhood.

The Port Royal invasion brought to South Carolina the man who ultimately would become the embodiment of Confederate courage and valor: Robert Edward Lee. For four months in the winter of 1861-1862, Lee was in charge of coastal defenses in South Carolina, Georgia, and eastern Florida, one of a series of short-term assignments given him during the first year of the war. These include command of Virginia state forces (April-July 1861), "coordinator" of Confederate troops in western Virginia (August-October 1861), the southeastern duty tour (November 1861-March 1862), and military adviser to President Jefferson Davis as "Commanding General of the Army" (March-May 1862). Only a shake-up in the top echelon of troops defending Richmond—one general (Joseph E. Johnston) was wounded and another (C. W. Smith) suffered a mental or nervous collapse—transformed Lee into an active field officer just before the famed "Seven Days" of June-July 1862.

The Robert E. Lee who set up headquarters at Coosawhatchie in the fall of 1861 was an imposing but hardly heroic or charismatic figure. This fifty-four-year-old man, a competent engineer who had spent all of his adult life in the United States Army, had done little to merit unusual recognition by civilians. When Confederate authorities took over Virginia troops in June 1861, he became, in effect, a leader without followers and played no part in First Manassas a month later. And the western Virginia affair turned out to be a disaster. The Confederate government, underestimating Union sentiment in that region, concentrated its attention upon operations east of the mountains. It further complicated matters by fielding troops led by two former Virginia governors (John B. Floyd and Henry A. Wise), ancient political rivals who were extremely ambitious but knew little about military tactics. Lee, who was supposed to "coordinate" the campaign, lacked clear-cut authority, yet with the loss of that region he became the scapegoat and was contemptuously referred to as "Granny" Lee or "Evacuating" Lee.

From Lee's point of view, this new assignment opened on a highly embarrassing note. His appointment was opposed by the governors of South Carolina and Georgia (Francis W. Pickens and Joseph E. Brown), both of whom thought he lacked vigor. There is a rumor that many South Carolina officers signed a round-robin protest against the general from Virginia.[3] In addition, Lee himself approached the task with misgivings. Shortly after arriving in South Carolina, he wrote to daughter Mildred

AN ACROSTIC

Abhored by all,
Both great and small,
Existing on Southern soil.
Lean, hungry,
Insidious,
Nefarious man,
Cunning and trying
Our ruin to plan,
Let Northerners bow to him,
No Southerner can.

The first letter of each line reveals the name of the individual being described. This acrostic appeared in Sumter's *Tri-Weekly Watchman*, 17 June 1861.

expressing irritation that he had been sent off on what he described as "Another forlorn hope expedition. Worse than western Virginia."[4]

But, despite protests and personal doubts, Lee, with the firm backing of President Jefferson Davis, arrived in Charleston on 7 November, the same day that the enemy finished mopping up the Port Royal-Hilton Head area. He left immediately for the front, ordered islands where enemy-held forts were located to be abandoned, and established headquarters at Coosawhatchie.[5] This new commander had at his disposal four converted steamers, each with two guns, and perhaps 12,300 men, most of them concentrated in or near Charleston and Savannah.[6] Opposing him was an equal number of soldiers and marines backed up by fourteen warships and some fifty supply vessels and transports. Bruce Catton tells in his three-volume *Centennial History of the Civil War* (1961-1965) how these men easily subdued two forts guarding the approaches to Port Royal. Once ashore, they found only a flock of turkeys (soon eaten) and hundreds of blacks baffled by their new freedom, all whites having fled.

The invaders were, it seems, equally confused, although some historians believe they could have enlarged their foothold with ease. This assumes, however, they had resources at hand for an extensive invasion, as well as plans for such an operation, and the Confederates would not summon reinforcements. In any case, it appears unlikely that 12,000 or so blue-clads, commanded by Brigadier General Thomas W. Sherman, could have gotten far inland unless they themselves were reinforced. Their true advantage lay in naval guns; separated from them they were simply a sizeable detachment adrift deep in enemy territory.

During the next ten days Lee was constantly on the move, touring Charleston and Savannah in an effort to evaluate the region's coastal defenses. The *Savannah Republican*, much impressed, commented on 19 November that Lee "seems to be giving close attention to every part of his command." While at Fort Sumter, he presumably was seen by poet Paul Hamilton Hayne, who subsequently wrote glowingly of the general's striking figure, his graceful, broad shoulders, and his knightly appearance. Yet it is far from clear just when (or even if) this sighting occurred; in addition, Hayne's pen portrait was not published until after Lee's death when his fame was much enhanced.[7]

On one of these fact-finding expeditions Lee covered 115 miles in a single day, thirty-five of them on "Greenbriar," a horse he had seen and admired in western Virginia. When its owner was transferred to South Carolina, Lee was able to purchase the animal, whose strength and endurance soon won him the better-known name of "Traveller."

While in Charleston, Lee met with Governor Pickens concerning manpower. Pickens insisted all new recruits remain within the state, but claimed he could arm only part of five regiments Lee wanted raised. Eventually they reached a compromise; Pickens would arm two regiments pledged to serve for the duration, and Lee would issue 2500 rifles, which had just arrived on a blockade runner, to other South Carolinians willing to enlist for the entire war. This subject—enlistment "for the war"—was much on the general's mind during these weeks, and he never lost an opportunity to speak up for any scheme assuring him of full regiments and a ready supply of men.

By 19 November, Lee had evolved a three-point plan that he would try to implement during the remainder of his duty tour.

1. Withdraw guns and garrisons from exposed islands to points that could be defended.
2. Strengthen approaches to major communities.
3. Construct an interior line in lower South Carolina and before Savannah so as to protect that city and the Charleston & Savannah Railroad, thus hopefully forcing the invader (if he came) to fight where naval guns could not be used effectively.

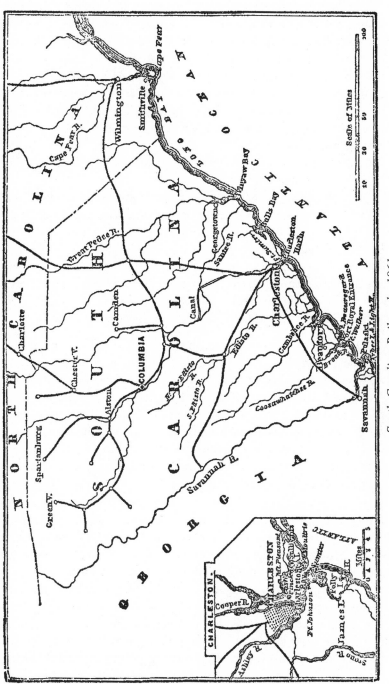

South Carolina Railroads, 1861.

According to Douglas Southall Freeman, Lee found conditions in Charleston better than elsewhere. The artillery detachments were well trained, but often lacked leadership, a deficiency he tried to rectify by shifting personnel about. Reports from some local citizens indicated the harbor forts were indeed in poor hands. Captain Alfred Rhett was said to be a gentleman but totally inexperienced, and Captain Thomas M. Wagner was accused of being incompetent, neglectful, and dissipated, "never spending the night in his fort, but coming to town to indulge in excesses with the common prostitutes."[8]

But Lee's principal problem was General Rowell Sabine Ripley (1823-1887), the Ohio native he put in charge of Charleston's defenses. Ripley, an able West Point graduate, married Alicia Middleton, widow of William A. Sparks, in 1852 and subsequently quit the military to become a local businessman. Somewhat pompous and a center of controversy throughout the war, he frequently was at odds with his superiors, though popular in Charleston, possibly because he always had that city's welfare uppermost in his mind and was a delightful raconteur. Early in 1862, Governor Pickens told Secretary of War Judah P. Benjamin that Ripley's attitude toward Lee was becoming harmful.

> His habit is to say extreme things even before junior officers, and this is well calculated to do great injury to General Lee's command. I do not think General Ripley means half of what he says in his energetic way, but others construe it differently.... Lee is a perfect head, quiet and retiring. His reserve is construed disadvantageously. I find him all that a gentleman should be, and all that ought to be expected of a thorough and scientific officer. The two are in contrast.[9]

Thus it is apparent that Lee soon overcame reservations expressed at the outset by Pickens and achieved similar success with Georgia's outspoken chief executive, although not without some bickering and compromise concerning men, arms, and terms of enlistment. As for Ripley, realizing the man did good work, he simply ignored his behind-the-scenes barbs.

On 21 November, Lee issued a general order to all personnel emphasizing they must not waste ammunition. Guards were to load their rifles only if the enemy was nearby, hunting parties were forbidden, and each man was "strictly accountable" for any bullets issued to him. He also warned against "the evil practice" of tearing down fences and other property to be used for firewood, reminding the troops they were both soldiers and citizens. Another general order (7 December) stressed that clean, dry camp sites, well-ventilated tents, and proper disposal of garbage and offal would promote healthy living conditions.

In mid-December, Lee went to Charleston for a visit that turned out to be much more eventful than anticipated. On the 11th, soon after he arrived at the Mills House, a great fire engulfed much of the business district, rendering hundreds homeless. Although the Mills House was saved, the general was forced to flee to the home of Charles Alston on the Battery. A short time later he contributed $300 to a relief fund that eventually swelled to nearly $400,000.[10] Then, on the 20th, the first anniversary of South Carolina's secession, a Union fleet appeared at the entrance to Charleston Harbor and sank some seventeen vessels loaded with stone in an unsuccessful attempt to block the main channel. Ironically, Lee, who was doing precisely the same thing on a smaller scale in order to prevent enemy craft from venturing into creeks and inlets dotting the coast between Charleston and Savannah, was furious. He quickly vented his anger to Judah P. Benjamin, while conceding this probably meant that the enemy did not intend to mount an invasion at Charleston.

> This achievement, so unworthy any nation, is the abortive expression of the malice & revenge of a people which they wish to perpetuate by rendering more memorable a day hateful in their calendar. It is also indicative of their despair of ever capturing a city they design to ruin, for they can never expect to possess what they labor so hard to reduce to a condition not to be enjoyed.
>
> I think, therefore, it is certain that an attack on the city of Charleston is not contemplated, & we must be prepared for assaults elsewhere on the Southern coast.[11]

On Christmas Day, the general wrote his wife a long letter from Coosawhatchie in which he touched upon many things, among them, loneliness, loss of her family home, and the *Trent* Affair.[12] "Arlington," he stated bluntly, was gone, adding "they cannot take away the remembrances of the spot, & the memories of those that to us rendered it sacred." He expressed the wish that he could purchase "Stratford," his birthplace, and make it their home. As for the trouble between Washington and London, Lee cautioned that Lincoln and his advisers were not "entirely mad" and, if necessary, would release the Confederate diplomats rather than risk war. "We must make up our minds to fight our own battles & win our independence alone. No one will help us."[13] Four days later he expressed similar sentiments to his son, G.W.C. Lee, adding these observations concerning the war in his sector.

> The enemy is quiet & safe in his big boats. He is threatening every avenue. Pillaging, burning & robbing where he can venture with impunity & alarming women & children. Every day I have reports of landing in force, marching &c. which turns out to be some marauding party. The last was the North Edisto [Inlet]. I yesterday went over the whole line in that region from the Ashepro [sic] to the Wad[m]alaw & found everything quiet & could only see their big black ships lying down the Edisto where the water is too broad for anything we have to reach them. They will not venture as yet in the narrow waters.[14]

On New Year's Day the Yankees launched a full-scale assault upon Confederate positions near Port Royal Ferry, their goal being to destroy but not to hold several mainland outposts. Although this account of the action, which appeared in the *Savannah Republican* on 6 January, is highly colored and inaccurate, it captures the intensity of feeling as hostilities became a reality along the South Carolina coast.

> When the great Lincoln Armada left the ports of the North, breathing slaughter and annihilation against the people of Carolina and Georgia, we gloried in the thought, and congratulated our readers, that Carolinians and Georgians were at last about to have an opportunity of vindicating southern independence on their soil. When the forces of Sherman, after a long delay, actually affected a lodgement, last week, on the Carolina main, and made a bold strike for the interior, we felt sure of a speedy realization of a hope long entertained. But Lincolnism is a deceitful and fishy thing. You cannot depend on it nowhere and for nothing. The revelations of the last day or two have cast down and discouraged us. After a thrashing in the first attempt at an inroad among a decent people, the

whole infamous pack have ingloriously taken to their heels. Reliable accounts Friday afternoon represented them as fortifying themselves at Port Royal Ferry under cover of their gunboats, but trust-worthy gentlemen who went over and returned the following day, report that every mother's son of the vile plunderers has pulled up stakes and fled to his island retreat on Hilton Head! The Ferry, Port Royal, Beaufort, have all been abandoned, and the places that once knew their onion-scented, puritanical, negro-stealing carcasses, now know them no more.

Despite these bold assertions, the Yanks still held strong to positions near the ferry, and two days later the *Charleston Mercury* reported this conversation recently took place at that site.

Yankee -'Halloo! over there.'
Southron -'Halloo! yourself.'
Yankee -'So you got LEE over there, eh?'
Southron -'Yes-sir-ee.'
Yankee -'Right smart man he is too. Ain't his headquarters at Coosowhatchie?'
Southron -'Well, he is some.'
Yankee -'Say! ain't his headquarters at Coosawhatchie?'
Southron -'Can't say, come over and see for yourself.'
Yankee -'How are you off for tobacco and liquor?'
Southron-'Got plenty of both.'
Yankee -'We want some tobacco, won't you trade some for whiskey?'
Southron -'Don't want any of *your* liquor.'

The following day this same newspaper waxed eloquent concerning the Charleston & Savannah Railroad, the "military backbone" of the Tidewater region. Without it, General Lee, said the *Mercury*, could not have progressed to the point where he could say confidently that both Savannah and Charleston were safe. Actually, this was not quite Lee's view; in his opinion, the two cities were secure against the existing enemy force *only* if all local citizens did their part by enlisting *for the duration*, furnishing supplies, and doing everything they could to aid the Confederate cause. The *Mercury* was closer to the truth when it made these observations concerning Lee's experiences on the rail line connecting Charleston and Savannah.

> When General LEE is whizzing along on a 'special,' at a speed of twenty-five miles an hour, doubtless, he involuntarily thanks his stars that he is no longer among the rugged and pathless winds of Western Virginia—than which it would be hard to imagine a place better adapted to wither the laurels of any military leader, in these times of steam and telegraph.[15]

But "whizzing along" or not, Lee's last weeks in South Carolina were dominated by fears of an attack upon that vital railway and perhaps even Savannah itself. In mid-January he made a quick trip to northern Florida where there was considerable dissension between civil and military authorities. He also stopped at Cumberland Island to visit the grave of his father, buried on the plantation of General Nathanael Greene when he died en route home from the West Indies. Meanwhile, more "stone" ships were sunk near Charleston, and the enemy began clearing channels leading to Savannah. As a result, on 3 February Lee moved his headquarters to that city.[16]

As important as these developments may have been, events much farther afield soon exerted greater impact. These include seizure of North Carolina's Roanoke Island by yet another amphibious force and disastrous reversals in Tennessee, culminating in the fall of several key forts to an army led by Ulysses S. Grant. Shaken by grim headlines, four days after President Jefferson Davis officially took office on 22 February, the *Mercury* attacked his administration as "lamentably shortsighted, and feeble, and unequal to the task of directing skillfully our affairs." It was obvious, it thundered, that Confederate citizens would have to use *state* governments to save their liberties and institutions since the men in Richmond could not do the job.

In the midst of this deep gloom, Lee was ordered by the War Department to withdraw his defenses to mainland positions and to virtually abandon Florida. At the same time, rumors began to circulate that the Virginian might soon head up that department. A report published in the *Savannah Republican* (27 February) speculated that Davis would move Benjamin from War to State, thus creating an opening for Lee. As it turned out, Benjamin did become Secretary of State, but the War Department post went to another Virginian, George Wythe Randolph, grandson of Thomas Jefferson.

Then on 2 March, Lee received a terse, noncommittal telegram from Davis ordering him to Richmond. When he arrived there, he discovered he was being nominated for the newly created office of "Commanding General of the Army," a bureaucratic position, which, in the opinion of many, meant that Davis (through Lee) planned to be his own Secretary of War.

On the day Lee learned that he was returning to Richmond, he wrote a long, introspective letter to his daughter Mildred. Things did indeed look grim, he conceded, but in his opinion the South had not yet "suffered enough, labored enough, repented enough, to deserve success."

> Our people have not been earnest enough, have thought too much of themselves & their ease, & instead of turning out to a man, have been content to nurse themselves & their dimes, & leave the protection of themselves & families to others. To satisfy their consciences, they have been clamorous in criticizing what others have done, & endeavoured to prove that they ought to do nothing. This is not the way to accomplish our independence. I have been doing all I can, with our small means & slow workmen, to defend the cities & coast here. Against ordinary numbers we are pretty strong, but against the hosts our enemies seem able to bring everywhere, there is no calculation. But if our men will stand to the work, we shall give them trouble & damage them yet. They have worked their way across the marshes, with their dredges, under cover of their gunboats, to the Savannah River, above Fort Pulaski. I presume they will endeavour to reduce the fort & thus open the way to their heavier vessels up the river. But we have an interior line they must force before reaching the city. It is this line we are working, slowly to my mind, but as fast as I can drive them.[17]

These words reveal a somewhat petulant Lee, quick to criticize others (especially civilians) and equally quick to assert that he, for one, certainly was doing his part.

So, what did the future hero gain from these months on the South Carolina-Georgia coast? Freeman tells us he learned how to handle a scattered command (some 25,000 men by the time he departed), acquired new appreciation for the value of rail communications, and had his faith in defensive earthworks reaffirmed. All of these things may be true, but this United States Army veteran also gained new respect for amphibious warfare and received a quick refresher course in the frustrating business of civilian-military relations. Yet there is a note of fatalism and resignation in his personal letters that bodes ill for the future. He talks not of victory but of sufficient suffering, labor, and toil to "deserve success." And success, according to Lee, would be possible only if *all* citizens pitched in and did their part, a desirable but very elusive goal.

Nevertheless, this gentleman from Virginia could take pride in his accomplishments in South Carolina. He came a question mark and departed with the respect of thousands. The *Charleston Daily Courier* (27 January) called him "our wise-headed and wise-hearted General." A month later, the *Mercury* (28 February), expressing regret that Lee might leave to join the Davis cabinet, said he had exhibited "great judgment, tact, and energy throughout his career in South Carolina, while his urbane manners and great dignity have heightened the favorable impression he has produced as commanding officer of this department."

Perhaps most important of all, his astute handling of coastal defenses erased memories of both "Granny" and "Evacuating" Lee. The hundreds of soldiers who dug the earthworks before Savannah— "the interior line" in which Lee took such pride—grumbled and griped as they shoveled and did menial labor they considered beneath the dignity of white men. But as they sweated and cursed, they also gave Robert E. Lee a new and very appropriate nickname: "the King of Spades."[18]

With one major exception—the intense bombardment of Fort Sumter and Charleston that began in August 1863—the sporadic clashes spawned by what Lee called "marauding parties" were typical of what would occur in South Carolina throughout the remainder of this struggle. On the local scene, this was a war, for the most part, of reconnaissance, small groups of armed men probing for weak spots in enemy lines and the inevitable encounters that resulted from such probes. On only two occasions would these confrontations flare up into full-scale operations costing the Union more than one hundred lives—at Secessionville on 16 June 1862 (107) and during an assault on Fort Wagner on 13 July 1863 (246).[19]

*"The Great Skaddle" of the inhabitants of Charleston, S.C., when
threatened by an attack from Union troops. From a sketch by
Lieutenant G.P. Kirby, 47th N.Y. Vols., while a prisoner in Charleston.*

Frederick H. Dyer's *Compendium of the War of the Rebellion*, source
of these totals, lists over one hundred skirmishes in this state, together
with eighteen affairs, fifteen engagements, fourteen actions, nine assaults, and four bombardments, as well as a handful of expeditions,
reconnaissance forays, demonstrations, sieges, and raids.[20] Even during
Sherman's eight-week march, Union casualties resulted largely from
minor skirmishes and were, according to Dyer, relatively rare: 450 killed,
2,043 wounded, 1,301 missing. And for this, Sherman perhaps should
thank (of all people) his adversary and outspoken critic, Wade Hampton. An Illinois officer, Major Charles W. Wills, says that, shortly after
leaving Columbia, his unit intercepted a message from Hampton to
Matthew C. Butler ordering the latter to cease destroying bridges and
dispense with tactics calculated to delay Sherman's progress: "For God's
sake let him get out of the country as quickly as possible." (And, one
might add, on into North Carolina.) Wills agreed—"Were I one of the
S.C. chivalry I'd be in favor of turning out en masse and building roads
for him."[21]

Late in March, now in Goldsboro, General W. T. Sherman wrote an
intriguing letter revealing the human side of civil strife. It was addressed
to a personal friend, Caroline Carson, daughter of the late James L. Petigru
of Charleston. Mrs. Carson, staunch Unionist like her father, left South

Carolina for Manhattan in the spring of 1861. While the general was in Savannah preparing to invade her native state, she wrote asking him to look out for the welfare of her mother (a refugee in Summerville) and a son, who—much against her wishes—had enlisted in the Confederate Army.

On January 20, the Union commander replied, promising to do whatever he could. Then, on 24 March, writing from North Carolina, again in his own hand, he noted he had not gone to Summerville but thought her son safe with rebel forces near Raleigh. Sherman expressed hope she was in touch with various family members and all soon would be reunited in "harmony & peace." But it is the opening sequence of this Goldsboro letter that most intrigues us today, an enigmatic phrase that says both a great deal and nothing: "I could tell you much of interest of South Carolina, but do not have the time."[22]

South Carolinians of postwar decades would like an expansion of these sixteen words...especially an explanation of the fire that engulfed Columbia on the night of 17-18 February 1865. This celebrated blaze, which sparked heated debate that still can be renewed with ease, swept through a thirty-six-block area destroying 458 structures, about one-third of the city, including virtually the entire business district. Southerners were quick to blame Sherman, charging he personally conceived and coordinated the entire affair; however, numerous attempts to prove such allegations have been unsuccessful.

Marion Brunson Lucas, author of *Sherman and the Burning of Columbia*, published in 1976 by the Texas A & M University Press, provides the most recent, in-depth analysis of this controversial episode. That confusion reigned as homefront became soil contested by rival armies should surprise no one. On the evening of the 16th, Wade Hampton informed Mayor Thomas J. Goodwyn that his forces would leave the next morning. At the same time, he made two fateful decisions. Richmond decreed that cotton be taken to the outskirts and burned, lest it fall into enemy hands. Thus, as a first step, the contents of various warehouses were dumped into the streets. However, Hampton was unable to complete the process and, fearing what might happen, ruled the cotton should not be set ablaze. Secondly, following consultation with General Beauregard (his immediate superior), he decided not to destroy substantial liquor supplies, both men taking the view such things were primarily private property and not under military jurisdiction. Meanwhile, departing Confederates and civilians began to plunder stores, shops, and railway freight. Motives undoubtedly were mixed—deny

Fleeing before Sherman's "Grand March."

goods to the invader, as well as settle scores with merchants who had been charging what they thought were exorbitant prices.

At about 10 a.m. on the morning of the 17th, the mayor and three members of the city council met a Union colonel north of town to whom they surrendered South Carolina's capital. As federal troops moved in, both blacks and whites greeted them with liquor in cups, bottles, and buckets. During the afternoon, Sherman set up headquarters, posted guards at some homes, if asked to do so, and tried to establish order. To sundown, the scene was chaotic, which was to be expected, but not especially alarming. Small fires burned here and there, some having been started by retreating Confederates, others by Union forces. Local firemen were able to contain all of these outbursts except one near the center of town, which, fanned by a high northwest wind that arose as darkness fell, quickly raced through the business district and adjoining streets.

Among those who tried to stem the flames were scores of blue-clad soldiers, including General Sherman himself. At the same time, other Yankees—often drunk—were torching homes and seizing whatever they could find. Civilians who lived through this night of horror have only utter contempt for the invader en masse, yet intermingled with their scorn are tales of individual generosity and heroism.

In the opinion of Lucas (a native South Carolinian and a graduate of the University of South Carolina), all of those involved must share blame for what happened. Confederate leaders, he says, failed to keep local citizens informed concerning the course of events and, by February 1865, their policy concerning the destruction of cotton made no sense whatsoever. He faults both sides for not destroying liquor and especially Sherman's officers for not acting decisively against drunken troops, who, in effect, mounted a riot in the midst of a raging inferno. And then there was the wind, which he believes probably made the task of fighting so many fires at once well nigh hopeless. Yet as horrifying as that night was, Columbia's experience should be put in context. Some two hundred buildings went up in smoke when the Confederates burned cotton as they withdrew from Charleston on 17 February, and during these weeks Hardeeville, Barnwell, Orangeburg, and several other South Carolina communities experienced chaos, flames, and terror.[23]

Some of the land action in and around Charleston, although it dragged on for several years, followed much the same pattern as the warfare waged by Sherman's men as they ravaged their way across the Palmetto State, that is, countless little shoot-outs as various patrols sparred for advantage. However, this snail's-pace maneuvering was augmented by Union bombardment from heavy guns (both army and navy), and shells bursting over ramparts or in city streets clearly are more eye-catching than lonely figures slogging through swampland and marsh. In addition, this spectacular type of combat blurred civilian and military roles in an alarming fashion. In short, homefront and battle lines often were one and the same.

Yet, as terrifying as federal shelling may have been at times, Charlestonians managed to adjust to such realities. Some left the city, but most simply moved out of range of Union artillery; and, if a Confederate report of 6 January 1864 is true and not mere bravado, the results were much less devastating than one might suppose. According to this summary, between 13 August and 31 December 1863, only five residents were killed and 126 buildings hit, forty-one of them sustaining merely minor damage. Observers stationed in the tower of St. Michael's Church, whose job it was to keep score, said 472 shells were lobbed into the city (21 August-5 January), but two-thirds of them failed to explode.[24]

Mrs. Henry A. DeSaussure told her sister that the initial bombardment in August 1863 caused "great excitement and indignation" and prompted most businesses to move "*much* beyond Calhoun St." The poor sought refuge at the race course and in open squares, she wrote, but she and her family remained at home. Mrs. DeSaussure maintained they felt reasonably safe since "their range is directed against all lofty Objects, and both nights that· they sheled [sic], the missiles passed beyond us. I take the precaution of having a tub of water in all the rooms. It is now three nights that we have slept in peace. None of us has been really alarmed, but it creates a solemn feeling to hear the screaming noise that some of the shells make." They were packed, she added, and ready to leave, but the railroads were jammed and it was nearly impossible to ship goods.[25]

Three months later, on 27 November 1863, fifteen-year-old Arthur Brailsford Wescoat of Monck's Corner visited the city and dined with "Uncle Washy," whose family was in Summerville. Shelling continued throughout the meal, he noted in his diary, but "the people seem not to mind it much." However, in January his father returned from Charleston and reported "the shells were bursting up town as high as Hudson Street where Uncle Washy's house is." As a result, the elder Wescoat left immediately for home and his daughter departed for Summerville.[26]

The most complete account of these hectic times—and even heavier shelling occurred in the months that followed—is found in E. Milby Burton's *Siege of Charleston, 1861-1865*, first published by the University of South Carolina Press in 1970 and now in its sixth printing. But even Burton concedes at the outset that Charleston's ordeal (587 days of intermittent shelling) differs from most sieges since, throughout all those weeks and months, "the back door was open." In other words, the city was not encircled by an enemy force, and communication and transportation links to the rest of the state remained intact. Meanwhile, by Burton's calculations, Fort Sumter was reduced to rubble during three great bombardments: 17 August-8 September 1863, 26 October-6 December 1863, and 7 July-8 September 1864. However, despite amphibious assaults as well, the brave little garrison stubbornly refused to give up. In fact, Burton believes the defenders actually were in a stronger position in September 1864 than at some moments during the previous year. And this, he writes, in the face of pounding by army and navy guns that would not be equalled until the World War I campaign at Gallipoli.

In addition to Charleston and coastal communities stretching south to Beaufort, there was one other focus of enemy activity, albeit minor, the Georgetown area to the north, site of South Carolina's third seaport town. In 1862 the Union blockade was extended to that region; and, in the absence of a substantial Confederate force, federal gunboats explored the rivers and bays of the area pretty much at will. The result was flight of hundreds of slaves to the enemy and transfer of still more to inland plantations to thwart such escapes. In the words of George C. Rogers, Jr., the Union navy and a covey of blockade runners played a "cat-and-mouse game" until 25 February 1865 when federal troops occupied

Georgetown, something they could have done with ease at almost any stage of the conflict.[27]

War exhibited various faces in South Carolina, 1861-1865. Shells bursting over Charleston Harbor and Sherman's march captured the attention of contemporary observers, as well as that of scores of historians and would-be historians, but this actually is the story of many small, seemingly inconsequential clashes. The participants might be Confederate and Union troops on patrol along the coast south of Charleston, the crews of federal gunboats exploring inlets and bays near Georgetown, or enrolling officers pursuing deserters and "Tories" in the hills of Anderson, Greenville, and Spartanburg districts. Yet much of the state was spared the sound of gunfire and the turmoil of sectional strife until the final months of the Civil War. Even then, some inland communities not in Sherman's path never heard a volley fired in anger. This is far from saying that the residents of these towns, villages, and farms were not affected by the tragic events of the 1860s, which, of course, gave birth to and created the homefront in South Carolina.

NOTES

[1] *War of the Rebellion: a Compilation of the Official Records of the Union and Confederate Armies* (130 vols.: Washington, 1880-1901), First Series, LIII, p. 13. Du Pont, head of the group that planned this operation, wrote these words to Secretary of the Navy Gideon Welles on 13 July 1861.

[2] Those interested in wartime life on South Carolina's Sea Islands would do well to consult Willie Lee Rose's award-winning *Rehearsal for Reconstruction: The Port Royal Experiment*, published in 1964.

[3] Douglas Southall Freeman, *R.E. Lee, a Biography* (4 vols.; New York, 1934-35), I, p. 607. The final chapter in this volume, pp. 605-31, discusses Lee's experiences in the southeastern states. Freeman could find no proof of the round-robin protest.

[4] Clifford Dowdey (ed.), *The Wartime Papers of R. E. Lee* (Boston, 1961), p. 86. Lee's fatalism and preoccupation with sin and suffering are apparent in this letter written in Charleston on 15 November. Commenting on the death of a relative's baby daughter, he observed, "Happy little creature to be spared the evil of this world." Three days later, in a message to his wife, he repeated his conviction that the dead child was indeed "happy." For a perceptive analysis of Lee's complex personality see Thomas L. Connelly, *The Marble Man: Robert E. Lee and His Image in American Society* (Baton Rouge, 1977).

[5] According to Freeman, Lee commandeered an abandoned structure (later destroyed), which probably was the home of Mrs. George Chisolm Mackay.

[6] The total coastal force reported by South Carolina authorities (which Lee later said was grossly exaggerated) included 13,000 men organized into twenty-six units. Only four of them, however, had more than a thousand men on their rolls, those stationed at Grahamville, Hardeeville, Huguenin's Neck, and Charleston. The overall figure included 125 cadets at the Citadel and sixty at the College of Charleston.

[7] Reverend J. William Jones, who published his *Reminiscences* of Lee in 1876, allegedly quoted this elegant description from a recent volume of Hayne's works. Citing Hayne, Jones says the poet saw Lee at Fort Sumter in the spring of 1861. Freeman, quoting Jones, moves the event to the summer of that year and then quickly adds that it probably occurred during Lee's visit in November.

[8] *War of the Rebellion*, First Series, VI, p. 320.

[9] Ibid., p. 366. For an analysis of Ripley's career, see C. A. Bennett, "Roswell Sabine Ripley: Charleston's Gallant Defender," *South Carolina Historical Magazine* (July 1994), pp. 225-42.

[10] The *Charleston Mercury* (25 December 1861) cites Lee among contributors. This was a rather liberal sum since his salary when he returned to Richmond in March 1862 was only $400 a month.

[11] Dowdey, pp. 92-93. The *Charleston Mercury* (21 December 1861) echoed these sentiments, emphasizing that only "a government mad with fury and revenge" would attempt such a dastardly deed. The *Mercury* agreed this indicated no attack upon the city was contemplated.

[12]This dispute concerning freedom on the high seas erupted when two Confederate diplomats (James Mason and John Slidell) were taken from the *Trent*, a British vessel, by an American captain, Charles Wilkes, and imprisoned in Boston. Although London talked of war, the matter was resolved peacefully and the men released.

[13]Dowdey, p. 96.

[14]Ibid., pp. 98-99.

[15]*Charleston Mercury*, 9 January 1862.

[16]Twelve days later, an overly ambitious Yankee colonel reported that he had landed at a point on Edisto Island only twenty-five miles from Charleston. Although surrounded by the enemy, he expressed the view that, given 10,000 men, "we" could be in that city "in less than three days." See *War of the Rebellion*, First Series, VI, pp. 89-90.

[17]Dowdey, pp. 121-22.

[18]Shelby Foote, *The Civil War: A Narrative* (3 vols.; New York, 1958-1974), I, p. 131. Writing from Savannah to his daughter on 19 October 1861, Langdon Cheves, Jr. (1836-1863), commented, "If coats of arms come in fashion again I think the family has earned the right to the shovel for its device" (Langdon Cheves West Papers, South Carolina Historical Society).

[19]The Secessionville clash occurred during an ill-fated Union drive to seize James Island. The fighting at Fort Wagner on Morris Island led to a successful siege that permitted federal troops to turn their big guns on both Fort Sumter and Charleston. One other encounter also exacted a heavy Union toll when 91 men died at Honey Hill (Grahamville) on 30 November 1864. For an account of this action see Leonne M. Hudson, "A Confederate Victory at Grahamville: Fighting at Honey Hill," *South Carolina Historical Magazine* (January 1993), pp. 19-33. Note: Since the Confederates usually were in a defensive mode, their losses generally were less than those of the Union during warfare that occurred in South Carolina.

[20]See Dyer, *A Compendium of the War of the Rebellion* (3 vols.; New York and London, 1959), II, pp. 831-36. This work is largely a summary of Union military activity, paying only passing attention to naval operations and Confederate maneuvers.

[21]Charles W. Wills, *Army Life of an Illinois Soldier* (Washington, 1906), p. 357. Distressed by drunkenness he saw as Union troops entered Columbia, Wills said before the famous fire began, "I think the city should be burned, but would like to see it done decently." When it happened, he and his colonel tried to restore order. Then, as Wills was about to leave South Carolina a few weeks later, he wrote in his diary, "I think she has her 'rights' now. I don't hate her anymore." Note: Matthew Calbraith Butler (1836-1909) was born in Greenville but went to live with an Edgefield uncle in 1850 and, as lawyer and politician, became associated with that community.

[22]This correspondence can be found in the James L. Petigru Papers in the Manuscripts Division, Library of Congress. In reply to Caroline's query as to why he did not migrate, her father replied he could not do so. He was getting $5,000 a year to

revise the South Carolina Code in the midst of war. As an emigré he would be a beggar. It might be noted that both Petigru and Benjamin Perry, despite their opposition to secession, won re-election as trustees of South Carolina College in December 1861.

[23]Sherman's army did not establish a military presence in February 1865; he and his men simply passed through. Only in May of that year were garrisons set up throughout much of the state. Thus, once the Yankees left on 21 February, Columbia residents were free to discuss and ponder their fate. The result fueled bitter public debate between Sherman and Hampton, each blaming the other for the fire. On the local level there appears to have been a sense of guilt or collective embarrassment at work, many well aware they had done little to impede enemy progress. So, if Sherman burned their city according to some preconceived plan, they reasoned that no exertions on their part could have prevented the disaster than ensued.

[24]*War of the Rebellion*, First Series, XXVIII, Part I, pp. 682-84. Major Henry Bryan, author of this report, conceded some shells that fell in burnt and deserted sections probably went unreported and a few missed the city entirely. "People are occasionally found living in the lower part of the city," he added, "apparently indifferent to the danger of the enemy's fire. I think there are a good many west of Meeting Street."

[25]Mrs. H. A. DeSaussure to Mrs. Joseph Glover, ? August 1863, Henry William DeSaussure Letters, Special Collections Library, Duke University.

[26]Nell S. Graydon (ed.), "Journal of Arthur Brailsford Wescoat, 1863, 1864," *South Carolina Historical Magazine* (April 1954), pp. 85-86, 88. In June 1864, Wescoat again spent a few days in Charleston. During that time he and his friends went up in the Orphan House "steeple" to get a good view of action taking place in the harbor and then strolled down to the Battery. A short time later a shell "dropped a short distance ahead of us striking S. Mikell's Church and cutting off a limb of a tree on Broad St. (p. 97)." Wescoat (1848-1941), who subsequently ran away and joined the Confederate cavalry, was Charleston's last Civil War veteran. The original manuscript of this unusual teenage diary is now in the Special Collections Library, Duke University.

[27]George C. Rogers, Jr., *History of Georgetown County, South Carolina* (Columbia, 1970), p. 410.

III

SHORTAGES, SPECULATION & SELF

In a nutshell, these three words sum up civilian life in South Carolina, 1861-1865. Because of war, many ordinary, even essential items became scarce, which gave birth to unscrupulous speculation and led all too often to displays of unabashed selfishness. There are, of course, other "s" words that come to mind such as substitutes (both for things in short supply and in reference to those donning uniforms in place of individuals who, when drafted, chose not to heed the call), and suspicion (haunting fear that one's family, neighborhood, town, or district was contributing more than its fair share to the war effort)…as well as three commodities that suddenly became worth their weight in gold: salt, shoes, and soap. One could add slavery and secession to the list, plus sex, which seemed to become increasingly blatant and exceedingly daring as the years rolled on.

The causes of shortages are perhaps all too obvious. Among them were the Union blockade, few manufacturing facilities in an overwhelmingly agricultural realm, and a ragged rail network that grew ever more tattered as war took its toll. In fact, the railroads had so many accidents and service became so unreliable that, when Mrs. Thomas Smyth talked in 1863 of shipping furniture to Summerton, her son advised leaving it in their Charleston home: "The risk from the yankees is less than the risk from the R. R."[1] Added to these factors were wartime speculation in and hoarding of scarce goods, the necessity to outfit thousands of men with clothing, shoes, blankets, guns, and ammunition (by a people possessing a minimum of such things, it might be noted), and a central government that impressed goods in random fashion and failed to deal effectively with either speculation or inflation.

The best analysis of this subject is, of course, Mary Elizabeth Massey's path-breaking work, *Ersatz in the Confederacy: Shortages and Substitutes on the Southern Homefront*, first published by the University of South Carolina Press in 1952 and re-issued in 1993 with a new introduction by Barbara Bellows. This book—expanding on the work of Frank Owsley, Bell I. Wiley, E. Merton Coulter, Charles Ramsdell, Ella

70

BLOCKADE GOODS,
JUST RECEIVED.

20 DOZ. Gent's White COTTON SOCKS.
20 doz. Gent's Colored   "   "
20 dcz. Ladies' Colored   "   HOSE.
20 dez.   "   White   "   "
25 doz. Ladies' Colored and Black Lisle Thread Gloves
35 dcz. Gent's Colored and Black Lisle Thread Gloves
50 lbs. Black Flax Thread
800 packs Pins
500 bundles Whalebone
50 doz. Bonnet Frames
20 dez. Colored Chenile Netts
25 doz. Dressing Combs
2,000 yards Homespun
Ladies' and Gent's Linen Cambric Handkerchiefs

ALSO,

A large and handsome collection of White, Grey and Black Straw Bonnets.

ALSO,

100 bundles Whalebone
30 gross English Tooth Brushes
20 dox. Whalebone Corsett Basks.
At   MADAME FILLETTE'S,
sep 30—3   Granite Range, Main street.

DRY GOODS ON COMMISSION

400,000 SUPERIOR NEE-
DLES
1 case English Pins
50 dozen Pen Knives
1 case Shoe Thread
100 Woolen Shawls
1 case Plaid, Domestic.
                    A. L. SOLOMON,
                    111 Richardson street,
          Auctioneer and Commission Merchant.
sep 30—4

500 BOXES

EXTRA FINE CHEWING TOBACCO in store
and for sale by   A. L. SOLOMON,
sep 30—4   111 Richardson street.

MARTELLE BRANDY.

1 CASK extra quality MARTELLE BRANDY,
50 doz. boxes superior OLD COGNAC for sale by   A. L. SOLOMON,
                    111 Richardson street,
          Auctioneer and Commission Merchant.
sep 30—4

$50 REWARD.

I WILL pay FIFTY DOLLARS to any person who will arrest and deliver my boy JOHN to the State Agent for Labor on the Coast I will pay the further sum of FIFTY DOLLARS for the proof and conviction of any white person who may harbor, conceal or employ him during the time he may be liable to labor on the coast defences.   J. H. WILLIAMS.
sep 30—6*

BLOCKADE GOODS!
DIRECT IMPORTATION!

4 BALES WHITNEY BLANKETS
2 bales All Wool ENG. KERSEYS
2 bales Packing TWINE
10 cases 4-4 ENG. LONGCLOTH

FANCY DRESS GOODS, &C.

1 CASE COLORED FANCY FALL GOODS
1 case Silk Warp POPLINS
1 case Saxony and Welsh FLANNELS
1 case Super Blk ALPACAS
1 case Assorted FLAX THREAD.

SUNDRIES.

BLK SEWING SILK
Coates' 200 yd SPOOL COTTON
Gent's Heavy MERINO SHIRTS
English PINS
Pearl Agate BUTTONS
CASSIMERES for Gent's wear
BLK LEAD PENCILS, NEEDLES, &c.

GROCERIES.

SUGARS—Brown and Crushed, wholesale and retail
Blk Pepper, Allspice, Mace, Cloves
Nutmegs, Rhine Wine VINEGAR
COFFEE, Tobacco, Starch, Cooking Soda
FINE SEGARS, Tallow Candles
100 boxes Stearine and Sperm Candles.

WINES, LIQUORS, &C.

MARTEL BRANDY
HENNESSEY BRANDY
BOURBON WHISKEY
CORN WHISKEY
APPLE BRANDY
SANTA CRUZ RUM.
All of our Liquors are guaranteed pure as imported. Domestic Liquors are selected with care and sold as low as can be afforded.

BRO. SHERRY AND LEACOCK
MADEIRA.

Having succeeded in purchasing the balance of these FINE WINES from one of the most eminent importing houses in Charleston, we can confidently recommend these for age and quality.
2 quarter casks Leacock MADEIRA.
1 half cask Newton Gordon SHERRY, imported 1858—vintage 54.

SILCOX, BRO. & CO.,
141, 143, 145 MAIN STREET,
nov 30   COLUMBIA, S. C.

Daily Southern Guardian
(Columbia), 1 October 1863.

Daily Southern Guardian
2 December 1864.

Table 1. Urban Population, 1860

Charleston	40,552	
Columbia	8,052	
Georgetown	1,720	
Camden	1,621	
Greenville	1,518	(slaves not reported)
Yorkville	1,390	(slaves not reported)
Spartanburg	1,216	(slaves not reported)
Sumter	1,119	(slaves not reported)
Orangeburg	897	
Pendleton	854	

As noted, four communities reported only whites and free blacks, not slaves. Only Charleston cited Indians (52). Three centers not listed in this Census Bureau summary—Beaufort, Greenwood, and Cokesbury—had about a thousand residents in 1850. All other towns and villages throughout the state apparently had fewer than 650 inhabitants on the eve of war; however, totals for communities such as Abbeville (592), Edgefield (518), Laurens (429), and Hamburg (404) are incomplete since slaves living within their corporate limits were not recorded.

Source: *Population of the United States in 1860* (Washington, 1864), p. 452; *Statistics of the Population of the United States* (Washington, 1872), pp. 258-60.

Lonn, and others—turned the spotlight of Civil War research to some degree from battlefield to homefront.

In a very general way, the most pressing shortage in urban South Carolina was food, not processed or manufactured goods; in rural areas, the reverse was true. If one lived in Charleston or Columbia, clothing, luxury items, even spices, sugar, and coffee—though costly—were available throughout the entire war, thanks largely to blockade runners. Those residing in smaller communities or in the countryside enjoyed a more varied diet but had limited access to many commodities once found on the shelves of local stores.

On 10 March 1864, for example, Harriott Middleton, a Charleston refugee living in Flat Rock, North Carolina, sent a recipe for simple potato soup to her cousin Susan in Columbia, who also had fled from the lowcountry.

> It is but disguised hot water, but like vice, though abhorred on that account, its victims finally end by preferring it to any thing else. Alice dined out the other day and had all kinds of delicious things to eat, but she confessed to having given a sigh to potato soup and she declared she had been so long debarred from luxuries she found she could not enjoy them! but to the recipe—a small piece of beef or a little piece of bacon two inches square—hot water—potatoes peeled and boiled in it, and then taken out and passed through a colander, and re-added—seasoned with herbs, pepper and salt, any scraps of vegetables I think would be an improvement. Isabella says the bacon is boiled in water for a long time [,] the potatoes only put in an hour before dinner.

Nine days later, Susan thanked her for the recipe but added, "...recommending us to eat potatoes now instead of something else reminds me of the French princess who wondered why the peasantry did not eat white bread when they could not get brown! We have not had potatoes for months and regard them as a first class luxury, entirely beyond our reach."[2]

During these same months Susan offered to shop for Harriott in a Columbia emporium filled with blockade merchandise, the so-called Bee Store, named for Charleston merchant, William Bee. She reported rather disdainfully on 13 January that goods were both inferior and costly, emphasizing she had not joined the crush trying to enter. According to a newspaper account, the rules for shopping were

> push, jam, squeeze, pinch, choke, stick with pins, stab with your elbows, and give as much impudence as possible. It spoils a woman's temper, patience, pride and clothes. Don't come if you can possibly stay away. Buy your goods by proxy, and let that proxy wear pantaloons. If you are frantic to try the experiment, however, rub your face with a brass candlestick before you start, with your pockets bountifully supplied with Confederate notes, a little silver on the tongue, iron in the heart, brass in the

face, and lead in your boots, you may venture forth, but these are indispensable.[3]

In late January, the excitement having subsided, Susan resolved to "venture forth." She found prices "absurd" but thought them perhaps one-fourth less than elsewhere and agreed to make purchases for her relatives in North Carolina. However, the money Harriott sent was counterfeit, and on 12 February Susan returned the bills with detailed instructions on how to recognize bogus currency. In succeeding weeks she told of going to the Bee Store to buy sugar, when, to her amazement, a woman arrived with a baby. But, once the mother was sent to the head of the line, there was a mad scramble for the child..."and the unhappy little thing was dragged about from one to another until it was nearly torn limb from limb."

Shopping, Susan admitted, was difficult and made even more so by counterfeit money and the government's decision to devalue old issues. Since all notes above $5 were to be taxed one-third after 1 April 1864, people in Columbia were hoarding $5 bills and spending larger ones, forcing the Bee Store to lay down a hard rule of *no change*. Instead, one had to take any amount over an initial purchase in soap, soda, and salt. Her friends, Susan commented in passing, "talk much more about the currency than the War."[4]

Of course, the fact that agricultural communities produced foodstuffs should surprise no one. South Carolina, although known for cotton, was growing substantial quantities of corn, wheat, rice, and sweet potatoes in 1860, and pressures (economic as well as legislative) quickly converted cotton fields to these and similar crops. William Elliott, Jr., writing to his mother from Manning in April 1864, described that county seat as a neat little town with plenty of hominy, bacon, and milk. But sixty days later he referred to it scornfully as "greasy bacon and corn country," complaining that chickens were becoming scarce since many residents, especially blacks, were spurning "Memminger trash" (Confederate currency) and taking their poultry to the railroads where they received higher prices.[5]

Similar conditions undoubtedly could be found in many parts of the state during the last years of the war, prompting refugees to move from place to place whenever possible. Sherman's famous march—accompanied by tales of smokehouses broken into and food and animals seized—is additional proof of full larders. Alonzo H. Quint, a Massachusetts chaplain who accompanied Sherman, recorded in his diary that the blue-clads found "forage aplenty" in the Robertville area and in Lawtonville "forage of all kinds was abundant. Men filled their haversacks with salt, fresh pork, and sweet potatoes." The same was true in Winnsboro and Camden; and, writing near Chesterfield on 2 March 1865, Quint noted foragers "found plenty of meat, flour, and bacon." However, they were, he recalls, less successful in and around Columbia, the population of which rose to nearly 20,000 during the war years.[6]

An Illinois man who also accompanied Sherman paints a similar picture. While in Georgia, S. F. Fleharty commented, "Talk of starving the Southern Confederacy! The idea is hugely ridiculous. The people have as much to eat as our own people have, and they raise a great variety of edibles."[7] A few days later, Fleharty remarked perceptively, "*We are fighting railroads.* When these are thoroughly destroyed, the rebel army will be in a sorry condition to oppose us."

As this young man and his companions entered South Carolina, they continued to find forage plentiful. At the same time, he tells how homes were torn down in the southernmost part of the state in order to construct "corduroys" across flooded swampland. Fleharty says nothing about the burning of Columbia; but, like Quint, he found great quantities of foodstuffs near Winnsboro. Then on 22 February he and his friends camped at Rocky Mount on the west bank of the Catawba River eight miles above Camden. "Forage was found in the greatest abundance," Fleharty wrote in his diary that evening. "The men brought in a great variety of edibles, including the best of hams and large quantities of flour. All the teams were loaded, and a large amount of forage was thrown away for want of transportation."[8]

This is not to imply that enemy incursions, as well as the depredations of Confederate deserters and renegade cavalry (such as General Wheeler's men) did not cause momentary hardship, for they certainly did...or, for that matter, that some soldier families and urban poor were not hard pressed, 1861-1865. Floride Clemson (John C. Calhoun's granddaughter), who returned to Pendleton in December 1864 after spending the war years in Maryland, found things a bit shabby and old-fashioned but saw "little real want." Luxuries were unattainable and sugar and meat "dear." Nevertheless, she found corn, flour, sorghum, poultry, and even salt plentiful, noting in her diary "& I believe there is little suffering off the tracks of the armies."[9]

Even after armies passed, all was not lost. On 6 April 1865, Edward McCrady, Sr., wrote from Stateburg to his wife, who was living temporarily in Chapel Hill, North Carolina. "The devastation in Sherman's

Mary Boykin Chesnut (1823-1886).

wake," he reported, "by no means came up to the idea I had formed from the newspaper accounts—and I cannot but believe that there is an abundance in the country yet to supply the wants of all, if it be not hoarded by those who have it." McCrady noted that Dick Richardson lost nothing and had contributed nothing to "our side." All of the Manning blacks except two had returned, and the family had lost neither provisions nor wagons, although some mules had been taken by the enemy. The following day McCrady told of smoking meat and looking for leather. If Sumter merchants would accept Confederate money, he added, he might seek some there.[10]

The truly bad times came *after* the war, not during, largely because of political chaos and poor growing seasons. In fact, South Carolina farmers had only one really good harvest between 1865 and 1870, and that was in 1868. Ben Robertson had it right when he wrote in *Red Hills and Cotton* (p. 71), "My grandparents never forgot Lee's surrender and the days of starvation in the South...."

As always, in times of peace or war, the wealthy fare best. In May 1862 garrulous Mary Chesnut hailed Columbia as "a place of good living—pleasant people, pleasant dinners, pleasant drives."

> Here in Columbia the family dinners are the specialty. You call or they pick you up and drive home with you. 'Oh, stay to dinner.' And you stay gladly. They send for your husband. And he comes willingly. Then comes, apparently, a perfect dinner. And they have not had time to alter things or add because of the additional guests. They have everything of the best. Silver, glass, china, table linen — damask — &c. &c. And then the planters live 'within themselves,' as they call it. From the plantation comes mutton, beef, poultry, cream, butter, eggs, fruits, and vegetables. It is easy to live here....[11]

It was easiest, one might add, for those such as Madame Chesnut describes who had one foot in each world, urban and rural. A year later, William Elliott told his fiancée of equally charming dinners in Camden. The first was a "grand" affair at Colonel John D. Kennedy's—"enough for four times the number of persons. The war don't trouble them much." This lavish display was followed a few days later by an impressive repast at the home of Colonel William Shannon. "Camden is perfectly crowded," he reported.[12] And, as we know, in September 1864 one of the Middletons refugeeing in Summerville, disgusted with a similar gathering of war profiteers, described a local party for "millionaires" where the guests flaunted homespun ($20 a yard), while the servants were dressed in broadcloth ($75 a yard).[13]

So, what were the most pressing shortages on the South Carolina homefront, 1861-1865? The two felt almost universally were salt and leather, followed by coffee, sugar, flour, meat, ice, and a variety of manufactured items such as soap, candles, paper, ink, cloth, thread, needles, cotton cards, medicine, and currency in small denominations...paper bills of $10 or less.[14] Salt was scarce because South Carolinians long had relied upon the cheap Liverpool product that came as ballast in vessels that carried away huge bales of cotton, and for generations animal skins had been discarded during slaughtering, not tanned and converted into leather. Two obvious sources of salt were the Atlantic Ocean and plantation smokehouses where the soil was impregnated with salt that had dripped from hams year after year. In December 1861, the General Assembly passed an act encouraging the manufacture of salt and subsequently published a pamphlet written by John LeConte (1818-1891) telling how to do it. While serving as state superintendent of lead mines, he investigated so-called salt licks in Lancaster, Edgefield, and Laurens district, concluding they were worthless.[15]

The ocean, it turned out, gave up its salt with great reluctance—salt boiling and drying proved to be a tedious, cumbersome process, but uprooting smokehouse dirt produced immediate results. Amelia Rainey of York District informed her daughter-in-law on Christmas Day 1862 that the family killed only eight hogs that season because of the lack of salt. "I think it is very doubtful whether we will have salt enough," she continued, "we made about four bushels out of the floor of the smokehouse. If I can succeed in getting any for you, will let you know right away."[16] On 16 December 1862, the *Charleston Daily Courier* described in great detail the operations of 120 salt-making firms in the city alone, which, it proclaimed, were producing 1,350 bushels each day. Nine months later, the *Mercury* could find only twenty-three. According to this editor's calculations, it cost $9 to produce a bushel of sea salt, which, delivered to the railroad, cost $3 more, yet was selling in the market for $20 to $25...why? More revealing than this query are frequent advertisements offering salt pans and drying equipment for sale, evidence that the process was not truly profitable even at inflated prices.

The leather shortage was especially troublesome since everyone— soldiers, slaves, and civilians of all ages—needed shoes; saddles and harnesses were almost as important, and, to a lesser degree, leather belting was required to transmit steam power. When Mary Dawkins of Union Court House told Jane McLure early in 1865 that boots and shoes were her "especial agony at present," she was giving voice to a cry heard throughout the entire war.[17] At about the same time, Philip Palmer informed his father that he could not get shoes and clothing for his company stationed near Mt. Pleasant. The men, he added, had not been paid since April 1864 and were "perfectly demoralized" and speaking "in a very disloyal way." If they got shoes, clothing, and money he thought they might quit grumbling, but many were threatening to quit if the enemy reached their homes since, in their view, there would be nothing left to fight for…"some have said that they did not care which side was victorious." They were especially critical of men of means who were moving their families to safety, something they could not do.[18]

Yet if Mary and Philip felt frustrated, others—early in the war—saw opportunity. Their ranks include men from Kershaw, Lexington, and Anderson districts who, sent to the coast in 1862, quickly realized an exchange of goods could be mutually beneficial, although none of them should be thought of as full-blown speculators. When John Cantey of Camden arrived in the Georgetown area late in 1862, he marveled at the beauty of the beaches (Myrtle Beach?) and the lovely live oak trees, but his eyes were on the salt works. He thought fleetingly of going into business himself; instead, he and a friend (Tom Ancrum) bought eighty-five bushels of salt to be delivered in ten days at a cost of approximately $10 a bushel. Early in December, while camped at Little River, he sent his wife precise instructions.[19] She was to sell eight to ten bales of cotton, give a man named Gray $600 ($20 in ones and some $10 bills since change was scarce, but all in new issue since the salt boilers would not accept old), and outfit two wagons with covers, mules, and the "best boys" to assist in crossing rivers. Gray, he said, should take care of Ancrum's wagon as well and bring two bushels of meal and at least thirty pounds of meat for himself and the wagon crews. In addition, Cantey requested two bushels of oats he had promised to give the salt makers and suggested this was an opportunity to send "a box of eatables"… perhaps "sausages, a ham, &c." Nevertheless, he assured his wife they were eating well and had plenty of pork, beef, oysters, and fish on hand.[20]

Henry K. Witherspoon, a Camden area resident serving with Cantey, was somewhat less impressed with the coast. In January 1863 he told cousin Ellen Tweed how he and his friends stole pigs and corn because "these plagued half bread yankeys down here will not sell any thing at a reasonable price." Two companions, Witherspoon added, paid $1.50 for a little pan of sausages, but local soap was somewhat cheaper than in Camden, a good turpentine variety selling for fifty cents a bar. Although salt was not mentioned, during these weeks he offered to send Ellen oysters, clams, fish, and perhaps even a turkey if she would dispatch a wagon from her plantation.[21]

Meanwhile, three Barkley brothers from Anderson District stationed near Charleston were shipping rice and salt to their parents, but the principal trade was in leather since at least two of the boys (George and Martin) were skilled shoemakers. In February 1862, Martin asked for still more leather from home: "I have sole all I braut with me and could a sole 100 pair if I had a had them [.] I have bin mending shoes all day to day and hant gut dun [.] my sole leather is almost gawn for I have dun a heap of mending sinse I have got back...."[22] As late as October 1863 this young man was continuing to ship salt and repair shoes: "I am shoe making Every day [.] I could get more to Do than 3 men could but I go on Picket duty Every other Night [.]"[23]

James Michael Barr of Leesville in Lexington District reacted somewhat differently. On duty near Pocotaligo and McClellanville in 1862-1863, he wrote to his wife of plans to buy salt and tan hides but did neither for several months, instead telling her how to trim peach trees, smoke meat, care for their children, and prepare his uniforms. Finally in June 1863 he shipped a barrel of salt to his family, expressing belief others should do the same. Then, a few weeks later Barr arranged to buy sixty bushels at $6 per bushel and reported that several neighbors had come to the coast to get salt, even though the price had increased to $10. Early the following year, much against his will, this young man was transferred to Virginia and in June sent home specific details concerning the cultivation of sugar cane. Wounded that same month, he died in a Charlottesville hospital in August 1864.[24]

Since postal and rail service were unreliable and grew increasingly so, whenever possible goods were transported under the watchful eyes of friends and acquaintances, perhaps a soldier going home on leave or a businessman en route from one community to another. In fact, personal correspondence indicates those who traveled usually were accompanied by letters, boxes of food, a bag of salt, perhaps a tanned hide, and so on...in addition to whatever luggage they might be carrying.

In their search for substitutes, South Carolinians experimented with rawhide and squirrel-skin shoes (really moccasins) and both wooden soles and wooden shoes. By the end of 1864, according to the *Carolina Spartan* (24 November), a factory near Bivingsville was turning out 600 pairs of wooden soles each day. Yet for every individual who scraped a smokehouse floor for salt or thumped about on slabs of wood, a hundred tried their hands at making imitation coffee. This was, above all else, the great food craze of the war. Ersatz coffee was made, at one time or another, from acorns, chinquapins, cotton seed, corn meal, peas, grape seeds, ground-nuts (peanuts), parched corn and rice, persimmons, beets, rye, sugar cane, sweet potatoes, and seeds produced by okra, benne, and milk-vetch plants—all of these ingredients toasted or roasted in some fashion. A Charleston man in July 1862 sang the praises of okra: "The Okra comes in finely for coffee, we take one half Okra to Same of coffee which makes a wholesome & fine drink for breakfast."[25]

But William Elliott, Jr., writing from Greenville a year later, blasted both imitation coffee and what he called "this extortion cursed country," for good measure demanding ten pounds of real coffee at any cost! "Every thing up here is so scarce and badly cooked when to be had," he told sister Emmie in Colleton District. "The only thing we have more of than we want is flies. How different from your fish and crabs, and tomatoes and squashes, and nice cream and clabber." The local rye coffee, he moaned, was "detestible & badly made at that."[26] Rye, on the other hand, got mixed reviews from William Neves, who in 1862 told his mother how to prepare a mixture that he and fellow soldiers had been drinking—"hit is a very good substitute for rio but it dont drink all together as well."[27]

Several factors help to explain this mad scramble. Between 1790 and 1860 American consumption of coffee soared from four million pounds a year to over 200 million, while tea imports only rose from three million to thirty-two million pounds. In the 1840s, for example, it was not unusual for the Charleston market to auction off two or three thousand bags of Brazilian (Rio) coffee in a single week. Not surprisingly, this upsurge in popularity created demand for "cheap" coffee long before 1860, and throughout the early decades of the 19th century various imitations were available. These include "coffee" made from acorns, potatoes, grape seeds, and chicory, each of these ingredients roasted and mixed with perhaps one-third to one-half of the real thing. On 20 November 1851, for example, the *Charleston Daily Courier* was praising the merits of "Essence of Coffee," which, it said, cost only 12½ cents, saving a housewife "4 lbs. of store coffee."

COFFEE! COFFEE! COFFEE!!

A very good coffee can be made, costing only 12½ cents, by mixing one spoonful of coffee with one spoonful of toasted corn meal. Boil well and clear in the usual way. I have used it for two weeks, and several friends visiting my house say they could not discover anything peculiar in the taste of my coffee, but pronounced it very good.

—*Tri-Weekly Watchman* (Sumter), 8 July 1861.

Take Rye, boil it, but not so much as to burst the grain; then dry it, either in the sun, on the stove or [in] a kiln, after which it is ready for parching, to be used like the real Coffee Bean. Prepared in this manner, it can hardly be distinguished from the genuine Coffee. The Rye, when boiled and dried, will keep for any length of time, so as to have it ready whenever wanted for parching.

—*Charleston Mercury*, 8 February 1862.

Take the common *Red Garden Beet*, pulled fresh from the ground, wash clean, cut into small squares the size of a coffee grain or a little larger, toast till thoroughly parched, but not burned, transfer to the mill and grind. The mill should be clean. Put from one pint to one and one half, to a gallon of water, and settle with an egg as is in common coffee. Make and bring to the table hot—with nice fresh cream (not milk) and sugar. I will defy you or anybody else to tell the difference between it and the best Java.

—*Laurensville Herald*, 20 September 1861.

According to the *Augusta Constitutionalist*, chinquapins are said to be a very fair substitute for coffee.

—*Yorkville Enquirer*, 30 September 1863.

Tea, on the other hand, obviously was less popular; but, of greater significance, raspberry leaves, various native herbs, and sassafras (leaves, bark, or roots) provided a reasonable wartime substitute. As a result, tea was taxed 10 percent under tariffs levied in June 1861; coffee was exempt from all import duties.

Most other shortages, as noted earlier, really are self-explanatory. The blockade, wartime dislocations, and an absence of manufacturing plants great and small created problems for all South Carolinians. However, it may be of some solace for their descendants to learn that Northerners faced shortages as well. They, too, because trade was disrupted, sometimes resorted to chicory seed coffee and sugar substitutes. Paper became scarce when rags were used for bandages, and farmers in some regions tried to grow cotton, while others increased their output of tobacco. And the Yankees also battled inflation as prices for most basic foodstuffs doubled between 1861 and 1863.[28] Yet their problems admittedly were minuscule compared with those faced by individuals living in the embattled Confederacy.

In addition to okra coffee and raspberry tea, South Carolinians experimented with pomegranate lemonade, portable soup cakes (bouillon cubes), peach leaf yeast, molasses made from figs and watermelons, bacon cured with hickory ashes and a minimum amount of salt (a Revolutionary War recipe), pepper made from wheat soaked in red pepper tea, and mustard concocted from walnut bark. Candles were fashioned from rosin, lard, myrtle berries, and mutton suet—although some people preferred lightwood chunks or simply performed all of their labor during daylight hours. James Pelot, working at the post office in Hodges in April 1863, told his sister of weighing, marking, and shipping over 250 bales of cotton and also keeping up postal records, all during the day since he had no candles.[29] And, by 1865, when Columbia's gas works no longer functioned, newspapers in that community adapted their publishing schedules to daylight hours.

South Carolinians made soap from mixtures of turpentine, potash, grease, corn shucks, lye, lard, cotton seed, and ley of wood ashes. Old ribbons, broom straw, bamboo roots, elderberries, and the bark of sassafras, beech, and willow trees yielded up various dyes. Sweet-oil bottles became lamp chimneys; wine bottles, tumblers. Ink was made from green persimmons and bark of the bay or dwarf magnolia, maple, and willow. The bean of the ordinary *palma christi*, really a weed, produced castor oil; prickly lettuce (*lactura virosa*), a form of opium. Small dogwood branches, stripped of bark, became toothbrushes, and dogwood berries were touted as a substitute for quinine. Cotton mixed with cow hair (to save wool) was woven into cloth—often with the aid of spinning wheels rescued from obscurity in some dark attic, harnesses were made of canvas instead of leather, buttons fashioned from gourd shells, and pins from various thorns...the latter yet another innovation inspired by Revolutionary War times. The clear gum of plum, peach, and cherry trees often was used to seal envelopes, some of which were turned inside out and recycled.

All of this may sound highly ingenious, but it really was not. As shortages developed, South Carolinians merely reached back into history or turned to less affluent neighbors for guidance, individuals who long had been using dogwood toothbrushes, drinking imitation coffee, making their own dyes and medicines, or perhaps doing without such things as candles and store soap. As noted, some substitutes were inspired by Revolutionary War experiences, and others by more recent conflicts. In June 1862, Mrs. James L. Petigru, who unlike her famous husband was a true Confederate, remarked in a letter to her grandson "that in the War of 1812 I remember well Rye coffee, was used, mixed with the other stuff."[30]

Liquor, as always, was in a unique class by itself, and whether it belongs in the shortage column depends upon one's point of view concerning imbibing, temperance, outright prohibition, and use of spirits as medicine. Demand for grain and corn as food for man and beast certainly was a strong argument against widespread distillation in wartime, and the General Assembly soon was receiving petitions advocating that all distilleries be closed. In December 1862, legislators enacted a law concerning "undue" distillation. Unless a distiller was fulfilling an existing government contract or producing for medicinal purposes, he was to cease operations. Those continuing to do so had to post bond and obtain a license.[31] But four months later all licenses were revoked and agents appointed in each district to supervise production and distribution to physicians and druggists. This ban did not include, however, liqueurs and cordials made from "ordinary fruits of their season."

In effect, this precursor of Ben Tillman's famous dispensary system of the 1890s meant all *legal* liquor was to be handled by the state.[32] Then, in December 1863, the law was amended to encourage production at a reasonable price. As before, each agent had to take an oath and post bond, and doctors and druggists were limited to fifty gallons of whiskey and five gallons of pure alcohol per year.

Since bars continued to flourish in Charleston, Columbia, and other centers throughout the state, these regulations appear to have been meaningless. Distilling, as before, was carried on illegally, at least part of the 500 gallons of alcohol produced each day at a vital medical laboratory housed at Columbia's state fair grounds never reached a hospital or anyone in pain, blockade runners brought in great quantities of liquor, and, at times, it was possible to drink northern whiskey that somehow made its way into South Carolina. In September 1864, a Columbia man advised James Earle Hagood, clerk of the Pickens District Court, that brandy

SPLENDID SUMMER DRINK.

Boil two pounds of mean tobacco in twelve gallons of water; add one bushel of mashed sour apples, and a pint of vitriol [sulfuric acid]—and you have a No. 1 article of whiskey—superior to any on the market. This is an old receipt which many have profitably used.

—*Tri-Weekly Watchman* (Sumter), 3 August 1863.

from his region would not sell well in the state capital because at the moment there was "a great quantity of good imported Liquors at very reasonable prices in the Market." However, he thought whiskey well packed would be welcome.[33] In previous years, as liquor laws were changing, Hagood dealt directly with several Columbia residents, all of them seeking "three gallons of good whiskey for medicinal purposes," these requests usually accompanied by proper documentation. And on the eve of Sherman's visit in 1865, twenty-two Columbia citizens (among them businessman J. H. Heise) were charged with selling liquor without a license. According to the *Daily Guardian* (10 February 1865), most paid a fine of $19.50 for each offense.

Money, much like liquor, was a special type of shortage. The real problem, apparent almost from the day Fort Sumter surrendered, was the absence of coins and small bills with which to make change. This was especially true in rural areas such as Chester District. In October 1861, writing from Lewisville, Isabella Wylie Strait told her son of the acute money shortage that was developing. Lots of people were willing "to do for themselves," but there was no money. "This is not the flourishing country we once had [.] *gone, gone* [.] I fear never to recover [.] in place of peceable Secession awful and horrible war. it almost makes my blood run cold, and where is some of our great men now [—] calm and silent as you please."[34] At about the same time, a neighbor, while relaying hometown news to Gilbert Lafayette Strait, confirmed that there was absolutely no currency in circulation. Folks could not get bills to buy groceries, he said, and merchants refused to sell on time. Even the wealthiest people in the Chester area could not get credit.[35]

Since metal was so scarce, Charleston banks began printing paper currency in the summer of 1861—the Bank of the State of South Carolina issuing notes worth 5¢, 10¢, 25¢, and 50¢; the Bank of Charleston, bills valued at $6, $7, $8, and $9. The following year the city itself announced plans to issue $1 and $2 notes; and in May 1864, in a unique departure, Charleston's Wayside Home, a facility designed to care for ill servicemen and those in transit, began distributing its own currency. These bills, worth one, two, and five dollars and backed by leading citizens, could be redeemed at the Bank of Charleston as soon as a new issue became available on 1 July 1864.[36] But, in a sense, this was one problem that solved itself. During the last year or so of the war, as small bills (and big ones, too) became virtually worthless, no one wanted them, and barter—agricultural produce for salt, cloth, shoes, etc.—became the accepted mode of exchange.[37]

There were at least two other shortages that should be mentioned, both closely related to the war itself. One was niter (saltpeter); the other, lead. Niter, mixed with charcoal and sulfur, creates gunpowder. Charcoal and sulfur were at hand, but niter was not; and, according to E. Merton Coulter, a niter craze was the first great fear to sweep the Confederacy.[38] In an attempt to produce it, many communities—Columbia and Charleston among them—dug pits that were filled with animal carcasses, stable manure, and other decaying matter. The plan was to stir the mixture occasionally, and then drain off the liquid to obtain niter. But the process took longer than anticipated and, in the opinion of many, yielded little save a very offensive odor. In all, according to a report on Columbia's "Saltpetre Plantation" filed in the South Carolina Department of Archives and History, the state spent $112,232.93 on the project before transferring the entire operation to the Confederate government early in 1864.

Lead was needed for bullets, and Spartanburg's Cameron Mine was activated for a time, employing a dozen or so miners. But it also was given to Confederate authorities in January 1864 along with the ill-fated niter experiment. *Reports and Resolutions* (1863) indicates the state spent $12,055 on the mine but obtained only 5,566 pounds of lead, less than one-eighth the return anticipated. More productive, however, were various salvage drives. In the summer of 1862, Columbia's principal Episcopal church (now Trinity Cathedral) presented Confederate authorities with seventeen tons of lead.[39] However, as fighting dragged on, salvage efforts gave way to looting as gangs (often men in uniform) systematically stripped abandoned homes of roof flashing, drain pipes, and plumbing. This was especially true in Charleston where advertisements by junk dealers eager to buy lead, copper, any and all kinds of metal undoubtedly encouraged such behavior. Eventually, in January 1864, local military authorities issued a formal order asking citizens not to purchase copper, brass, zinc, etc. from soldiers.

But, unlike efforts to produce niter, the lead campaign seems to have achieved results, at least until the final months of the war. South Carolinians also tried to manufacture weapons at their State Military Works in Greenville. This facility, organized in 1862 with the aid of men and machinery brought from Nashville when that community fell to Union forces, was supposed to make and repair small arms and produce gun carriages, carbines, shells, and rifle bolts. By October 1863, it had cost taxpayers $252,546.03—largely because of new construction—but had turned out military goods worth only $67,513. According to an army spokesman, the plant was beset with problems. The buildings were shoddy, steam power was expensive, and iron and coal had to be hauled from great distances. In November 1864, when the Confederate government refused to assume control, the governor was authorized to sell the works, but no buyer ever was found.[40] Each of these undertakings— niter production, lead mining, and arms manufacturing—reveal how very difficult it was to develop essential industries from scratch in the midst of war.

Pilfering lead from homes is, however, only one example of widespread theft that plagued communities big and small as shortages became apparent. Slaves often were blamed, hauled into court, convicted, and duly whipped. But, in retrospect, they do not appear to have had any monopoly on petty theft, larceny, burglary, or house breaking. Prime targets were smokehouses, animals, clothing, and leather. The *Camden Confederate* (5 April 1862) vowed robbery was so rampant that the community needed either a special patrol or martial law. In September 1862, saddle skirtings were stolen in broad daylight from horses standing along Yorkville's main street, and in succeeding years mill owners in Greenville and Camden offered rewards for the return of leather belting. Meanwhile, horses disappeared in Abbeville, cows in Charleston, and, for good measure, Sumter's village bulletin board vanished.[41]

In December 1862, $24,000 (soon recovered) was taken from the Confederate Printing Office in Columbia. Two years later, a wounded Louisiana soldier who stopped briefly at the Charlotte Depot in that same city was relieved of most of his belongings, which included an artificial leg wrapped in a blanket.[42] In February 1864, Mrs. William Mason Smith described with horror conditions in Augusta. "...Swap was stolen from the stable yesterday. Men & women are robbed in these streets daily, also in the cars. Clothes stolen out of the tubs & off the ironing table. Our whole world is demoralized—turned topsy turvy."[43]

The following summer, W. W. Walker, owner of Spartanburg's Walker House, offered $1000 for the recovery of goods presumably taken from his hotel. According to the *Carolina Spartan* (21 July), the items included eight pieces of sole leather, a calf skin, eleven gallons of corn whiskey, sixty yards of jeans cloth, sixty pounds of bacon, ten pounds of candy, ten bunches of cotton yarn, a bag of rice, twenty-two plugs of "good" tobacco, a bed quilt, a large blue blanket, and small pair of hand steelyards (weighing apparatus).

Two types of theft—both of which occurred close to the battle lines along the coast—were especially irritating, the first committed by Confederates in uniform, the second by civilians. William John Grayson (1788-1863), a well-known literary figure who defended slavery but was no admirer of secession, railed in June 1862 against the "infamous" plunder to be seen almost everywhere, a circumstance he blamed upon "democratic soldiery."

> War with these people is a season for license. The camp is a barbecue ground with the additional convenience that the parties assembled may plunder any neighbour's house, shoot his pigs and help themselves without scruple to whatever they may fancy in his field or garden. On John's island, during the winter, every house abandoned by the planter was gutted by our troops and the furniture that was not carried away was wantonly destroyed. Pictures served as targets for pistol shots or objects for bayonet practice; the window sashes were smashed and the doors, window shutters and out houses converted into fuel. One gentleman of John's island saw his chairs on the rail road cars. No destruction of Lincoln's men could be more complete and unsparing. We are realizing the adage that laws are silent among arms even where the arms are in the hands of our own people.[44]

Arthur Brailsford Wescoat, a teenager living near Monck's Corner, was equally frustrated, though for somewhat different reasons. His family had been driven from Edisto Island early in the war; and, despite tender age, Wescoat occasionally joined an older brother on army patrols through their old neighborhood. In contrast to Grayson's observations, he found family property in reasonably good shape in January 1863, noting, however, it was painful to see what the Yankees

How to get rid of extortionists.
Southern Illustrated News (Richmond), 19 September 1863.

and blacks had done to John F. Townsend's mansion. The object of his wrath in June 1864 were white squatters who took over abandoned homes in the Monck's Corner area, stole indiscriminately from white and black, and often beat up the latter. In this instance, a Wescoat slave was told to go fishing and, while there, was accosted, beaten, and robbed by one of these white freebooters. As a result, young Wescoat hunted down and berated "the old wretch," threatening to shoot him if he ever dared to do such a thing again. "It is hard for the law to reach these people," he wrote in his diary on 4 June, "and they steal your cows and hogs and beat up your negroes and you can scarcely do anything with them unless you take things in your own hands." [45]

It would be wrong to blame this wave of lawlessness solely upon shortages. Wartime conditions—men away from home and police departments in cities such as Columbia and Augusta overtaxed by transient populations—created the perfect milieu for such activity, as did the stationing of soldiers in regions to which they had no personal ties. And there is always the possibility that simple gain through re-sale—not need nor hunger—was what motivated many to steal. During the final years of the war, Confederate deserters and so-called Tories became exceedingly bold in the upper Piedmont, sometimes pushing homeowners aside (or perhaps shooting them), packing their belongings into wagons, and driving away during daylight hours. A startled Winnsboro family suffered such a fate in January 1865, though it is unclear whether the intruders were deserters or escaped Yankee prisoners. However, chaos inspired by the imminent demise of governmental authority as defeat looms is something quite different from taking goods stealthily for one's own use or with the intent of realizing quick profit.

Turning to speculation, it hardly seems necessary to point out that scarcity quickly attracted the attention of the ambitious, shrewd, foresighted, and unscrupulous, for there was money to be made. In 1861, residents of several communities asked the General Assembly to prohibit speculation in salt, bacon, and other basic foodstuffs, but the question of reasonable profit in wartime was a hard nut to crack. A petition emanating from York District won House approval, even though that body's Committee on Commerce and Manufacturing thought a request for legislation against "extortion in the sale of the necessaries of life" was "inexpedient." The issue for some may have been the difference between *speculation* (buying and selling with expectation of profit through price fluctuations) and *extortion* (wresting goods by illegal means or sheer ingenuity, in effect, stealing). In any case, not until February 1863 did lawmakers take a firm stand. By the terms of legislation passed at that time, anyone convicted of extortion could be imprisoned for up to a year and fined up to $1,000, with half of the sum going to the informer and the rest to the relief of soldier families. However, this law did not apply to foreign imports or goods from other states sold at prevailing prices, nor did it actually address the problem of speculation. But this made little difference. By that date, both crimes—speculation and extortion—were one and the same in the lexicon of most South Carolinians.

> Quoth Meade to Lee,
> 'Can you tell me,
> In the shortest style of writing,
> When people will
> Get their fill
> Of this "big Job" of fighting?'
>
> Quoth Lee to Meade,
> 'Why, yes, indeed,
> I'll tell you in a minute—
> When legislators
> And speculators
> Are made to enter in it.'

—*Charleston Mercury* (18 April 1864), quoted from the *Charlottesville Daily Chronicle*.

Almost any diary or collection of letters details the upward spiral of prices during the war years. In November 1861, David Harris, who lived near Spartanburg, took some hides to be tanned, noting "leather has got to be so high that I prefer this to selling." Two months later he remarked that coffee and salt were not available at any price and cotton cards now cost from $5 to $10. On 9 March 1862, he wrote, "The war is assuming a rather ugly appearance. The people are becoming alarmed. I think that war is not the game of fun that they did at the commencement." [46] The following month salt was selling for $20 a sack, and in October 1862 Harris noted the price had jumped to $125.

Thoughts recorded in the diary of John B. Patrick, a mathematics instructor at Columbia's Arsenal Academy, tell a similar story. On 21 December 1861 he was shocked when he had to pay $16 for a sack of salt: "How men can remain quietly at home, attending to their own business, and thus extort from the families of those who are serving their country, I should be at a loss to imagine were it not that I know human nature is utterly depraved and weak." Six days later Patrick discovered the price had risen to $25 and by October 1862 stood at $100. This produced an angry outburst against speculators, followed by this entry on 29 October after failing to secure shoes for Negroes and clothing for himself: "I find everything in that line selling at three or four prices—the inevitable result, when the demand is great and the supply small. It is

SPECULATORS (For the *Watchman* by F. Gamewell Puckett)

In lies they're adepts, in deceit they're fiends,
From every virtuous thought and honor weaned,
In meanness, graduated at its school,
Of every avaricious thought a tool.
In perjury, well versed (though some are young),
Blasphemies in crowds hang on their tongues.
RAPE, MURDER, ROBBERY, their delight,
Friends—to 'old Nick' they love the Night,
Could their black hearts be seen within,
'Twould fright a devil from his den.
The orphan's tears, the widow's moan,
A country's suffering, bleeding groan
All fall alike, unheard, before
His vile, black heart, and's heard no more.
Though hell of miscreats, vile and mean
With hearts of horrid, fearful mien
Is composed, yet the sign board's there,
NO SPECULATORS ENTER HERE.
Far less their chance is to obtain
A seat in heaven, where free from pain
Repose their victims saved from strife
And 'portioned to eternal life.
O, righteous ROPE why dost thou sleep
While orphans, widows, DEVILS weep
And crimes in black confusion roll
O'er our country's troubled soul?
O let the joyful, glorious day
Of JUSTICE be not far away
When our bright, peaceful land shall be
From such vile imps and villains free.

—*Tri-Weekly Watchman* (Sumter), 2 February 1863.

probable, however, that heartless speculators have had a great deal to do with creating these fabulous prices, for such they are."

There was one man who, throughout 1862, fought to stem the tide, although he may not have understood "Economics 101" as well as Patrick. Charlestonian John Bachman (1790-1874)—Lutheran pastor, amateur naturalist, friend and benefactor of John James Audubon—was stirred to action as a result of his work in behalf of soldiers in both camps and hospitals, and in the spring of that year he composed a rambling, five-part treatise attacking "Monopolizers, Forestallers and other Extortioners."[47] Incensed by the price of food in the wake of what farmers and planters boasted had been the best provision crop in history, Bachman expressed alarm at "the spirit of selfishness and avarice which has exhibited itself within the last few weeks in our Southern country...." Yet he conceded on 23 April that not *all* farmers and planters were guilty of extortion.

Target number two was the manufacturer, especially the operations of William Gregg of Graniteville and the well-known Saluda Factory of J. G. Gibbes near Columbia. Both men were, he claimed, paying one-third less for cotton, yet their prices were up 100 percent! Gregg, Bachman noted, at least published a price list; Gibbes did not.

For target number three, the speculator-extortioner, Bachman saved his special scorn. These were the men who, after pleading exemption from military service, stored vast quantities of salt that they sold for many times the original cost, ran up prices at auctions, unloaded old stocks of dry goods they once were unable to sell, and sent agents scurrying about the countryside to buy up bacon in order to corner the market and create a monopoly.

> They are the Shylocks that creep along our Rail Roads, purchase up the poultry and eggs, and compel us to pay a hundred per cent. as a contribution to their cunning and niggardly exploits. These men, however clamorous for the rights of the South, have not a spark of patriotism in their ignoble souls. Whilst the mass of the community are laboring and suffering in their country's cause, they are the slaves of avarice, and if they can only succeed in their speculations, they are content, although the country may be ruined, and the patriotic, the virtuous, and the good, may be reduced to beggary by the success of their nefarious schemes.

Bachman then harked back to the dark days of the American Revolution, from which he tried to draw encouragement, ending with lavish praise for southern womanhood—unselfish, patriotic, courageous—"Blessed woman, thou wilt yet save the country!" [48]

Part IV, which appeared on 30 April, called for an immediate return to pre-war prices, creation of charitable committees to aid the poor, and a more cooperative spirit among all of those involved: farmers, planters, manufacturers, merchants, government officials, railroad directors, and "ladies." "A united people who resolve to be free," Bachman thundered, "cannot be subdued." This probably was the conclusion to the original essay, but on 28 April the *Courier* published an anonymous letter signed "Fact" stressing that price was simply the result of supply and demand. Nothing done by governments, armies, or legislatures could, in this writer's opinion, change "the law of trade." How, he asked, could anyone be expected to sell at one-half of the market value? If the poor cannot pay the price, they must do without or resort to charity. If the choice was charity, then "Fact" advised Bachman to go forth and help the poor with good works, but to cease heaping blame upon "those who happen to live by selling the article in question."

Meanwhile, J. G. Gibbes wrote to Columbia's *South Carolinian* defending his actions and furnishing a brief history of his company, words reprinted in the *Courier* on 29 April. He and his associates, he said, bought the Saluda Factory in 1855, spent a considerable sum renovating it, and up to July 1861 had lost $20,000. Why? Largely because of "want of home patronage" while South Carolinians bought northern products. At the moment he was selling yarn to local residents for less than he could have gotten for it in New Orleans and for which he obviously was getting little thanks. And, Gibbes added, he *had* contributed to the support of the poor since the fighting began.

Bachman's Part V, published in the *Courier* on 10 May, was a direct assault upon Gibbes, during which he praised Daniel McCollough of Fairfield District and Joseph Starke Sims of Grindall [sic] Shoals, Union, who, in contrast to Gibbes, had not raised the price of their cotton yarn. Three days later, the sharp reply of Gibbes appeared in that same daily. In essence he charged Reverend Bachman clearly had lost his temper, perverted facts, and really did not know what he was talking about. "Your idea of Christian charity," Gibbes observed caustically, "seems to be to practice the opposite of what you are told to teach—to judge and condemn others, whose business you profess to know better than themselves."

There matters stood until Bachman, writing from Columbia after returning from the Virginia battlefields, published a letter in the *Courier* (18 October 1862) telling of horrors committed by Yankees. In the process he alluded to harm being done to the Confederate cause by "unconscionable extortioners," three-fourths of whom, he vowed, were Jews. Four days later, L. I. Moses answered Bachman with a short note that included this stinging phrase: "Your motive surely cannot be to prepare the public mind for religious persecution...." [49] Then on 7 November yet another "supply and demand" letter appeared in the *Courier* signed by "Domestic Industry." And on 12 November, Bachman published a final volley, much of it Scripture, designed to prove that extortion was indeed a terrible sin.

During the war various stratagems were tried in an effort to alleviate conditions that so distressed this well-meaning clergyman. In April 1862, for example, the Sumter town council passed an ordinance calculated to curb speculation. This decree, which appeared in the *Tri-Weekly Watchman* on 11 June, forbade shipment of basic foodstuffs except to fill government contracts. This ban did not apply, however, to whatever relatives and friends sent in good faith to men in uniform. If convicted, an offender might be fined $50 and goods involved given to the family of a local soldier.

At about the same time, Charleston opened its Free Market for military dependents. By April 1863 it was supporting 800 families at a cost of $10,000 a month. [50] Patterned after similar benevolent organizations in New Orleans, Mobile, and Savannah, this institution undoubtedly was a godsend to many but always teetered on the brink of disaster, about to shut down for lack of funds. Then in April 1864, the city council passed a complex ordinance designed to limit sale of foodstuffs to a single site, the municipal market, where transactions could be more easily supervised. Columbia tried yet another approach, setting up a Mutual Supply Association in which individuals bought shares. Anyone who owned a $100 share could buy up to that amount in goods at the association store each week, presumably at more attractive prices than found elsewhere. If a member did not use up his $100 allotment, then those too poor to purchase shares could acquire goods equal to the balance. The Columbia city council also tried to prevent re-sale of foodstuffs until they had been displayed for at least two hours. In addition, Richmond published official price schedules for the entire nation, which, as "Fact" predicted, had little impact. In October 1863, the citizens of Robertville in Beau-

---

SUMMARY OF CHARLESTON'S FREE MARKET RULES

1. Recipients shall be wives, widows, and families of soldiers, sailors, and those in "the privateering Service."

2. Market days shall be Monday, Wednesday, Friday, and Saturday, 8 am to 1 pm.

3. Applicants must provide clerk with vital information such as residence, marital status, number of children, etc. If married, shall furnish marriage certificate or certified copy; if single, a certificate of character endorsed by two respectable citizens. Upon approval, clerk will issue a ticket indicating how many rations an applicant may receive.

4. Rations are to be distributed in accordance with the number of persons in a family.

5. Property owners and those with sufficient income to maintain a family shall be debarred from the Free Market.

6. Members of the General Committee are to be present each market day (in rotation) to supervise distribution of supplies.

7. Any applicant "using indecorous language, being inebriated, finding fault with the quantity or quality of provisions, or being in a riotous or unbecoming manner" may forfeit privileges for one or more market days. Every applicant is expected to appear "in cleanly and decent attire, under like penalty."

8. Clerk shall keep a roster of applicants and the number of rations to which they are entitled, fill out tickets, record contributions, and summon committee members as necessary.

---

fort District formed the Confederate Society for the Reduction of Prices, citing several very laudable objectives:

1. Deliver produce (tax in kind) to the government promptly and sell any surplus at or below official prices, investing the profit in Confederate bonds.

2. Receive Confederate money at par.

3. Concede to merchants and manufacturers a just, legitimate profit.[51]

Two weeks later, a Greenwood farmer vowed the only way to check extortion ("the best army Lincoln has in the field") was to buy *direct* from the grower. In his view, city folk had polluted the country with avarice, and the only solution was to form associations like the one in Robertville and on sale day purchase nothing through middle men, instead dealing only with the farmer himself.[52]

The most widespread form of assistance to the poor—and hence a break of sorts on speculation—were boards of relief formed by legislative act in 1861 to aid soldier families.[53] These bodies (one in each district or parish) were given power to levy taxes, which might be in the form of money or agricultural produce. At that time, most state officials saw this issue as a community problem to be addressed with local funds. But when only about $200,000 was raised, the program was revamped in 1862 with a state appropration of $600,000 to be divided among needy families on the basis of the white population recorded in the 1860 census. Still more appropriations followed, coupled with various taxes in kind and levies on manufactured goods, all in an effort to aid those in need.

Reports issued by these boards, often incomplete, reveal great disparity from one area to another both in how relief was administered and in the amount granted. York District applicants, for example, had to file written appeals endorsed by some well-known citizen who would vouch for them, and in 1863 the annual amount received per person (usually in goods, not money) ranged from $29.73 in Charleston District to $5.16 in Horry. Yet the next year, without citing specific details, the Marlboro board painted a rosy picture indeed. Soldier families were "substantially" provided for and many lived "as well or better than they did in time of peace." The board members said they always were given produce, not currency, to protect them from "their own want of thrift." They were, it was claimed, better clad than ever before, "this resulting from the necessity of spinning & weaving their own garments. Not being obliged to work in the field, they have much time to work in & around the houses, in spinning & weaving & raising little crops of vegetables, & fattening a few hogs, & chickens for their own consumption." The board thought all of the families "well satisfied," emphasizing they had heard few complaints.

Even when a well-meaning individual tried to help he sometimes merely increased his personal woes. Early in 1863, cotton manufacturer William Gregg began exchanging cloth for agricultural produce...so many yards of sheeting for a pound of bacon, barrel of flour, bushel of

William Gregg (1800-1867).

corn, bucket of lard, etc. This was not pure altruism since Gregg needed the foodstuffs to feed his operatives and especially oil obtained from lard to grease machinery.[54] But, as soon as wagoners refused to sell as before and drove on to Gregg's mill to obtain by barter what they could not get with money, former customers were furious. What right has Gregg, Aiken residents asked, to be charitable at the expense of our community? He was, they complained, disrupting normal channels of commerce and increasing suffering.[55] This dispute continued to fester until 10 February 1865 when a mob broke into Gregg's store and made off with 33,000 yards of cloth—perhaps the most striking example of mass civil disobedience that occurred in South Carolina during the war years and certainly an expression of blatant selfishness.[56]

After mid-1863 several factors tended to shift the spotlight from speculation to other matters. These include growing concern for military affairs following the fall of Vicksburg and the decision at Gettysburg, the increasing prominence of barter—an economic process that stripped items in short supply of their monetary value, and, above all else, the fact that virtually everyone was involved to some degree in speculation. Also, it might be noted that truly successful speculators had their admirers. In March 1862, writing from an army camp near Goldsboro, North Carolina, Edward McCrady, Jr., rejoiced that another of George Trenholm's blockade runners had arrived in port. Yet he conceded not everyone was cheering; in fact, men just outside his tent were at that very moment "abusing" Trenholm. "But neither Trenholm or Memminger need ever expect thanks for any thing," he added. "They are too successful and the world to[o] jealous."[57]

One of the most surprising turnabouts on the subject of speculation is found in the letters of Theodore Honour, the young man who in April 1863 lectured his wife concerning the "terrible vice" that he believed was contaminating her family. Five months later, stationed near Charleston, he urged his mother to send him three bushels of sweet potatoes, noting he could sell two bushels, pay all costs, and get one free. That, of course, is petty stuff, but in October he asked his wife if they should not sell their front room carpet. He thought they could get $1,000 for it. And in 1864 he ordered her to go to the Bee Store, buy the largest and best calf skins available, and ship them to him...probably with an eye to resale.

A more explicit profit-making scheme is found in the letters of George C. Mackay, an Orangeburg youth who died in Virginia in 1864.

The previous year he wrote these words to sister Jessie Elvira from that state:

> I would advise you all, as there is likely to be a large army in South Carolina, to buy up all the cloth you can and make up clothing to sell to the soldiers. For I think in a very short time after the army has been in South Carolina, and particularly should there be a fight, everything will be sold for four times its value. Why not make envelopes and such things to sell? For this small speculation get Willie to collect what money is owing me, sell Fanny, and use the money as you all think best. I would advise Willie, if his crop is short, to buy corn at once. I have a large and fine gold watch. If the small amount of $150 would assist in buying or providing for the family in any way, it would please me to sell the watch and send this money.[58]

The line from shortage to speculation to selfishness is direct and clear, much like the clean, swift flight of an arrow to its target. Isabella Strait found the shelves of Chester District stores stripped clean in the fall of 1861. In succeeding years, John Bachman and others tried to help Isabella and thousands like her, but without much success. And in 1865, after Sherman had ravished Barnwell, Sarah Jane Sams, furious when a local merchant who had lost nothing refused to sell her provisions unless she had something to barter, uttered this anguished cry: "Can the people of the Confederacy ever be purged of their selfishness?"[59]

Midway through this struggle, Greenville's Benjamin F. Perry, a Unionist who nonetheless went with his state and supported the Confederacy, on 12 May 1863 gave voice to similar pain and frustration in his private journal.

> Yankees never acted more meanly than have Southern men in taking advantage of the necessaries of their fellow creatures to make fortunes for themselves. Those who opposed the Revolution have done more for the war than those who advocated it—Yancey was the arch fiend in breaking up the peace & happiness of the Union, & yet he has never thought of going into battle. The other

Benjamin F. Perry (1815-1885).

leaders have done the same—Barnwell Rhett—But I cant go on as I intended—I feel too bitter.[60]

But Perry did go on, at least for a few more weeks, during which he wrote of defeat, bloodshed, horrendous prices, and a land filled with "extortioners and unprincipled speculators." At length, on 4 September he made one final entry that closes with these words concerning his fellow South Carolinians.

> Instead of that self-sacrificing spirit which should actuate our people & make them give up all for their country, they are devoting themselves to speculation, money making & extortion, to any entire forgetfulness of the great cause in which our country is involved! Shameful & criminal! They who were loudest in secession & revolution are now at home making fortunes! skulking the army & seeking exemptions.
>
> The war has bourne particularly hard on the Poor! They have had to leave their wives & children without food & go to fight! whilst the rich are at home speculating & refusing to sell provisions to their famishing families! Oh Shame! Shame! on the farmers & planters who are now asking four or five dollars per bushel for corn & seven & eight dollars for wheat per bushel! Such a people do not deserve success! God will punish them in some way & I fear it is by the emancipation of their slaves!
>
> The Confederate money is fast depreciating & these high prices are rapidly increasing their depreciation— Never did a people play so palpably into the hands of their Enemy.[61]

NOTES

[1] Augustine Thomas Smythe to his mother, 3 November 1863, Augustine Thomas Smythe Letters. (Smythe appended an "e" to this family name.)

[2] Isabella Middleton Leland (ed.), "Middleton Correspondence, 1861-1865," *South Carolina Historical Magazine* (January 1964), pp. 41-43.

[3] *Camden Journal*, 11 March 1864, quoting from a recent issue of Columbia's *South Carolinian*.

[4] "Middleton Correspondence," pp. 33-39. A letter in the Thomas Burden Papers at the South Carolina Historical Society dated 18 March 1864 indicates that Winnsboro almost got a "Bee Store." However, when half of the goods shipped from Columbia were stolen en route, the local railroad agent refused to accept the remainder, which was then returned to Columbia.

[5] William Elliott, Jr., to mother (3 April 1864) and to sister Emmie (16 June 1864), Elliott-Gonzales Papers. This young man also told his sister of plans to spend the summer in nearby Summerton, which reportedly had even more food and gayer society than Manning.

[6] Alonzo H. Quint, *The Record of the Second Massachusetts Infantry, 1861-65* (Boston, 1867), pp. 259-64.

[7] S.F. Fleharty, *Our Regiment: A History of the 102d. Illinois Infantry Volunteers....* (Chicago, 1865), p. 117.

[8] Ibid., pp. 146-47.

[9] Ernest M. Lander, Jr., and Charles M. McGee, Jr., (eds.), *A Rebel Came Home: The Diary and Letters of Floride Clemson, 1863-1866* (Columbia, 1989), p. 74.

[10] Edward McCrady, Sr., to his wife, 6-7 April 1865, McCrady Family Papers, South Caroliniana Library.

[11] C. Vann Woodward (ed.), *Mary Chesnut's Civil War* (New Haven and New York, 1981), pp. 346-47.

[12] William Elliott to Isabella Elliott Barnwell, c. 26 and 30 September 1863, Elliott Family Papers. They were married in December 1863.

[13] Annie Middleton to her mother (Mrs. Henry De Wolf) in Rhode Island, 19 September 1864, Nathaniel Russell Middleton Papers. After bewailing the wickedness and extravagance of the times, she noted that her daughter was "very desirous" of writing a letter to Lincoln, which she was certain would convince him "that it is right and *therefore best*, that the war be *stopped* immediately."

[14] Ice, usually packed in sawdust or similar protective material, traditionally had been imported from the North. For a discussion of problems caused by this shortage see Massey, *Ersatz in the Confederacy*, pp. 150-51. Sumter's *Tri-Weekly Watchman* (31 May 1861) said ice could be delivered for $1.50 a barrel anywhere along the Wilmington-Manchester railroad line. A month later the price rose to two cents a pound; and, twelve months after that, Colonel Blanton Duncan, writing from Columbia, told the *Charleston Mercury* (1 July 1862) that reports of government officials using ice for juleps were untrue. It was kept for the sick and dispensed

from a central ice house in maximum units of ten pounds at 6¢ a pound.

[15]LeConte's pamphlet, *How to Make Salt from Sea-Water*, was printed in Columbia in 1862. Documents relative to his investigation of salt licks in May 1862 and October-November 1862 can be found in the State Auditor's Papers, South Carolina Department of Archives and History.

[16]Amelia T. Rainey to Jane McLure, 25 December 1862, McLure Family Papers. Note: The best work on this subject is Ella Lonn's *Salt as a Factor in the Confederacy* (University, Ala., 1965); however, South Carolina plays a very minor role in her story.

[17]Mary Dawkins to Jane McLure, 16 February 1865, McLure Family Papers.

[18]Philip Palmer to John Saunders Palmer, 4 January 1865, Palmer Family Papers. In the same letter, Philip asked his father if he was planning to move in the face of the Union advance.

[19]John Cantey to Camille Cantey, 7 December 1862, John Cantey Papers, Special Collections Library, Duke University.

[20]Like many officers, Cantey subsequently expressed hopes of settling down, securing a house, and sending for his family.

[21]Henry K. Witherspoon to Ellen Tweed, 7 December 1862, 1 January 1863, Henry K. Witherspoon Papers, Special Collections Library, Duke University.

[22]Martin V. Barkley to Josiah Barkley, 26 February 1862, Barkley Family Papers, Southern Historical Collection, University of North Carolina.

[23]Ibid., 18 October 1863. It would appear that Josiah Barkley also was a shoemaker. In a letter in the same collection dated 23 December 1863, W. W. Slaten—"barefooted" in the snows of Virginia—asked his son to go to Barkley, get him "No. 11" shoes, and arrange payment.

[24]See Ruth Barr McDaniel (compiler), *Confederate War Correspondence of James Michael Barr and Rebecca Ann Dowling Barr* (Taylors, S.C., 1963). En route to Virginia, Barr was disgusted with Union sentiment evident in Greensboro, N.C. The people there, he thought, were so tired of war that they wanted peace on any terms.

[25]S.S. Roberts to William Birnie, Sr., 26 July 1862, William Birnie Papers, Southern Historical Collection, University of North Carolina.

[26]William Elliott, Jr., to sister Emmie, 5 July 1863, Elliott-Gonzales Papers. He also noted that all of his handkerchiefs were ragged and asked for six new ones, two of them colored.

[27]William P. Neves to Mrs. A. A. Neves, 14 February 1862, Neves Family Papers, South Caroliniana Library.

[28]George Winston Smith and Charles Judah, *Life in the North During the Civil War: A Source History* (Albuquerque, 1966), pp. 196-201.

[29]James Pelot to Lala Pelot, 5 April 1863, Lala Pelot Papers, Special Collections Library, Duke University.

[30]Mrs. James L. Petigru to James Carson, 26 June 1861, Vanderhorst-Carson Papers, South Carolina Historical Society. Ten letters from this collection (1861-1863) have been published. See Joseph T. Holleman, "The Carson Through the Lines and

Blockade Correspondence," *Confederate Philatelist* (July-October 1981), pp. 95-103, 131-38.

[31]A collection of permits issued under this statute is available in Executive Department Papers at the South Carolina Department of Archives and History. Most individuals sought permission to distill, while others wanted to expand their operations to another district, dispense liquor at their hotel, or transport it from one place to another. Some promised not to sell spirits to those in uniform, and three men in the Pickens-Pendleton area and another in Richland District sought permission to distill in order "to feed hogs." Orangeburg's James Garvin simply expressed a desire to produce liquor because the current price of $7-$8 per gallon was beyond the reach of those of "limited means."

[32]Throughout South Carolina from 1893 to 1915, liquor could be purchased legally only at state stores called "dispensaries," a controversial and often corrupt enterprise that was the bane of Prohibitionists and a boon to bootleggers.

[33]R. Grestel (?) to J. E. Hagood, 1 September 1864, Haygood Papers. See also correspondence from William R. Hunt to Hagood, 18 August 1862 and 26 May 1863.

[34]Isabella Wylie Strait to Gilbert Lafayette Strait, 8 October 1861, Gaston, Strait, Wylie, Baskin Papers.

[35]J. C. Hicklin to Gilbert Lafayette Strait, 7 October 1861, Gaston, Strait, Wylie, Baskin Papers. Hicklin, who predicted Union forces soon would land on the South Carolina coast, advised against any invasion of Maryland. That, he thought, would only arouse "the conservative party of the north (those that desire peace)." The following month Strait's mother remarked in a letter to her son (24 November) that Jules Milles [Julius Mills] was trying to raise some kind of company…"I suppose a company to stay at home." By this, she meant a home guard unit or a similar group that would not actually go to war.

[36]See the *Charleston Daily Courier*, 2 May and 16 July 1861, 10 April 1862; *Charleston Mercury*, 24 August 1861, 5 May 1864. Also, on 9 December 1861 the Georgetown town council sent a petition (#44) to the General Assembly suggesting that local governments be permitted to issue notes from $1 "downward."

[37]On 9 March 1864, R. A. Black published this notice in the *Yorkville Enquirer* to all physicians and druggists: "As I cannot buy CORN with money, you are hereby notified, that you or your patients are required to furnish me with THIRTY BUSHELS of CORN, each, otherwise I will be unable to furnish you with with WHISKEY." In addition, several individuals cited in Chapter 1 underscore this phenomenon. Jane McLure of Union District told her husband in August 1864 she had to give corn for "*every* thing that I buy." At about the same time, the Macdonalds—mother and two daughters—were making straw hats that they exchanged for foodstuffs.

[38]E. Merton Coulter, *The Confederate States of America, 1861-1865* (Baton Rouge, 1950), pp. 205-206.

[39]*Charleston Daily Courier*, 4 August 1862.

[40]See H. L. Sutherland, "Arms Manufacturing in Greenville County," *Proceedings*

and Papers of the Greenville Historical Society (1971), pp. 46-60. Sutherland says, in all, perhaps $500,000 was expended on this facility; but, according to *Reports and Resolutions* (1863), the state spent only about half that amount.

[41]For information on these and similar examples of theft, see the *Yorkville Enquirer*, 17 September 1862; *Southern Enterprise*, 12 March 1863; *Camden Journal*, 11 March 1864; Columbia's *Daily Guardian*, 7 September 1863; *Charleston Daily Courier*, 16 May 1863; Sumter's *Semi-Weekly Watchman*, 13 March, 24 November 1863; and the *Charleston Mercury*, 16 December 1863, 18 January 1864.

[42]*Tri-Weekly South Carolinian*, 13 July 1864.

[43]Mrs. William Mason Smith to her daughters, 16 February 1864, quoted in Daniel E. Smith, Alice R. Huger Smith, and Arney R. Childs (eds.), *Mason Smith Family Letters, 1860-1868* (Columbia, 1950), p. 83.

[44]Richard J. Calhoun (ed.), *Witness to Sorrow: The Antebellum Biography of William J. Grayson* (Columbia, 1990), pp. 227-28. Earlier versions of Grayson's diary were published in the *South Carolina Historical Magazine* in July 1947-April 1950 (edited by Samuel G. Stoney) and July-October 1962 (edited by Elmer L. Puryear). Thomas Elliott—in the army but on the staff of a general who let him tend to plantation affairs—told his father on 4 February 1862 that he was glad to have a Virginia regiment on his land near Pocotaligo since they conducted themselves properly: "The South Carolina and Tennessee Regts. are rascally fellows, they plunder hen roosts, & burn fencing at a great rate—if Dunnovant's Regt. are near you, I should advise you to keep a guard over your Turkeys—" (Elliott-Gonzales Papers).

[45]Graydon, "Journal of Arthur Brailsford Wescoat," p. 96.

[46]Philip M. Racine (ed.), *Piedmont Farmer: The Journals of David Golightly Harris, 1855-1870* (Knoxville, 1990), p. 236. The originals are available at Winthrop University, Rock Hill, S.C.

[47]See the *Charleston Daily Courier*, 23, 24, 25, 30 April and 10 May 1862.

[48]Ibid., 25 April 1862. Throughout these years, South Carolina editors frequently sought hope and solace in the grim days of 1776-1783. On 5 June 1862, for example, the *Mercury* published an annotated version of the "Original Journals of the Siege of Charleston in 1780." Hailed as "a text-book of patriotism for all coming ages," it covered seven columns or over one-fourth of a four-page issue. The following day the *Mercury* began appearing as a single sheet of only twelve columns, six to a page.

[49]Ibid., 22 October 1862.

[50]Ibid., 15 April 1863.

[51]Ibid., 16 October 1863. Six months earlier (1 April), the *Courier* reported that a local tobacco store owner refused to accept a Confederate note, asking instead for bank bills or city currency. This was immediately denied by Jose Jara, who thought he had been maligned. However, by October such reports were becoming more common.

[52]Ibid., 28 October 1863.

[53]See William Frank Zornow, "State Aid for Indigent Families of South Carolina Soldiers, 1861-1865," *South Carolina Historical Magazine* (April 1956), pp. 82-87. Zornow stresses that the trend throughout the war was from local to state involvement and from money to relief in kind. Data on the work of some individual boards is available at the South Carolina Department of Archives and History.

[54]For an example of Gregg's advertisements seeking produce, see the *Charleston Daily Courier*, 24 December 1863.

[55]*Charleston Daily Courier*, 11 March 1863. Records of John Forsythe Talbert of Edgefield at the South Caroliniana Library reveal he sold farm produce for cash throughout 1863. In January of the following year, however, he exchanged bacon and eggs for 205 yards of cloth at Gregg's mill and by November was paying for shoes with corn.

[56]Gregg warned readers of the *Edgefield Advertiser* (22 February 1865) that these goods actually belonged to the wives and children of soldiers and he was prepared to prosecute those who stole them.

[57]Edward McCrady, Jr., to Edward McCrady, Sr., 26 March 1862, McCrady Family Papers. On 12 February 1863, William Birnie, Jr., writing from Columbia, remarked to an uncle in Greenville, "The gardener here tells me Trenholm is going to lay out $100,000 in beautifying the place he has bought near this city. He is to have a splendid lawn, water works, fish ponds &c." (Birnie Papers).

[58]J. Skottowe Wannamaker (compiler), *The Wannamaker, Salley, Mackay, and Bellinger Families....* (Charleston, 1937), p. 275.

[59]Mrs. Randolph Sams to her husband, 22 February 1865, Sams Family Papers, South Caroliniana Library. It was the Yankee cavalry, she wrote, that did the most damage: "They behaved more like caged tigers than human beings, running all over town, kicking down fences, breaking in doors and smashing glasses [,] also stealing and tearing up clothing." Yet she conceded some of the men were kind and helpful. By comparison, the army, 24,000 strong, that arrived two days later created virtually no disturbance, and finally on 9 March merchant James Patterson relented and sent her some grits and potatoes.

[60]Lillian Adele Kibler, *Benjamin F. Perry, South Carolina Unionist* (Durham, 1946), p. 365. Perry refers, of course, to Alabama's William Lowndes Yancey, who once studied law in Greenville under his guidance, and Robert Barnwell Rhett, editor of the *Charleston Mercury*.

[61]Ibid., p. 370. A short time later, the *Edgefield Advertiser* (23 September) echoed these sentiments: "Speculation, extortion, and the *grab game* are stalking abroad with more unblushing face than ever; southern gentlemen are forgetting themselves so terribly as to be systematically out-jewing the Jew, and out-trading the sharpest Yankee traders."

Francis W. Pickens (1805-1869).

IV

THE DRAFT, DESERTION & DISSENT

Contrary to what one would expect, the convention called to take South Carolina out of the Union in December 1860 did not simply fade away when that task was accomplished; instead, it conducted business intermittently for the next two years and, through an executive council, often wielded great power. During the first year (1861), this body was largely advisory, assisting Governor Pickens in various ways during difficult times, but a re-invigorated panel virtually replaced his excellency throughout much of 1862. There are at least two reasons for this change. Many thought Pickens tactless, inept, and unable to cope with emergency situations; and, secondly, the Union foothold at Port Royal shocked South Carolina into the reality of war.

Historians such as David Duncan Wallace and Charles E. Cauthen give the council high marks; rank-and-file South Carolinians of that era did not.[1] Yet much of what the five-member council did in the opening months of 1862 was precisely what should have been done. Actually a "committee of safety," these men revamped the military arm of the state, declared martial law in some communities, began the manufacture of war supplies, impressed slaves to build coastal fortifications, instituted conscription, curtailed liquor sales, tried to defend the Georgetown area after Confederate forces withdrew to fight elsewhere, initiated a policy of appointing officers in lieu of soldiers electing their superiors by ballot, and announced plans to confiscate gold and silver for coinage. The result was a storm of protest centered largely on the charge that the council was a despotic concentration of executive, legislative, and judicial power in a single body, and on 18 December 1862 it was abolished by the General Assembly.

Except for the scheme to seize gold and silver (quickly abandoned), all of these measures seem reasonable enough, perhaps even necessary, and the general reaction raises questions concerning how committed the average citizen was to the war effort once the initial cheering and bombast subsided. Nevertheless, some aspects of the state manpower draft

109

(which preceded that of the Confederate government) raised real concern, and an attempt to establish a military presence inland from Georgetown stirred up a hornet's nest.

As C. G. Memminger (Secretary of the Confederate Treasury) stressed on 4 April 1862 in a letter to W. W. Harllee, the man trying to mount this operation, General Lee and others urged withdrawing troops from coastal regions that could not be defended. As a rule, those affected thought such a policy lacked merit, yet Memminger urged planters to remove their slaves and form them into work gangs. These laborers, hired by railroads or perhaps the state, would provide income equal to any crop and "a great public work would be accomplished." "Depend on it," he said forcefully, "any dispirited attempt to defend Georgetown will only produce the same vain confidence among the planters which lost the negroes in Beaufort District."[2] In theory, this sounded fine, but area residents failed to cooperate and the campaign—as Memminger feared—certainly was "dispirited."

What happened in eastern South Carolina in the spring of 1862 is unclear, except that many men did not respond to the call to duty issued by the council. Some of them, members of the 4th Regiment of the South Carolina Militia, were thrown into prison but soon escaped, probably with the connivance of local officials. It is possible, this is merely a guess, that Harllee, a seasoned Marion District politician, made enemies during his long career, hence creating one possible source of opposition to his leadership. The *Marion Star* (6 August 1862) turned the disaster into a frontal assault upon the Executive Council, calling that body nothing more than a five-governor "pentarchy." Instead of being flattered by a scheme to fortify the Pee Dee region, this editor claimed the council was using tax dollars to defend an area the enemy already had reconnoitered and spurned.

> One of the governors with some voluntary aids who know as much about military fortifications as a jackass does about christianity, surveyed the Pee Dee swamp and found a bluff—the last place where Lincoln and Seward would ever dream of sending a gunboat and there 'FORT FINGER' sprung into existence. Five companies were thrown in for defence of this impregnable work for three months—two thirds of the whole remaining at home all the time, in fact we have been informed by a commissioned officer of one of the five companies that since the

middle of June no one company could have mustered a platoon, and thus the Governor and Council have immortalized themselves by this masterly piece of strategy from which no good can eventuate and for which the people of the State of South Carolina *have to be taxed.*

A few months later, still seething, citizens of eastern South Carolina peppered the General Assembly with hot complaints. Some were distressed by an apparent decision *not* to defend Georgetown after all, Horry District residents wanted their men sent home (needed there, they said), and members of the famed 4th Regiment still wanted to elect their officers, not have them appointed by government officials. A Marion petition asserted that, as a result of this fiasco, the spirit of the country was poor and so few volunteers appeared that the community had to resort to a draft. In addition, some men had gone into hiding and, worse yet, now were predatory outlaws living along the banks of the Pee Dee. And local residents were alarmed as other men were arrested, handcuffed, and forced into the reserves.[3]

James Chesnut, Jr.—head of South Carolina's Military Department, a member of the much-reviled Executive Council, and husband of Mary Boykin Chesnut—graciously placed part of the blame for what happened upon unfortunate timing, not any want of patriotism. This operation, he noted, was launched just as spring planting began. But Chesnut then turned his full wrath upon an "uninformed" press, which, in his opinion, used the ill-fated campaign to attack the council itself: "Thus, sir, were ignorance, indolence, selfishness, disaffection, and, to some extent, disappointed ambition, combined and made, unwittingly, to aid and abet the enemy, and, in like manner to become coadjutors of Lincoln and all the hosts of abolition myrmidons."[4]

In February 1863, the General Assembly reacted with equal warmth by censuring Chesnut's remarks concerning the 4th Regiment. The legislators vowed those living in eastern districts of the state were doing their full duty. If any area seemed reluctant to respond to requests issued in Columbia, it was not from any disregard for sovereignty or want of spirit but common conviction that "the extraordinary authority by which the calls were made was unconstitutional and oppressive."[5] However, by that date the hated council had disappeared, an event applauded by virtually every editor in the state and a majority of his readers.

Much of this maneuvering resulted from sudden realization by both state and national leaders early in 1862 that they were locked in a real

James Chesnut, Jr. (1815-1885).

struggle and faced serious manpower problems. About one-third of the entire Confederate Army consisted of those who had signed up for only a year. Anticipating a short war, few made provision for their families and assumed they would go home as others came forward to take their place. The military scene was further complicated by waning enthusiasm, increasing danger, and grim news from the Mississippi Valley. To counter these trends, in December 1861 the Confederate government began offering special inducements to those who would re-enlist for two or three years or even for the entire war. These included a $50 bounty, a 60-day furlough, transportation to and from their homes, and the opportunity to reorganize companies and elect officers.

On 2 February, President Davis set South Carolina's troop quota at 18,000, six percent of the white population. According to the Secretary of War, 6,000 South Carolinians already were in uniform, which meant the state had to raise at least five regiments and re-enlist as many of the twelve-month men as possible. Unlike the blandishments of the central government, South Carolina's leaders tried a two-pronged approach— an appeal to patriotism accompanied by threats that volunteering would cease on 20 March, to be followed by conscription of all white males, 18-45. At first, they did not use the word "conscription," preferring to experiment with drawing so many men "by lot" from various militia companies. This system was used in Charleston in mid-February when about 1400 men—some volunteers, others chosen at random—signed up for twelve months in the Confederate service. Among them were seven volunteers from the *Courier* staff.[6] It should be noted, perhaps, that miscellaneous records at the South Carolina Department of Archives and History indicate the state sometimes was offering bounties to those who would re-enlist ($20-$25) and, at that juncture, officially enrolling men into "the Army of the State of South Carolina and the Confederate States."

This campaign proved to be generally successful, yet the *Yorkville Enquirer* (27 February) could not resist spirited comment concerning events taking place in the "Holy City."

> It is remarkable that on the coasts, or near the scenes of action, force has often to be resorted to, to secure the public defence, while the interior pours forth its hosts, too often to fall the prey of heartless speculators, if not to Yankee vandals. Charleston has had to resort to a draft, while most of its Yankee and counter jumping popula-

tion is sporting fancy uniforms, and the famous blood-
less Fourth Brigade, numbering some 38 officers and
three privates, guarded the Washington race-course. But,
we suppose such things must be. 'God made the country, the people made the town.'

Although what transpired in Charleston was not an official draft,
conscription, both state and Confederate, was on its way. Soon local
authorities were insisting that (a) volunteers enlist for the entire war and
(b) officers be appointed, not chosen by ballot. All of these pressures
worked splendidly, coupled with fears of being labeled a "conscript"
and widespread female persuasion...one might even say persecution. So
many came forth voluntarily (even if pushed) that the date for conscription was delayed several weeks to 15 April, at least that was the official
story. What really happened was sudden realization the draft machinery
could not possibly be in place on 20 March, hence the postponement. In
any case, on 28 April Colonel James Chesnut proudly announced that
nearly 22,000 South Carolinians had entered the Confederate service
for the duration of the war, 4,000 more than the established quota. In a
report issued some months later, however, Chesnut said the draft was
used only in Charleston "where the Adjutant General encountered every
species of harassment and delay."[7]

This strange assertion, perhaps meant to boost morale while taking
a jab at Charleston, is a bit suspect since numerous accounts indicate
individuals in all parts of the state sought to stay out of uniform. Both
state and national drafts recognized the right to secure substitutes, and
official records reveal about 120 young South Carolinians did so in 1862.
Most of those who became substitutes were German aliens, although a
few hailed from Maryland. During that same year nearly a thousand
Palmetto State citizens won exemptions as overseers.[8] Of the latter, 210
(22.2%) had the same last name as their employer, strong evidence that
an occupation long scorned and reviled suddenly gained remarkable
prestige and allure...at least to many it seemed more attractive than
marching and fighting.

The day after state conscription became official policy on 15 April
1862, the Confederate Congress initiated compulsory, three-year service for all young white men ages 18 to 35. These "conscripts" (the
word did not appear in the act) were supposed to fill vacancies in units
recruited from their own state. Anyone who volunteered before being
drafted would be permitted to select the company in which he wished to

serve, and those reluctant to don uniforms could secure substitutes from among those "not liable for duty." Six months later, the draft age was increased to 45 and in February 1864 expanded to 17-50, although only those 18-45 could be asked to serve outside of their state.

The levies of 1862 were followed by complex legislation creating long lists of exemptions, those who did not have to serve, such as Confederate and state officials, legislators, firemen, mail carriers, telegraph operators, railroad and river workers, miners, clergymen, factory hands, editors, professors, teachers, and so on. Most were relieved of any obligation to shoulder arms because of their occupations, men thought vital to a functioning society. The first exemption act passed by the Confederate Congress concentrated upon industrial workers; the second, an expanded list designed to fit regional needs, included the controversial provision exempting any planter or overseer responsible for twenty or more slaves. These loopholes quickly were exploited by the unscrupulous as they sought out "safe" havens, what their contemporaries called "bomb-proof," and help to explain why so many South Carolinians suddenly became overseers.

From the outset, Richmond's draft caused considerable outcry in South Carolina because of blatant differences between *state* and *national* conscription. Twenty-four hours after Congress acted, the Adjutant and Inspector General replied in this fashion to an individual who asked which policy to follow: "Conscription being ordered by the Confederate government, the State authorities until otherwise directed do not feel authorized to assign conscripts."[9] To begin with, those from 36-45 were, for several months, subject to the local draft but not the Confederate. Of much greater importance was the question of overseers, an anomaly not resolved until the fall of 1862 with passage of the "twenty-nigger law."

On 2 January 1862, several months before either government endorsed conscription, South Carolina's on-going convention passed an ordinance exempting some overseers from active militia duty. This group included all those in charge of fifteen or more "working hands" if the owner was absent in the service of the state, over sixty years of age, decrepit, or female. The convention did not excuse these individuals from local militia musters, patrol duty, etc. A reference to this ordinance (but not the specific provisions themselves) was incorporated into the state conscription law, as well as a clause exempting military cadets, another bone of contention with Richmond.

Soon after Confederate conscription became operative, James Chesnut suggested the state organize men not affected into two corps—

those 36-50 to be called into service anywhere in the state and men 16-18, 50-65 who would perform patrol and police duty in their own communities. Hardly had these units begun to take shape when the Confederate government expanded the draft age to 45 creating still more confusion. As a result, buffeted by conflicting rules and decimated by conscription and recruiting of volunteers, by 1863 the once-proud state militia virtually ceased to exist.

Nevertheless, the warmest issue in state-national relations between April and October 1862 was not age groups but the status of South Carolina's overseers. In June the Executive Council advised those seeking exemptions under state law to apprise Confederate enrolling officers of their situation and subsequently talked of issuing a "countervailing" order in respect to Richmond's policies.

Truly alarmed, on 3 September 1862, President Jefferson Davis dispatched a long, thoughtful letter to Governor Pickens and the council.[10] His words were, above all else, an attempt to nip in the bud what could become a very embarrassing confrontation between state and national rights. First he appealed to patriotism and then stressed the inherent dangers in South Carolina's stand.

> If a State may free her citizens at her own discretion from the burden of military duty, she may do the same in regard to the burden of taxation, or any other lawful duty, payment, or service. In other words, the assertion of such a right on the part of a State is tantamount to a denial of the right of the Confederate Government to enforce the exercise of delegated power and would render a confederacy an impractical form of government.

Davis said this dispute really was a matter for the courts to decide and suggested those distressed seek redress there. South Carolina, he noted dryly, once nullified an act of the United States Congress "but on no occasion did any portion of her citizens ever maintain the right of the State to modify an order of the General Government." The president concluded with the observation, which was true, that the ordinance in question referred to service with the state militia, *not* army duty. It was, he emphasized, enacted before any conscript law was passed and "by its terms it has no relation to the armies of the Confederacy." Passage of more liberal exemptions on 11 October 1862, especially the "twenty-nigger law," tended to relieve tensions, although not until December

1863 did South Carolina officially withdraw its claims to state exemptions.[11]

Yet if Confederate exemption of overseers eased one problem, as this letter reveals, at the grass-roots level it created still more. Late in October 1862, Mrs. Lucy Sheldon of Newberry poured out her anger and dismay to Milledge L. Bonham, then a congressman and soon to become governor.

> You will be astonished to get this letter from me but owing to the act that has passed there in Congress the people here don't like, especially the poorer class, that is exempting all men that have twenty negroes. There is a great many buying up to make the number up so they won't have to go to the wars. If you had passed the act that they would have to pay one thousand dollars for the poor men's wives that has been killed, that is on the field of battle, it would have been all right. But it is not right as it is and I would not be surprised if there is a rebellion in the camp on that very account.
>
> I have seen men from Georgia; they say that there will be trouble there about it. If you know that them very men are buying up everything to specolate on, that cotton is rising and that the poor men's widdows can't hardly get a garden to tend. Call that to the floor again and make amends on it for the benefit of the poor men's wives that has been killed and are in battle. I think we are depending on them for the safety of our country.... Do try to re-enstate things to benefit the poor. I tell you if it is not done there will be trouble in the camp.
>
> Write me. I love to hear from my old friends. There is great specolations going on here. I think they ought to [im]press all the flour that the specolators has for the solders. There is plenty here at [$]30 a barrel....[12]

One might ask if the fate of a thousand men, South Carolina's exempted overseers, was worth all of the fuss and fury expended in the summer of 1862. A better question would be, perhaps, was conscription a success? For historian E. Merton Coulter the answer was an emphatic "no." Never resorted to in previous U.S. wars, he viewed such a policy as foreign to American thought and especially to states-right dogma. In

Milledge Luke Bonham (1813-1890).

his opinion it destroyed one of the Confederacy's most potent weapons—the cooperation of state governments and their citizens. Conscription was not unconstitutional, he writes, but unworkable: "A modified system of conscription, managed by the several states, would have recognized state pride and responsibility and have worked much more efficiently than the system that was adopted."[13] It did, Coulter concedes, force many young men to volunteer, those eager to avoid the stigma of "conscript." Yet, over-all he brands the program a failure. In addition, implementation of conscription was public admission that thousands of Southerners were not rabid secessionists and, in turn, ignited passions detrimental to the cause, as Mrs. Sheldon's letter so clearly demonstrates.

Albert Burton Moore, another historian who has studied Confederate conscription, agrees it soon became ineffective, and the most lamentable feature, in his opinion, was substitution. Some men took the money and then deserted, while others—newly enriched—served alongside those getting only $11 a month. It benefited those with money, stirred up class hatred, and created a disturbing chain effect: men in uniform began searching for substitutes and those who became substitutes went looking for a way out...or perhaps departed and began the process all over again with yet another payment in hand. By the end of 1863 when substitution was ruled illegal, Moore believes the Confederate conscription program was a mess. He points specifically to low morale, confusion over a dual system of conscription and voluntary enlistment (those facing conscription often could volunteer to serve in local units), and failure to back up conscription officers with armed might.[14]

As late as February 1863, despite a year of grim warnings, South Carolinians "liable for conscription" still could sign up voluntarily and win a $50 bounty.[15] For whatever reasons, men seemed to don and discard uniforms with ease...joining up, coming home for a spell, going back, perhaps transferring to new company, then taking a tour of duty in the reserves before marching off to war once more under yet another command. The valiant attempt of A. S. Salley, Jr., to list all Palmetto State soldiers by name—*South Carolina Troops in the Confederate Service*—ended in 1930 after only three volumes were published, possibly because he had to deal with so many transfers, discharges, re-enlistments, re-organized companies, and special details. Small wonder that the *Charleston Daily Courier* (2 April 1863) complained editorially that conscription was not being carried out properly. Thousands, it said, were shirking their responsibilities; and, were they at their posts, the Confed-

SUBSTITUTES WANTED.

THE undersigned wants two SUBSTI-
TUTES, who are between 16 and 18
years of age, for which a liberal price will
be given. Apply through the Columbia
Post Office.   JAMES CAMPBELL.
Aug 21   3*

Daily South Carolinian (Columbia), 21 August 1863.

erate Army would be much larger: "We should all feel it our duty to make them suspend their lucrative avocations and participate in the labors, dangers, and privation of their brethren in the field." This was by no means the last such outcry, which, to a large degree, was fueled by an inept system of recruitment that was poorly administered, lacked enforcement power, and did not actually *conscript* since those called could pay someone else to take their place.

Ads for substitutes, always discreetly phrased, appeared in numerous South Carolina newspapers. Typical is this item in the *Charleston Mercury* (7 March 1862): "Substitutes can be furnished, and good references given, by application to Box 492, Post-office. Communications confidential. Persons desiring immunity from the present and coming draft should apply at once." A month later, the *Mercury* (2 April) published an ad seeking substitutes. Ironically, those interested were to write "Volunteer" in care of the paper. And in December 1862, Columbia's *Southern Guardian* carried a notice from a Raleigh concern (Thomas Jones & Company) eager to dispel confusion concerning the conscription law. Jones advised all who thought they should report to do so; however, if they believed they were exempt, he would supply the law on their case for $5. He vowed he did "nothing but legitimate business" but could not act until the retaining fee was in hand.

On the same day that the *Mercury* published the "Volunteer" plea for substitutes, the editor expressed amazement that 600-700 foreign nationals residing in Charleston were seeking exemption from the draft. "We had not imagined," he wrote, "that the European Powers had so many true and loyal subjects—*arms* bearing men—under the shade of the Palmetto. It becomes an interesting query how far these exemptions will diminish the number of our 'voters.'"

One of the obvious by-products of conscription was desertion, although some impetuous individuals did not wait for such laws to take effect. The *Charleston Daily Courier* noted on 13 January 1862 that four men from a coastal installation who got permission to go for oysters instead went out to join the Union blockade fleet. Also, throughout the first year of the war there was considerable disagreement as to whether volunteers could be required to serve outside of the state. Perhaps the result was not *true* desertion, but it comes close. Two examples will suffice.

On 20 April 1861, one week after the fall of Fort Sumter, Maxcy Gregg left for Virginia in response to a frantic call for help. With him were some 350 to 500 men, perhaps half of the men enrolled in the First South Carolina Volunteers. In a letter to the *Darlington Southerner*, Captain F. F. Warley of the Darlington Guards, explained what happened.[16] He and his men, he said, took up arms on 3 January before the Confederacy was formed and entered state service for one specific reason—to defend Charleston. "We never dreamed of leaving our own State," Warley insisted, "one acre of whose soil is dearer to many of us than the balance of the continent—the *possibility* of being required or asked to do [so], had not been hinted to us by those in authority." According to Warley, Gregg, without any warning, suddenly asked those willing to sail for Norfolk at daybreak to step forward. When only about one hundred men responded, Gregg denounced those hesitant to join him and, with the assistance of liquor, rounded up another 250 or so. Warley, in turn, denounced Gregg as a bachelor tyrant with no family ties who had the audacity to sign himself as "Colonel, 1st Regiment, S. C. Volunteers."

Two weeks later, Edgefield Riflemen accompanying Gregg replied from Richmond with a tepid defense of their commanding officer that appeared in the *Edgefield Advertiser* on 29 May. Deploring rancor that could only harm the Confederate cause, they refused to blame directly those who remained in South Carolina since they did so in "*the defence of their country*," words that may or may not have been intended as a reproach. They did, however, resent the assertion their choice had been influenced by ardent spirits, a charge Warley subsequently diluted ever so slightly. The following week, the *Advertiser* (5 June) printed his statement to the effect that he did not mean officers coerced the rank and file with liquor, merely that the men were asked to choose while drunk.

A somewhat more blatant but similar incident, which also involved the Edgefield community, took place in Aiken and Augusta in April 1862 when hundreds of South Carolina soldiers jumped from cars bound for Corinth, Mississippi. These men, members of the 19th Regiment, asserted the same familiar claim, that, as volunteers, they could not be sent beyond the borders of the state. In this instance, Governor Pickens acted more forcefully and on 19 April ordered the sheriffs of Edgefield, Lexington, Sumter, and other districts to arrest any men of that regiment found without proper papers. They were, he directed, to be considered deserters and jailed or turned over to Confederate authorities.[17] A few days earlier, the *Edgefield Advertiser* (16 April) put the best face possible on what the editor conceded was an "awkward" situation. While admitting almost all of the local men in the regiment had simply come home, he mounted a half-hearted defense. Edgefield, he said, weeps over "the mistaken conduct of her children," adding it would be best if in some way they could ward off the stigma that perhaps would be attached to her good name. That "some way" apparently was to return to duty as soon as possible.[18]

Throughout the middle years of the war (1862-1864), South Carolina newspapers published bits of information concerning substitutes, conscripts, and deserters. These often appeared in the form of ads or official notices. One item, however, was a humorous spoof copied from a northern journal. On 24 August 1864, the *Charleston Mercury* printed the following notice indicating, in the words of the editor, that the gentleman was "tired of his boarding house."

> Wanted, a substitute to stay here in my place. He must be thirty years old; have a good moral character; all digestive powers, and not addicted to writing poetry. To such an one all the advantages of strict retirement, army rations and unmitigated watchfulness to prevent them from getting lost, are offered for an indefinite period. Address me at Block 1, Room 12, Johnson's Island, Military Prison, at any time for the next three years, enclosing half a dozen postage stamps.
>
> Asa Hartz.

But much of this news was altogether different. A handful of men serving in the Charleston area were shot for desertion, undoubtedly as an example and warning to their comrades. Among them was a corporal executed on Sullivan's Island in August 1862, a Georgia man (Jacob Adams) put to death at the Washington Race Course in May of the following year, and Private Henry Jerome of Chester, who met his maker at the same site in May 1864. Jerome's demise is a bit puzzling since, by that date, straggling, desertion, not being where one was supposed to be were all too common; however, Henry had deserted *twice*.[19] By the end of 1864, some South Carolina commands were urging men simply to return to duty (no questions asked) or officially classifying as "absentees" many of those who failed to respond when roll was called.[20]

Ads for deserters usually offered a $30 reward, although an Anderson District man was valued at only $10, perhaps because he had been missing for nearly a year.[21] On 6 December 1862, the *Charleston Mercury* published an extensive list of deserters being sought, most of them natives of Anderson, Spartanburg, Marion, and Barnwell districts. Ten days later, the *Courier* noted that the *Mobile Register* had produced a similar accounting, the names of fifty men, nearly all of them from Edgefield District, who were absent from General Bragg's command. At about the same time, the *Yorkville Enquirer* (14 January 1863) told of the arrest of an entire company in Columbia. These men, who hailed from Pickens, Anderson, and Greenville districts, had arrived in the state capital from Virginia, some sources said to recruit infantry, others claimed to desert. Since the authorities had no place to lodge so many bodies (the local jail was being used to house Yankee POWs), they paroled the enlisted men temporarily and held the officers in a local hotel. The following morning only the latter could be found.

Especially revealing is an official roster of delinquent conscripts published in the *Daily Southern Guardian* on 8 September 1862. Those named were warned to show up soon or they would be treated as deserters. The totals by district were as follows:

District	Count	District	Count
Abbeville	166	Kershaw	5
Anderson	22	Lancaster	24
Barnwell	13	Laurens	30
Charleston	3	Lexington	42
Chester	11	Marlboro	58
Chesterfield	21	Marion	145
Clarendon	17	Newberry	13
Colleton	7	Orangeburg	17
Darlington	37	Pickens	70
Edgefield	110	Sumter	13
Fairfield	11	Spartanburg	81
Georgetown	1	Union	25
Greenville	111	Williamsburg	10
Horry	53	York	37

This adds up to 1153 men and nearly 60 percent of those listed are from six districts: Abbeville 166, Marion 145, Greenville 111, Edgefield 110, Spartanburg 81, and Pickens 70. According to the 1860 census, Abbeville had 1646 white males ages 20-40. This means approximately 10 percent of that age group were dragging their heels, the highest ratio in the state, followed by Marion (.094%), Horry (.068%), Greenville (.056%), and Edgefield (.051%). Others such as Spartanburg, Pickens, Darlington, and Lexington weighed in at about .033%.

That the Pickens-Greenville-Spartanburg area figures prominently— fewer slaves and from the outset less enthusiastic about secession—is no surprise. Spartanburg's David Harris stated in January 1861 that some of his pro-Union neighbors had decided not to organize a company. It was not that their politics had changed, he confided in his diary, but that they feared being hanged. A year later he observed that volunteers departing in crowded railway cars "boo-hooed desperately."[22] And in July 1864 the local enrolling office published the names of nearly a hundred area deserters and absentees in the *Carolina Spartan* (21 July), an announcement followed in succeeding weeks by scattered denials.

What is surprising is the continuing pattern of disenchantment in the Edgefield-Abbeville area and, to the east, similar conditions in Marion and its environs. Perhaps Maxcy Gregg's impetuous orders in April 1861 and the campaigns of the following year to reinforce Mississippi and the Pee Dee offer partial explanations, but evidence is really too fragmentary to provide definite answers. In July 1863, William Birnie told his uncle of comparable troubles in Charleston as that community was organizing home guard details. Many men, unwilling to volunteer even for sentinel duty, were, he writes, arrested "at church doors & bulletin boards on Sunday." Others were plucked from a crowd attending the launching of a gunboat on the following day.[23] A few weeks later, Sumter's *Tri-Weekly Watchman* (24 August) complained that deserters were everywhere, killing stock and arousing resentment.

As the year came to a close, a letter to the editor of the *Courier* (10 December), signed simply "H," bewailed absentism in the army: "Every paper almost in the Confederacy teems with accounts of numbers of this class of our people among us. Every village, every neighborhood, can furnish its quota of delinquents." Most, "H" said, seemed to be junior officers, not enlisted men, who "*occasionally visit the army*" but whose regular place was "*out of it.*" Early in 1864, Allen J. Green, enrolling officer in Columbia, announced plans to raise six local companies of mounted men to arrest deserters, track down delinquent conscripts, and resist any raid or invasion by Abolitionists.[24]

However, the region of greatest concern was the upcountry, especially the hills above Greenville stretching into North Carolina, a hotbed of discontent. In April 1863, William Elliott, Jr., told of rounding up twenty-five conscripts in that area and expressed amazement at the lack of patriotism evident on all sides—"a mean Yankee population" filled with mechanics and overseers who swore to falsehoods in order to escape the draft.[25] Fifteen months later, stationed in Manning and busy arresting deserters, Elliott remarked it was "a burning shame that our discipline has been so lax." If corrected, he thought army ranks could be increased by 25,000 to 30,000. "Much of the evil," he emphasized, "comes from the *election* instead of the appointment of officers, who will not do their duty by those to whom they owe their positions."[26]

There is little doubt that Major John D. Ashmore, Elliott's commanding officer while he was in Greenville, mounted an all-out campaign against desertion in the summer of 1863. Early in August, he warned Colonel James Chesnut that there were 600 to 1000 deserters in the region, their numbers were increasing daily, and scores of civilians were coming to their aid. "Very many of the Deserters are armed; are bold, defiant and threatening. Nothing but extreme measures can accomplish anything. What shall we do? Advise me."[27] The answer was to get tough, shoot to kill if necessary, and the *War of the Rebellion* gives a detailed account of what ensued.[28]

On 7 August, Ashmore poured out his tale of woe to Major C. D. Melton, the man in charge of state conscripts. He told how on 13 July he issued "an earnest appeal" that was treated with ridicule and contempt, only four or five individuals coming forward, men already sent to Columbia. Deserters, gathered in small bands, were spread along a 150-mile frontier, "every foot of which is a mountain country and much of it almost inaccessible." Spies and signals give warning whenever strangers appear, and he had been unable to contact any of their leaders. Some loyal citizens vowed only force would bring "these deluded men back to their duty." Yet those who deserted often were being sustained by others who, while not openly hostile to the Confederacy, thought speculation and extortion so rampant that those in uniform were not being properly supplied. Ashmore agreed this was, unfortunately, all too true and could not be denied. The deserters swear they will die at home rather than be dragged forth again to battle for such a cause.

In a word, if one-tenth part of the information lodged with me be reliable, and I do not believe that it is exaggerated in the smallest particular, there is a most lamentable condition of affairs in the mountains of Greenville, Pickens, and Spartanburg. Their chief points of rendezvous in Pickens are the mouth of Brass Town Creek, on Tugaloo, the passes west and northwest of Tunnel Hill, Choehee, bordering the Jocassee Valley, and Table Rock. Almost every intermediate pass and valley, however, is occupied by a deserter's cabin, who on the approach of a stranger flies to the rocks and ravines where, taking his perch, he sees and observes all that is going on, safe from the eye of his pursuer (if pursued) until a call or halloo from wife or child assures him of safety. In Greenville their chief points are at Caesar's Head, Potts' Cove, Solomon's Jaws, Turnpike, Saluda Gap, on the headwaters of the Tyger, Howard's Gap, and Hogback Mountain, as well as intermediate points. In Spartanburg they seem to have no special rendezvous in the mountains, but occupy their farm-houses in the valleys and on the hills, and by a well-arranged system of signals give warning of the approach of danger.

Ashmore went on the say that, if enemy cavalry came with money, not guns and swords, they "could and would command whatever they wanted." The deserters, he added, work together in gangs, congregate at stills and houses where liquor is sold, and "swear vengeance against any one who approaches with the intention of molesting them. The true and loyal citizens are afraid to turn out to aid the officers, as not only their lives, but the destruction of their homes and property is boldly threatened if they dare to give aid and assistance to the authorities in arresting them and punishing these offenders."

Several weeks later, Melton summarized conditions in Greenville, Pickens, and Spartanburg districts in a report to Colonel John S. Preston, his superior in Richmond. These communities had produced some of the best companies in the state, he wrote, but the people are poor, ill-informed, little identified with "our" struggle, and thus "easily seduced from their duty." Desertion was so widespread that it was no longer a reproach to be known as a "deserter." As an example, Melton told what had happened a few months earlier when a brigade commanded by

General Nathan B. Evans was en route from Charleston to Jackson, Mississippi.

> ...one regiment, the Sixteenth South Carolina Volunteers (Colonel McCullough), was made up almost exclusively of companies from these districts.[29] They had been nearly two years from home; had but recently closed an arduous campaign in North Carolina; were ordered to Charleston, where they hoped to remain. The order to go forward to the west was the signal for a general desertion. These took their arms with them, intending, as I am satisfied, to return to their commands after a hurried visit to their families. But finding among their friends and throughout the country a change of tone, a weariness of the war, a readiness to counsel and encourage desertion, they have with but few exceptions remained at home. And now from other regiments others are coming out; letters are written from home giving deplorable pictures of the destitution of families. Some few persons of property and some social position are advising and inducing new desertions, and I am informed that it is not uncommon for squads of ten or fifteen to come in from the army, having made their way across the country on foot, and generally bringing their arms.

A much more down-to-earth account of these same events is found in the letters of A. A. Neves of Greenville District's Mush Creek community to his sons serving in the army near Charleston.

> [11 September] Capt Mcguire is in the mountains with fifty men all mounted [.] he is taking up Dezerters & conscripts. I saw him yesterday & think him pretty smart [.] he has taken some 8 or ten & killed one or shot him so that he is sertain to dye [.] it is William Roberson [.] I have not heard from him since yesterday [.] he was still a live then but no chance of getting well [.] I think a few more to get the same fare will bring the tories & Dezerters to there sences [.] if the last one of them was dead I mean torys & Dezerters was dead the country would be a heap better off than it is [.] There is some of

the old men that ought to be shot where ever they are found & I expect old bill Roberson is one [.]

[11 October] Mcguire is getheren men [.] I suppose he has got the most of them that was in the mountains [.] he got fifty seven in the neighborhood of Cashvill last week [.] he is gone now to Reedsvill [.] he is the perseveringest man I ever saw [.] he told me the other day that he sent off 284 since he come up [,] shot 2 & hung one [.] the name of Mcguire is a turer to the tories & deserters [.]

[18 October] I under stand that some of those men that is taking Deserters shot one of the Lindseys ded Thursday last & one of the Pruets Friday & wounded two others but I have forgot the names [.] I understood that the Deserters had got to think that they would not shoot to kill but per haps they may conclude that some of them is fool enough to kill a deserter or tory [.] I would be glad that every ball shot at one of them would go plum through there heart [.][30]

But this crash program failed to have the desired results. On 20 January 1864, a Charleston officer acknowledged a letter from Ashmore concerning a Union meeting to be held three days later in Anderson District, led by Nathan McAlister.[31] He was ordered not to interfere; instead, he was to have at least two "reliable and discreet" witnesses present, preferably disguised, who could tell the governor what happened. Discontent had progressed from grumbling to armed resistance and public protest. All the Confederates could do was watch, report, and hope.

Desertion is, of course, an extreme expression of dissent, personal affirmation of unhappiness with things as they are. The justification for quitting the army usually was the safety of one's family—*family before country*—an argument, according to historian Malcolm C. McMillan, hard to refute.[32] Yet diverse elements other than military service were fostering widespread disaffection during 1863 and after, among them, shortages, speculation, extortion, the twin blows of Vicksburg and Gettysburg, and impressment of slaves and crops.

Rounding up blacks to work on coastal defenses became an especially troublesome issue in 1862-1863. The General Assembly first debated the matter behind closed doors and in December 1861 passed a secret resolution permitting the governor to spend up to $20,000 either

Slaves building fortifications on James Island. According to Leslie's (31 January 1863), this sketch was made by Private Asa Palmer, late of the 21st South Carolina Volunteers, a thirty-two-year-old Georgetown resident. The following week Leslie's published three more Charleston sketches by one who, "although a native of that state, had seen the 'error of his ways'" and changed sides.

to hire or impress slave labor as required by Confederate authorities. According to the *Charleston Mercury* (8 August 1862), this program began three months later, largely among blacks ousted from areas seized or threatened by Union forces. But some fled to enemy lines and others failed to appear, often because their masters refused to release them. In July 1862, Colonel James Chesnut presented the Executive Council with a plan to impress 2 percent of the slave population as "axmen, spadesmen and ditchers" to help build fortifications. Those summoned would serve thirty days, receive soldier rations, and their pay ($11 a month) would go to their owner or agent. This scheme, loosely based on the road-duty system, was approved by the council on 28 July.

As soon as the plan was announced, the upcountry seethed with resentment. Abbeville, for example, mounted a strong protest (by no means the last). Planters in that region insisted labor was needed at home and expressed fears of disease, lax discipline, and contaminating influences. Chesnut acknowledged their concerns and promised efforts would be made to overcome such objections.

With the demise of the council, the General Assembly turned its attention to impressment, this time in public debate. In December 1862, lawmakers approved a bill designed to increase the flow of Negro labor that fixed upon the central government responsibility for all aspects of the operation—transportion, housing, compensation, liability, etc. Even the state agent hired to regulate the program was to be paid by Richmond.

A few weeks later, General Beauregard and Governor Bonham exchanged letters concerning this perplexing issue.[33] Beauregard conceded on 7 January that blacks called for thirty days service often were detained two or three times as long because no replacements arrived and pleaded for a more orderly system. On the 15th, Bonham expressed regret but said Congress really was to blame since it refused to assume responsibility for any slaves lost while in state service. The governor said he was eager to abandon the present scheme: "It has created more dissatisfaction and discontent than any other duties the Citizens have had to perform whilst at the same time they have desired [,] I think, Every man to discharge his whole duty."

Eight weeks later, the General Assembly passed new legislation designed to alleviate this problem. Each judicial district in turn was to supply for one month one-third of its slave labor liable for ordinary road duty, which, in theory, would provide 3,000 able hands. All were supposed to appear with shovels and spades, but again many did not. Instead, their owners were willing to risk payment of a small fine ($1.50 per diem for each delinquent slave).[34] Planters said the coast was both unhealthy and unsafe, blacks were neither properly cared for nor well supervised, and they also were exposed to "bad" influences.[35] But the principal objection, as before, was that slaves were needed at home on their plantations.

Reaction in Yorkville was typical of what happened in many upland communities. In this instance, those attending a public meeting held in April 1863 vowed the call for labor beginning on 4 May was "inopportune" and drafted a formal protest to the governor.[36] Two months later, stung by the *Charleston Mercury's* continued demand for upcountry slaves, the editor of the *Yorkville Enquirer* gave voice on 1 July to a myriad of wartime frustrations. Lowcountry blacks, in his opinion, often were a nuisance—much too "non-chalant," not humble enough. They demonstrate, he said, "a non-chalance at once in keeping with their fugitive masters." And, as for those masters and their cries for assistance, they should turn "their own shoulders to the wheel, then call for Hercules, if help be needed." Upcountry farmers now had good crops but few on hand to gather them. "…we are again called on," he added, "to protect the untided rice fields, while the negro marts are crowded with plantation negroes, for the block. We are not disposed to grumble, but we do insist, that the coast has slave labor enough to suit its purposes, and they have neither right or title to any assistance in that respect from the upcountry. We will fight their battles, as we have done, but we will do it as freemen, while they may save their negroes, and we protect ours. We have no negroes to spare for the coast; in fact, but few freemen. If the *owners* will go, we have no objection."

These thrusts hit home, and on 15 July the *Enquirer* printed a refugee's angry reply. It opened with a brief defense of lowcountry blacks, a quiet reminder that all South Carolinians should be brothers, and acknowledgment that refugees were not always well received, although this was not true, the writer emphasized, in the community of Yorkville.

> If we could be brought to believe that the desire you manifest to get rid of us, was shared by many others, we would feel it our duty as well as our interest to seek some other home. Our 'non-chalance' seems to offend you. I am not sure that this is a habit with us. If it is, I would ask if it is not better than lugubrious countenances and doleful complaints? You insinuate that the Parishes are not taking a sufficiently active part in the great battle for liberty and independence. Now, sir, there is nothing more true than that no part of the State has sent more fighting men to the field than the Parishes, in proportion to the population. You insinuate that the whole work of fortifying the sea-coast should be done with low country labor. Here we differ. It is obvious, if the enemy get possession of the coast, Charleston included, the whole State must suffer; it may be entirely overrun, or, at least indispensible supplies—salt, for instance—cut off. The heaviest work has already been done by Parish labor, and a great deal of it *without pay or rations*. You propose to fight our battles whilst we labor. We decline this, and prefer, as we have heretofore done, to do our part in the battlefield, as well as in the trenches. You are displeased at the sale of so many negroes. But what is an unfortunate refugee to do in the terrible emergency? Many of them are not only driven from their plantations, and their products de-

stroyed for the good of the country, but have no possible
way of maintaining their families than that of disposing
of such property as may be left in their possession. Mr.
Editor, let there be peace, good will and forbearance,
within the borders.

In a brief disclaimer, the editor agreed it was time for good will
and—in view of recent events (Vicksburg and Gettysburg)—also a time
for action, not words. Nevertheless, he maintained that (a) feeding an
army was almost as important as its fortifications and (b) blacks already
acclimated to the region should be used as labor on the coast, not those
unaccustomed to such conditions.

It would appear, then, that impressment of upcountry slaves to work
on lowcountry defenses stirred old regional animosities, while seizure
of goods—much like conscription—activated class differences as various individuals thought they were being treated less fairly than others.
Those living near Union-held territory, Confederate installations, and
railroad lines undoubtedly suffered most. Whether crops, chickens, and
animals were simply stolen by troops, legally impressed by government
officials at ridiculously low prices, or seized under "tax in kind" regulations approved by Congress in April 1863 (1/10th of various commodities
held by farmers and planters), they were gone. Six months later, the
Chester Standard said impressment, as operated, was "eminently unwise, unjust and calculated to bring odium upon the Government and its
agents and result in nothing but harm to the Confederate cause."[37] A
planter, this weekly complained, would agree to exchange corn for cloth
to clothe his slaves (perhaps with a manufacturer such as William Gregg);
but, once the corn got to the depot, it was seized by the government and
the planter given only $2 a bushel, much less than true market value.

Columbia's *Tri-Weekly South Carolinian* (9 December 1863) said
it first thought tax in kind a good idea, but outright seizure of goods
demonstrated bad faith on the part of the government. Individuals frequently offered up their 1/10th only to be told the authorities were not
prepared to receive it. Then, within a short time, agents would appear
and take everything but what that person's family needed for its own
use and order the household not to sell to neighbors. This was "ridiculous," the editor cried.

Near the close of the year, overseer S. H. Boineau of Combahee
began to detail his problems to owner Edward B. Heyward. On 28 December 1863, a government representative said he must have one-third of

the cattle at once, agreeing to pay 35¢ a pound for beef and leaving only enough animals for family use. In January, thirty-four more animals were taken and in October, another twenty-seven, followed shortly by two thousand pounds of fodder.[38] In August of the same year, Barnwell District agent T. P. Counts proposed to buy all of the surplus corn held by Lewis Malone Ayer, Jr., and pay "in Treasury notes at scheduled prices." If Ayer chose not to sell, Counts stated in writing, then "you may consider the same impressed for the use of the army in this Military Dist."[39]

Despite angry protests, the state government could do little to stem such practices. In September 1863, the General Assembly's Committee on Confederate Relations—successor to a little-known body that for decades monitored the activities of the federal government—officially deplored impressment.[40] Agents sometimes seized goods, members complained, when the same items could be purchased a few miles away. They suggested that, if supplies were scarce in a district, farmers be permitted to pay in money and any goods collected used for relief of soldier families.

In December, alarmed that impressment woes were continuing to increase, they spoke out sternly against the seizure of horses, "a subject of general and loud complaint.... Horses have been taken in the public streets, from carriages in which there were ladies, and while valuable animals much needed by their owners have been taken from those who made no effort to withhold them, persons have been suffered to conceal their horses, and no pains have been taken to prevent this evasion of the law." The text of their protest, couched in carefully chosen words, talked of patriotism yet warned of trouble: "The citizens of this State will give up freely and cheerfully whatever may be with propriety be demanded of them during the war, to the maintenance of which they are devoted with remarkable unanimity. But tyrannical and ruinous demands, arrogantly made and enforced by its agents, must engender disaffection to the government, and stir up a spirit of resistance."[41] This sounds fine, but the truth is—as many living in the hills of South Carolina could attest— "unanimity" to the cause was hardly "remarkable" and demands being made already had created something much more potent than mere "disaffection."[42]

Yet another type of dissent—perhaps more insidious—appeared much earlier, a phenomenon one might call "personal patriotism." Only a handful of South Carolinians displayed this strange brand of selfishness, but they were, almost without exception, experienced, well-to-do community leaders, the very men a new government waging war sorely needed. These individuals loudly proclaimed their devotion to "the cause" and were among the first to march off to battle; but, within a year or so, miffed because they failed to get some position they sought, they returned home and immersed themselves in various homefront activities.[43]

While pondering the root causes of disenchantment, one should not lose sight of the "big" picture. South Carolina was basically an agricultural realm and farmers are notorious complainers. The weather is always too hot or too cold, too wet or too dry, and the common foot soldier probably comes close to the tiller of the soil as a chronic fault finder. Thus an army of farmers' sons is a recipe for trouble. Ask that same army to march, fight, and face death in one campaign after another, following fire-eater assurances of peaceful secession and no war, and problems mount.

But, you say, the enemy had farm-grown troops, too, which is true. However, the boys in blue rarely were fighting on their own soil, their nation was not at the same time trying to create the industrial base needed to wage war, their homefront was not being strangled by a blockade, shortages, speculation, and runaway inflation, and—despite impressive Confederate battle maneuvers and innumerable defensive heroics—they were winning. By the summer of 1862, the Stars and Stripes were flying somewhere in every Confederate state, but the reverse was not true and never would be.

Therein lies the rub. A few solid *offensive* victories, perhaps only one, would have done much to relieve homefront pressures throughout South Carolina and the rest of the Confederacy.[44] Sacrifice can be tolerated if shared equally and so long as it holds promise of achieving desired goals. What many rank-and-file South Carolinians were saying after July 1863 is patently clear. The Confederate war effort, in their opinion, was a failure on both counts. It was not being conducted fairly, and apparently no amount of sacrifice could put on firm footing a national structure based upon the institution of slavery.

Thus a manpower draft, though obviously necessary by the spring of 1862, increased dramatically both desertion and dissent. Differences between state and national conscription, further sources of discontent, were exacerbated by an ill-advised substitute system. Impressment of slaves and foodstuffs (tax in kind) only added to smoldering resentment in scores of South Carolina households. Not surprisingly, more and more citizens were beginning to question both state and national policies. In effect, not only were they beginning to wonder if a separate path was possible, was it—under these conditions—worth fighting for?

NOTES

[1] See David Duncan Wallace, *The History of South Carolina* (4 vols., New York, 1934), III, pp. 172-74, and Charles E. Cauthen, *South Carolina Goes to War, 1860-1865* (Chapel Hill, 1950), pp. 139-63. Cauthen also edited the records of this body, which were published by the South Carolina State Archives in 1956.

[2] C.G. Memminger to W. W. Harllee, 4 April 1862, Memminger Papers, South Caroliniana Library. Memminger added, "If the planters cannot be brought to concur in such an organized effort as that which I have suggested, at least, let them retire their negroes from the reach of Yankee gunboats. Their reign cannot be long, and by organising the Militia further in the interior, our defence is certain."

[3] Documents relative to these matters can be found in Petitions to the General Assembly (1862), South Carolina Department of Archives and History—Horry (#8, 30 November), Marion (#3, no specific date), Marlboro (#4, 8 December).

[4] *Report of the Chief of the Department of the Military of the State of South Carolina....* (Columbia, 1862), p. 9. This pamphlet, which covers events from January to July 1862, refers to numerous attached documents that were not printed and presumably have been lost.

[5] *Reports and Resolutions* (Columbia, 1862), p. 321. Although the General Assembly spoke out in 1863, these remarks are bound in a volume bearing date of 1862.

[6] *Charleston Daily Courier*, 20 February 1862.

[7] *Report of the Chief of the Department of the Military....*, p. 7.

[8] See "List of Draft Substitutes, 1862" and "Overseers Exempt from the Draft, 1862," South Carolina Department of Archives and History.

[9] Wilmot G. DeSaussure to W. A. Courtenay, 17 April 1862, Letters Sent, Office of the Adjutant and Inspector General, South Carolina Department of Archives and History. This statement appears to mean that Confederate conscription, at least for the moment, took precedence over state.

[10] *War of the Rebellion*, Fourth Series, II, pp. 73-75.

[11] However, at the end of 1864 the state reversed policy and began to claim exemptions from Confederate service once more. This change undoubtedly was prompted by rising opposition to Davis, failure of Richmond to send reinforcements to counter Sherman, and conviction that the state should marshal its remaining manpower in the face of a Union invasion. When Sherman arrived early in 1865, 5,839 South Carolinians enjoyed exempt status (Cauthen, *South Carolina Goes to War*, pp. 170-71).

[12] Mrs. Lucy Sheldon to Milledge L. Bonham, 28 October 1862, quoted in an unpublished biography of Bonham (p. 625) in the Bonham Papers, South Caroliniana Library.

[13] Coulter, *Confederate States of America*, p. 328. See Chapter XV, "Raising Troops," pp. 308-22. Of course, locally managed conscription was precisely what South Carolina had in mind in the spring of 1862.

[14] Albert Burton Moore, *Conscription and Conflict in the Confederacy* (New York,

1924), pp. 49-51.

[15]*Tri-Weekly Watchman* (Sumter), 2 February 1863.

[16]Reproduced in the *Edgefield Advertiser*, 15 May 1861, at the request of some members of the Edgefield Riflemen. Note: Since many wanted to be *first*, at least three regiments laid claim to priority—Gregg's, Hagood's, and First Regiment of South Carolina Infantry.

[17]See the *Camden Confederate*, 2 May 1862, for a copy of this order.

[18]Samuel Langley of Aiken, writing to Lewis Malone Ayer, Jr., on 15 April, remarked that "twelve months men organized for State defense were ordered to Corinth, and en route to Augusta, their libations being rather potent, mutinied and about one or two hundred I understand, returned home. They were mostly from Edgefield. Several however have repented their folly, and I am happy to learn have determined to go on" (Lewis Malone Ayer Papers, South Caroliniana Library). When the 17th Regiment was ordered to Virginia in June authorities sent upcountry men by the Wilmington railroad; those from the Pee Dee, via Columbia and Charlotte.

[19]These executions are noted briefly in the *Courier*, 29 August 1862, 19 May 1863, and the *Mercury*, 30 August 1862, 3 May 1864.

[20]See the *Charleston Daily Courier*, 2 May 1863; Columbia's *Daily Southern Guardian*, 10 August 1863; and the Columbia *Tri-Weekly South Carolinian*, 29 November, 12 December 1864.

[21]*Daily Southern Guardian*, 10 August 1863.

[22]Racine, *Piedmont Farmer....*, p. 222.

[23]William Birnie to his uncle (William Birnie) in Greenville, 13 July 1863, Birnie Papers.

[24]*Camden Journal*, 12 February 1864.

[25]William Elliott, Jr., to his mother, 12 April 1863, Elliott-Gonzales Papers.

[26]Ibid., 7 July 1864.

[27]John D. Ashmore to James Chesnut, 3 August 1863, Ashmore Letters, South Caroliniana Library. About two weeks later, Ashmore told superiors Elliott and a sergeant had been fired upon twice in the mountains and reported deserters were constructing a heavy log building near Gowensville, "loop-holed and prepared for defense." He requested more arms and a small cannon, adding the ranks of the deserters were being augmented by men from South Carolina's 22nd Regiment who had walked cross-country from Augusta.

[28]The Ashmore-Melton-Preston correspondence that follows can be found in its entirety in the *War of the Rebellion*, Fourth Series, II, pp. 769-74.

[29]William Elliott, Jr., told his mother on 17 August 1863 that 74 deserters from this regiment alone were known to be in the mountains (Elliott-Gonzales Papers).

[30]A. A. Neves to his sons, William John and G. W. Neves, Neves Family Papers.

[31]*War of the Rebellion*, First Series, XXXV, Part I, p. 536. On 30 December 1863, the General Assembly passed legislation designed to prevent desertion. It was the duty of each sheriff, lawmakers said, to arrest deserters. Those who did not might be fined up to $1000. Also, it was unlawful to aid deserters. Anyone convicted of doing so could be fined up to $500 and spend up to a year in jail.

[32]Malcolm C. McMillan, *The Disintegration of a Confederate State: Three Governors and Alabama's Home Front, 1861-1865* (Macon, 1986), pp. 42, 127. McMillan sees desertion as the "main cause" of the collapse of the homefront and emphasizes that, if an individual was needed at home, his decision to leave the service was widely condoned.

[33]See Milledge L. Bonham Papers, South Carolina Department of Archives and History.

[34]On 30 September 1863, failure to supply labor became a misdemeanor; and, upon conviction, an owner could be fined $200 for each slave not sent when requested.

[35]In 1864, for example, when Francis Pickens sent seven slaves to the coast, he asked Charleston resident James Reid Pringle to contact them: "They have been raised carefully, and it would be a great comfort to me to know there was some one to look to for protection." Pickens to Pringle, 21 June 1864, Pringle Papers, Special Collections Library, Duke University. In addition, some slaves used the opportunity to develop or perfect their reading skills. See Jacob Stroyer, *My Life in the South* (Salem, Mass., 1885).

[36]*Yorkville Enquirer*, 8 April 1863.

[37]Quoted in the *Charleston Daily Courier*, 10 October 1863. The following day, Columbia's *Daily South Carolinian* published the letter of a soldier shocked by food prices in that city. He also recounted rumors that impressing officers were preventing farm produce from reaching urban markets.

[38]Heyward Family Papers, 28 December 1863, 25 January, 6 October, 17 November 1864.

[39]T. P. Counts to Lewis M. Ayer, Jr., 23 August 1864, Lewis Malone Ayer Papers.

[40]*Reports and Resolutions* (Columbia, 1863), pp. 272-73. In addition, South Carolina and Richmond were bickering over funds expended in defense of Charleston, most of them before the Confederate government was formed on 8 February 1861. Of about $1.3 millions, the latter refused to honor $267,432.32, claiming vouchers were not in good order.

[41]Ibid., pp. 319-20.

[42]Even lawmakers were affected. On 1 December 1863, Benjamin F. Perry penned a gloomy letter to his wife from Columbia. Colonel Beaufort Watts of Laurens, he related, declared "it was time to think of being subdued" and expressed the wish that Judge John Belton O'Neall, ex-governor James Henry Hammond, and Perry "could go to Washington to treat for terms—I told him such a proposition would be treason—He said he knew it would not do to talk about or to mention" (Perry Papers, Southern Historical Collection, University of North Carolina).

[43]James B. Griffin of Edgefield and duelist E.B.C. Cash are prime examples of this type of behavior. See Judith N. McArthur and Orville Vernon Burton, *A Gentleman and an Officer: A Military and Social History of James B. Griffin's Civil War* (New York, 1996).

[44]According to Susan Middleton, who attended meetings of the convention held in Columbia in September 1862, in answer to criticism, Confederate Senator Robert W.

Barnwell said "the defensive policy of the government was *mere myth... no* one *ever* adhered to it." Sickness alone, he maintained, "has kept our armies on our own soil." Susan to cousin Harriott in Flat Rock, 14-16 September 1862, "Middleton Correspondence," *South Carolina Historical Magazine* (July 1962), p. 171. Although Susan thought Barnwell by far the best speaker, she did not find this statement convincing. Robert Barnwell Rhett, she remarked, was "like a whole volley of cross *Mercury* editorials."

V

SLAVES & FREE BLACKS

The Institution of Slavery.—Just, humane, wise and Christian; one of the earth's greatest blessings to the benighted African, and essential to the prosperity and welfare of the South.

For generations the Fourth of July had been celebrated in a grand manner throughout South Carolina, a colorful panorama of parades, patriotic speeches, feasting, and toasts, but 1861 was different. Some communities, Columbia among them, took a low-key approach, studiously avoiding any display that might evoke Union memories. The *Southern Guardian* (4 July) told readers that banks would be closed, there would be an eleven-gun salute at sunrise, and the Richland Volunteers would march through town. Also, by order of the mayor, the city bell ("Secession") would be rung, but generally the day "would be observed as a mere holiday, without jubilant demonstration."

Charleston tried to do the same; however, local military units fired occasional salutes, as did the federal blockade fleet at daybreak...a total of thirty-four salvos, one for each state. These volleys moved the editor of the *Courier* to comment on the 6th that the Yankee commander should not have wasted powder on eleven of them! The Society of the Cincinnati held a picnic, some folks enjoyed excursions on the harbor, and the '76 Association met under confusing circumstances. Alfred H. Dunkin, the gentleman scheduled to address the group, declined to do so, pointing out in a curt note that it was a time for action, not words. Taking heed, members agreed that 20 December, not 4 July, henceforth would be "Independence Day." Nevertheless, a delegation of Cincinnati faithful showed up at the Association meeting and delivered an onslaught of effusive rhetoric as banners were presented to the Charleston Riflemen and the ladies who made the flags hailed as paragons of honor, virtue, and sacrifice.

Yet old customs die hard, and some regions held the usual ceremonies. These include Georgetown District, where citizens met in the Pee Dee muster shed to hear patriotic orations, and St. James, Santee, scene of an enthusiastic military display featuring riflemen, cavalry, infantry, and even a coast guard unit. There was a parade, speech-making, food, liquor, and toasts—thirteen of them. And, after saluting King Cotton, Jeff Davis and the Confederate States of America ("true to the spirit of '76"), and Governor Pickens and the state of South Carolina ("the first to throw off the yoke of corrupt and fanatical government"), as well as the late United States ("we mourn over its corruption and death by Northern fanaticism and misrule"), came formal toast number twelve, the homage to slavery that opens this chapter—"just, humane, wise and Christian...a blessing to the benighted African...essential to the prosperity and welfare of the South."[1]

Unwittingly, perhaps, these words cut to the heart of the fury that would burst forth at Manassas a few days later, for much of the nation (and the world, for that matter) did not agree that slavery was just and humane or that it was a vital part of any healthy economy. Hence the struggle that would kill some 600,000 men, ruin millions of lives, and change the course of our history. No one at St. James, Santee, said anything about "states rights."

Table 2, "State Population, 1860," offers a summary of population district by district on the eve of war. Significantly, enumerators found South Carolina to be 58.6% black, and they also recorded mulattoes and Indians.[2] Ten of the thirty districts had white majorities: Anderson, Chesterfield, Greenville, Horry, Lancaster, Lexington, Marion, Pickens, Spartanburg, and York. The greatest concentration of free blacks was found, of course, in Charleston (3,622), which also was home to fifty-two Indians. Three regions (Horry, Lexington, and Williamsburg) reported less than fifty free blacks, while Darlington and Lancaster had fifty to one hundred. All other districts had at least a hundred, although Beaufort (809) and Barnwell (640) lagged far behind Charleston.

Hostilities, as well as events leading up to the outbreak of war, focused considerable attention upon South Carolina's blacks. In 1860-1861, legislators considered numerous bills and petitions designed to restrict their movement. Some individuals wanted to force free blacks into slavery, banish them from the state, prohibit them from carrying guns, or compel them to enlist as cooks in the army. Others wanted to deny blacks the right to ride in carriages or become merchants and tradesmen. The practice of masters leaving standing orders for liquor at shops

Table 2. State Population, 1860.

District	White	Free Black	Slave	Indian
Abbeville	11,516	367	20,502	0
Anderson	14,286	162	8,425	0
Barnwell	12,702	640	17,401	0
Beaufort	6,714	809	32,530	0
Charleston	20,136	3,622	37,290	52
Chester	7,096	156	10,868	2
Chesterfield	7,354	132	4,348	0
Clarendon	4,378	151	8,566	0
Colleton	9,255	354	32,307	0
Darlington	8,421	52	11,877	11
Edgefield	15,653	173	24,060	1
Fairfield	6,373	204	15,534	0
Georgetown	3,013	183	18,109	0
Greenville	14,631	212	7,049	0
Horry	5,564	39	2,359	0
Kershaw	5,026	197	7,841	22
Lancaster	6,054	93	5,650	0
Laurens	10,529	129	13,200	0
Lexington	9,333	44	6,202	0
Marion	11,007	232	9,951	0
Marlboro	5,373	168	6,893	0
Newberry	7,000	184	13,695	0
Orangeburg	8,108	205	16,583	0
Pickens	15,335	109	4,195	0
Richland	6,863	439	11,005	0
Spartanburg	18,537	142	8,240	0
Sumter	6,857	320	16,682	0
Williamsburg	5,187	43	10,259	0
York	11,329	189	9,984	0
Total	**291,300**	**9,914**	**402,406**[3]	**88**

Source: *Population of the United States in 1860* (Washington, 1864), p. 452.

and permitting slaves to procure it for them came under fire, as did the common custom of allowing slaves to "hire" their own time, a constant irritant year in and year out. Still others appealed for laws banning slaves from public gatherings such as musters and political rallies. However, the only such act passed in 1861 related to travel permits ("tickets") issued to slaves. Henceforth "general" passes were forbidden; instead, a master was to state in specific terms the date, time, and place of any visit by a slave. (This did not apply to urban slaves in the course of a normal work day.)

These pressures were not new, simply intensified by the threat of war and war itself. In the spring of 1859, for example, a Newberry District grand jury—after appealing for more hitching posts around the town square and making the annual plea for full enforcement of laws relating to slaves hiring their time—lashed out at free blacks.

> The existence of the Free Negro,—their known want of thrift and the mischievous influence they exert on the slave, render them almost a nuisance to any Community in which they may happen to be located. And their rapidly increasing numbers, make some Legislative enactment in the case highly necessary. We, therefore, think that the existing laws should be so altered or amended, or such new laws enacted as would compel the Free Negro to Choose a Master, in a certain period of time, and in failure to make such Choice, each and every Free Negro so failing should be sold into slavery. And in the case of such sale the proceeds thereof should be paid to the Clerk of the Court and be equally divided between the different Boards of Commissioners of the District.[4]

Under these conditions, a handful of free blacks flowed with the tide and initiated legal steps to become slaves. Among them was Lucy Andrews of Lancaster, an eighteen-year-old woman with a four-months-old daughter, who lived with Henry Duncan (white). In a petition filed with the General Assembly in 1861, Lucy claimed she was excluded from both black and white society and sought the protection of slavery. That same year a Laurens youth asked permission to give himself to W. G. Gore and his heirs: "I, William Jackson, a free boy am tired of freedom and wish to become a slave." Two years later, Lucy, now mother of two small children, again appealed to the General Assembly, vowing she never had a permanent home until she began living with Duncan some six years ago.[5]

One suspects that both Lucy and William were seeking to perpetuate relationships endangered by their current status or perhaps were being offered special inducements by Duncan and Gore. The 1860 census reveals that Duncan (37) was a relatively well-to-do farmer with an eight-year-old daughter and a wife (Susan), Lucy ostensibly existing as a household servant. Whatever the relationship between Duncan and Lucy, it seems quite possible that Susan may have been pressuring her husband to convert Lucy into a slave. W. G. Gore (46) also was comfortably situated in 1860—a wife, seven children, eleven slaves. Since Jackson's name does not appear in the Laurens census of that year, his motives remain wrapped in mystery; but, whatever the true circumstances, lawmakers took no action, simply filing these various petitions for posterity to ponder.

In their quest to become slaves, Lucy Andrews and William Jackson were in a distinct minority. Most free blacks reacted quite differently to white pressure, especially in Charleston, where, in the summer of 1860, local officials went from house to house demanding *proof* of free status. As the secession drumbeat increased, many feared that in a new nation they would become light-skinned slaves instead of dark-skinned free and fled to other regions such as Philadelphia and Haiti.[6] On 11 February 1861, a correspondent of the *New York Tribune* stationed in Charleston estimated that at least 2,000 free blacks had left the city within the past month. Most were laborers, tradesmen, carpenters, bakers, tailors—men without much property and few ties to bind them, individuals who could scrape up funds to transport themselves and their families to a safe haven.

But more affluent free blacks were unable to liquidate their assets and depart so easily. This was especially true in the winter of 1860-1861 as the local economy stagnated and shipping declined to a trickle. The *Tribune* (9 February 1861) reported that only 141 vessels entered Charleston Harbor in the thirteen-month period ending 31 January 1861, compared with 269 in 1859. During the same months, cash duties dropped from $60,000 to $14,000, and the value of foreign exports fell from $3 million to $900,000. A few days earlier, this New York daily noted on 29 January that a business boom in nearby Savannah, not troubled by a dispute over federal installations, was causing considerable consternation on the local scene.

Under these conditions, unable to flee, well-to-do blacks in two communities—Charleston and Columbia—decided to make the best of a bad situation. In what obviously was a coordinated effort, on 10 January 1861 they presented memorials to key officials stressing their South Carolina birth, the white blood flowing in their veins, their loyalty, and their dependence upon the good will of white friends. Thirty-seven leading freemen of Charleston sent a memorial to Thomas J. Gantt, clerk of the Court of Appeals, while twenty-three of them signed a similar statement forwarded to Governor Pickens and another twenty-three presented Columbia mayor J. H. Boatwright with an identical document. (No memorial went to Charles McBeth, mayor of Charleston, the man who led the recent assault upon free blacks.) "Our attachments are with you," they told Gantt, "our hopes of safety & protection from you. Our allegiance is due to *So. Ca.* and in her defence, we are willing to offer up our lives, and all that is dear to us."[7] They asked only that, if ordered to duty elsewhere, the state would provide for their families and that any such orders be subject to the approval of certain leaders.

This offer, skillfully phrased, said nothing about giving money or property to the cause, instead it stressed a common birthright, loyalty to the state, and dependence upon carefully nurtured ties to white benefactors. It was, of course, refused, Governor Pickens saying he would come to them only as a "last resort." Nevertheless, this proclamation of loyalty was of vital importance to the free black community. It won reassurance that, for the most part, they would be left alone, and subsequent efforts on behalf of the Confederacy—volunteer work on harbor defenses, purchase of war bonds, and benefit performances for soldier relief—tended to curb any attempt to restrict the status of South Carolina's free blacks during wartime.[8]

Early in September 1861, Charleston's free colored formed a committee with the mayor's permission and collected $450 to aid soldiers in Virginia. (Emma Holmes noted in her diary with satisfaction that this act was indeed "very creditable.")[9] Two months later, on 12 November his excellency issued a general appeal for assistance in defending the city, at the same time ordering all free black males (18-45) to report to the engineers in charge of public works with tools and implements in hand. Since this plea was repeated several times during the next few years (as well as the order to free blacks), we can assume neither race came forward with alacrity or in the numbers anticipated.

Nevertheless, on 10 December 1861, the Committee on Colored Population in the lower house of the General Assembly turned aside with soft words a suggestion from Laurens District residents that all free blacks be compelled to enlist as cooks or render "such other service" as soldiers might require. The committee said members had considered the matter

> and recollecting with gratification the many examples of patriotism and loyalty exhibited by the Colored Population since the commencement of our troubles, and believing that the people as a class are anxious to contribute every thing in their power towards the public weal, think it would be unwise and impolitic to pass a law of compulsion to effect the same object which is now obtained, by the free will offering of those referred to....[10]

Thus, despite a flurry of anti-free black activity on the eve of war, this campaign was much less apparent during the conflict that followed, possibly because some dark-skinned individuals made certain their patriotism was highly visible and evident to all. Yet another non-event was slave insurrection. White South Carolinians often attribute this to innate loyalty and affection for "good ole massa," but a better reading might be simple pragmatism. Why pile revolution on top of revolution and risk life and limb while men in blue were fighting to set you free? Let them do the job for you.

Newspaper editors frequently boasted of the devotion of South Carolina blacks to the Confederate cause. Shortly after the fall of Fort Sumter, the *Abbeville Banner* told of the great joy evident among those thronging railroad depots from Greenville to Columbia: "There is today more humbleness and good feeling, more contentment than in any period in our history."[11] However, shortly before that fortress fell, a northern journalist said Major Anderson was a hero to Charleston blacks. "When not in attendance upon the Chivalry," he wrote, "they chuckle and caper with delight 'cos Sumter ain't took.'"[12]

But there are scattered hints of black protest. In the summer of 1862 a Georgia runaway was lynched in Williamston, a small community in Anderson District, because he allegedly was fomenting rebellion. Trial records indicate that Alfred, who claimed Abraham Lincoln knew of his crusade, vowed he was a disciple of Jesus Christ...who, he said, soon would appear. Although this young slave cautioned blacks to obey their masters, he promised that, once Christ came, there would be no difference between the races. Alfred was lodged in the district jail for a time and then taken to Williamston for trial where he was seized by the townspeople and hanged.[13] Had Alfred been the property of a South Carolina resident and possessed of intrinsic monetary value easily recognized by the community, it seems unlikely that he would have been so summarily dispatched. Eighteen blacks accused of listening to his words were merely whipped, and those involved in other rumored insurrections of the early 1860s in Spartanburg, Union, and Sumter (as well as another incident in Anderson District) received varying degrees of legal punishment. A few were found innocent, others imprisoned or whipped. The most serious of these affairs, which resulted in execution of three slaves and incarceration of fourteen more, took place in Sumter in 1862.[14]

In addition to the overt patriotism displayed by some free blacks and virtually no organized slave protest, there are two other factors—often overlooked—that contributed to produce relatively stable race relations during wartime. First, white South Carolinians needed desperately the skills their slaves possessed; and, second, for the most part, the day-to-day life of blacks (both slave and free) was improving. According to the 1860 census, the state had 703,708 residents; and, of that number, 81,631 reported specific occupations. This was the lowest total found in any Confederate state except Florida, which had a population of only 140,424. But even there occupations were proportionally more numerous than in South Carolina—15.6% compared to 11.6%. Arkansas, with about two-thirds as many people as South Carolina, cited 85,001 individuals with occupations; Louisiana, with virtually the same number of residents (708,002), reported 107,498 occupations.[15]

What this means, since technically only whites and free blacks had occupations, is that thousands of South Carolina slaves were shoeing horses, making barrels, repairing machinery and tools, and performing scores of tasks done elsewhere by free men, white and black. And when those white workers marched off to war, local economies throughout the South suffered. Looked at another way, a preponderance of skilled slave labor meant South Carolinians experienced less internal disruption than other Confederate states during the war years, which may help to explain why loyalty to the cause persisted even as North Carolinians, Georgians, and others were abandoning the fray.

It is obvious, then, with thousands of men in uniform, that South Carolina's white population was extremely dependent upon blacks, both skilled and unskilled, even more so than in peacetime. Perhaps it would

Adele Petigru Allston (1810-1896).

be folly to expect this dependence to translate into better treatment; but, for a variety of reasons, that is what seems to have happened. Among them were lax supervision (or none at all), demand for farm produce and other goods that slaves and free blacks could furnish by fair means or foul (no questions asked), and the specter of impending freedom. If nothing else, the turmoil of war created unique opportunities for blacks whether they stayed put, sought haven behind enemy lines, or were moved inland to temporary quarters.

When eighty-four slaves belonging to John Berkeley Grimball of St. John's Parish, Colleton, fled to Union-held Edisto Island in March

FAITH COMETH BY HEARING...

When a group of Georgians petitioned their legislature to permit owners to teach their slaves to read and thus remove "this foul blot" upon
the civilization of both Georgia and South Carolina, Columbia's *Confederate Baptist* (8 October 1862) reacted sternly: "Faith cometh by
hearing, and all the benefits of revelation may be communicated to
them by what always has been the great means of conversion, the
preaching of the Word. Oral communication has ever been God's chosen method of saving sinners."

1862, he was, according to his wife, "quite unstrung by it."[16] Seven
months later, the Robert F. W. Allstons, who lived near Georgetown,
were equally shocked when the head carpenter and eighteen of Francis
Weston's "finest, most intelligent and trusted men" took the family boat
and sailed away to join the enemy. Adele Petigru Allston told her son on
30 October 1862 that the circumstances were indeed "very painful" and
revealed "quite a widespread feeling not only among Mr Westons people,
but throughout the neighbourhood."[17] In March 1863 another boatload
of local slaves disappeared, and in July of the following year the Allston's
Stephen vanished. His mistress found this especially distressing since
he was married to the daughter of Mary, a highly favored servant, who
had command of the house keys. Since half of Mary's children had "gone
off," she wondered whether their slaves were acting according to some
prearranged plan. Should the authorities be told and near relatives held
responsible for such conduct?[18] A subsequent report by the Allston overseer confirmed that Stephen was armed and took others with him: "I
Can see since Stephn left a goodeal of obstanetry in Some of the Peopl.
Mostly mongst the Woman a goodeal of Quarling and disputeing & telling lies."[19]

Numerous reports in the *War of the Rebellion* volumes reveal how
frequently slaves such as Stephen joined forces with blue-clad troops,
often serving as guides for Union patrols near Georgetown, Beaufort,
and other coastal communities.[20] When a band of ex-slaves attacked Confederate troops on Jehossee Island in January 1862, several were captured
and sent to Charleston's work house. Confederates who raided Hutchinson
Island six months later found 125 blacks attending flourishing crops
thought to have been laid out by white Northerners who had departed.
The wife of the Yankee overseer presumably was maintaining a school
as well. In June 1863, a Confederate captain (J. H. Mickler) led an expe-

dition to Daufuskie Island where he discovered a dozen elderly blacks living in the lap of abandoned luxury. Their "remarkable accumulation" included gold and silver coin, furniture, clothing, dry goods, etc. that once belonged to white residents who had fled. The loot was so vast that Mickler could not carry it all away in two small boats; however, he and his men secured blankets, clothing, and supplies worth at least $2,000; the money ($188) was sent to aid the suffering people of Fredericksburg, Virginia.[21]

Early in 1862 a commission was established to coordinate the evacuation of slaves from coastal areas. The initial scheme was to use various church campgrounds as temporary havens with railroads providing half-fare transportation to those sites. But this plan quickly ran into trouble because the rail lines already were crowded, distribution of foodstuffs proved nearly impossible in a time of shortages, and some individuals insisted on taking virtually all of their possessions with them, that is, in addition to their slaves.[22]

More typical than movement to temporary quarters was the wholesale transfer of a well-to-do planter, slaves, food, and equipment to an inland plantation. On 12 March 1862, Henry W. Swinton of St. Paul's Parish, Colleton District, intent upon moving to Orangeburg, received a $200 draft from the commission. A printed form, now in Executive Department records at the South Carolina Department of Archives and History, lists the names of thirty-five slaves and four implements to be transported by rail. Other drafts (actually loans to be repaid) include those of Colleton neighbors, as well as residents of Beaufort and Georgetown citing slaves, corn, rice, and various agricultural equipment. However, General Beauregard's decision in mid-1863 to evict all non-combatants from Charleston overtaxed this already inadequate evacuation system and altered the basic nature of the program. The truth was, as some members of the commission observed, many individuals—especially poor urban whites—would not move unless forced to do so at the point of a gun.

South Carolinians residing fifty or a hundred miles inland faced other problems. In mid-1861 the *Edgefield Advertiser* expressed concern about slaves living alone on isolated farms and fears that some of them might be trading in poultry and eggs without proper permits from their owners. One lady, the editor noted on 19 June, recently had lost thirty chickens in this manner. The following year, Sumter officials passed an ordinance entitled "For the Better Maintenance of Good Order Among the Colored Population." No black vendors, slave or free, were to sell goods at stands without specific permits costing $7 per quarter. If convicted, an offender might receive fifteen lashes, and any owner permitting such commerce could be fined $10 for each offense; significantly, these rules did not apply to house-to-house sales.[23]

And on 1 September 1863, Columbia's *Tri-Weekly South Carolinian* published a rambling complaint from a reader distressed by "disorderly and riotous" conduct that prevailed each night on Main Street and "the almost complete monopoly of our market by negro venders, who intercept and buy up the supplies as they approach the city, and thus compel the citizens to purchase from them at their own prices." Many women, according to this writer (who recommended sales be restricted to whites), were reluctant to visit the local market because they had to trade with blacks "and to mingle with the crowds which they usually gather about them."

The rival *Daily Southern Guardian* quickly took up the cry. On 17 September the editor asked Columbia police to preserve good order and prevent "the confusion worse confounded, occasioned by loud talking, laughing and whistling of negroes upon the public streets, both in the day and in the night." Six days later, the same gentleman complained of black youths who filled up benches near the telegraph office at Taylor and Main and "sally forth at intervals, into either street, and upon either pavement, cracking whips, throwing stones, and yelling at the top of their lungs." One would think, he added, that they were free and the streets belonged to them. A stranger might even suppose the town occupied "exclusively" by Negroes! What this editor did not say was that some of those gathering at the telegraph office may have been listening for war news. A few weeks later, a reader observed that blacks were talking with Yankee POWs lodged in the local jail and even exchanging Confederate currency for greenbacks ($15 or more in rebel money for $10 U.S.)...bills that obviously would be useful if a prisoner escaped. Perhaps, he suggested, the police should put an end to this cameraderie.[24]

By the spring of 1864 a full-scale campaign against Columbia's "idle blacks" was under way. The *Guardian* (11 May) urged they be heavily taxed and banished to the countryside, where, under white control, they could produce goods badly needed by the army. Without such supervision, this editor said, blacks inevitably "ran into idleness and dishonest" practices such as

> huckstering, speculating in the necessaries of life by meeting country wagons out of town and buying up provisions

to resell them again at a heavy advance—and even travelling on the railroads far and near for this purpose. The negro, like the monkey, whom he so much resembles, is an imitative animal. We regret to say he has the white man as his example in this thing of speculating in the prime necessaries of life. He is the blockade runner in the home department, and, much like his more distinguished prototype, nothing but large profits will satisfy him.

As consumers, he warned, idle blacks continue to require food, clothing, and warmth. In cities they often stole goods, gambled, hired their own time, and were "comparatively under no control." In the country, properly guided, blacks would, in his opinion, become productive members of society.

Two years earlier, under the guise of a martial law decree dated 30 May 1862, Charlestonians also tried to banish idle blacks from their city and its immediate environs. Any not employed or under the supervision of a white resident were to leave within ten days. Those who did not could be arrested and assigned to a public works project or removed at their owner's expense. However, these regulations did not apply if an owner was in the service or a slave had been left in charge of a city dwelling. No slaves were to be brought into the community except in transit.[25]

There is no indication these rules were honored, and this angry outburst from an unidentified resident appeared in the *Courier* on 1 August, undoubtedly in reference to free blacks.

A Gross Nuisance

Colored women roll in carriages through our streets in high revelry, and their performances are such as to render it impossible for any lady to use her own carriage for recreation in the suburbs of our city, without having her sensibilities shocked; and, as occurred in the past week, one of these nuisances alighted from her coach in which she had been flounting, and entering a store inspected a pair of shoes for which $11 had been asked. I like them so well she said that I will take two pair, while a lady, who stood by trying to find something within her means, not only failed to do so, but was expelled from the store by the insolent behavior of the purchaser of two pair of shoes. We have a city police and martial law prevailing, yet such outrageous proceedings are permitted. Shall such things continue? [26]

On 30 September, the *Mercury*, following an almost obligatory condemnation of Jeff Davis and his "defensive policy," pointed its finger at

A Growing Evil

The free people of color in Charleston are, in general, an orderly and very respectable class; but the present anomalous condition of our city affairs is, and for some time has been made, the occasion for daily promenades of colored street-walkers in the most public streets.[27] It is high time they were summarily checked. Some of these women are riding about the city in hired carriages, making purchases at the stores, and occasionally have gone so far as to have hacks at church to ride from the services.

We have been repeatedly requested to bring this nuisance to the attention of the city government, and to urge, for the sake of decency, the nuisance be abated.

Soon even small communities such as Sumter were becoming distressed by "over-dressed" blacks, especially "wenches" who crowded the depot on Sundays to hear the news from Charleston. "But the gayest plumage which the jackdaw can borrow," the *Tri-Weekly Watchman* warned on 28 August 1863, "does not make him a peacock—he is a jackdaw still; and these darkies must remember that even broad cloth and flounces fail to change their *social* status." This evil, the editor emphasized, must be nipped in the bud.

Rural whites also were disturbed by trends they found unnerving. In November 1863, Mary Milling of Camden District wrote to her husband in Louisiana expressing concern over the manner in which the army was treating slaves it commandeered. Her father already had lost two blacks, as had his neighbors. "It is very difficult to know what to do with them now [;] they are more an expense than a profit," she added, giving voice to personal fears that the state was being flooded with blacks as they flowed in from western regions threatened by Union armies.

Four months later, Mary moaned that she saw no end to the fighting: "I wish the South had given up the negroes to *Old Abe* rather than so much trouble and distress."[28]

One could present more examples, but the message is clear. Black people, focus of this struggle, were becoming a liability instead of an asset. Increasing numbers in the upcountry were causing unease. Free blacks, often enriched by the war, were "putting on airs"; and, while whites went off to fight and die for slavery, the slaves they left behind were not acting like slaves and, in many instances, were living much more comfortably than their masters in various army camps. In addition, not only were they ignoring time-honored rules and regulations, some were fleeing to and even aiding the enemy. Along the coast this assistance took the form of active cooperation; further inland, slaves helped Yankee POWs reach federal lines beyond the mountains in Tennessee. Nearly every journal written by escaped prisoners tells of aid given them by blacks and "outliers" (whites hiding in isolated regions in order to evade the Confederate draft). Some tales seem to possess a healthy dose of swagger and braggadocio, but rarely did slaves turn a northern soldier over to local whites. Instead, they provided food, shelter, and advice concerning routes to be followed.

Hannibal Johnson, a Maine lieutenant who fled from Columbia's Camp Sorghum in November 1864, had an especially interesting, seven-week journey. After tarrying in Lexington District for a few days, he began eating his way through one chicken dinner after another as he headed west, usually traveling at night and hiding during daylight hours. On the morning of 4 December he had a bountiful breakfast on the plantation of the late Preston Brooks, who gained fame by caning Massachusetts senator Charles Sumner. This estate, located near Ninety Six, was, he observed, "in first class condition" and did not seem to have felt the effects of war "as much as the rest of the country we have passed through."[29] After the family had departed for church, a slave produced the famous cane, now broken into three pieces. Johnson wanted to keep them, but the servant protested that the house was in her charge and such a loss would be hard to explain.

W. H. Shelton, who escaped twice from Camp Sorghum—first on an ill-fated foray toward Charleston and then westward into the mountains—tells of entering an isolated Tennessee cabin inhabited by "outliers." When informed that Yankee visitors had arrived, an elderly woman huddled by the fire asked, "Be they selling tablecloths?"[30]

The account of Pennsylvanian Isaiah Conley in the Manuscripts Division of the Library of Congress is an unusual, twenty-eight-page saga. He and two fellow officers jumped from a train near Columbia in October 1864 and, misled by rumors that blacks would turn them over to the enemy, avoided all contact for several days. Finally, desperate for food and directions, they cautiously approached a slave who said he would ask his overseer to help them. When they objected, thinking he was white, the black replied, "No, sah, we's got a culled oberseer here!" Wade, the overseer, quickly provided food, advised them to associate only with field hands (not house servants), and headed them toward railroad tracks leading to Spartanburg.

Several evenings later, the trio—now dressed in homespun—had a long chat with a group of slaves owned by a Colonel Fenner. This plantation also was run by a black overseer, who greeted them with these words: "God bless you, I never seed no Yankees before." Many questions followed concerning the war, freedom, and "Marse Lincum & emancipation." Their new-found friends had to be assured that Lincoln actually was white—"Our folks all say dat he is a nigger." Conley at length produced a greenback bearing the likeness of the president as proof that he indeed was a white man. Then, following a sumptuous chicken dinner complete with tablecloth, plates, and silverware, still more slaves gathered to ask more questions. The women, according to Conley, tended to hang back, not come close, and merely listen to what was being said.

Another federal officer, Colonel John Azor Kellogg of Wisconsin, tells a similar story. While en route from Charleston to Columbia in October 1864, he and several friends jumped from a train when it stopped near Branchville and made their way (helped by both blacks and whites) to Chattanooga via Georgia. Despite difficult moments, Kellogg bore no grudge. During months spent in Charleston's Roper Hospital, he ate reasonably well, was not guarded once he promised not to escape, was treated in a civil manner, and even received mail while incarcerated there. "Although Charleston was the scene of the inauguration of hostilities," he observed, "there is a warm spot for it in my heart, since my imprisonment there in 1864."[31]

Johnson, Shelton, Conley, and their companions may well have spent a night or two on the property of Spartanburg farmer David Harris. On 16 December 1864 his wife noted in the diary she continued whenever he was away in uniform that several POWs reportedly had lived in their gin house for a few days. This information, she added,

Escaped POWs being fed by slaves.

came from blacks in the neighborhood but failed to say if the informers were her slaves.[32] Actually it made little difference. By the end of 1864 all was gloom in the Harris household, and whatever mistress-slave relationship existed was unraveling fast. Beset by problems on every hand, Emily Harris—furious when deserters and blacks stole food and animals—exploded in anger on 18 November: "The Confederacy! I almost hate the word."[33]

During the Christmas holidays, several of her slaves left without permission to celebrate with friends. Then on 3 January 1865 she penned this entry: "Old Will came to me and asked me to give him 'a paper' and let him go and hunt him a new home. York has given him a whipping and he wishes to leave the place. I'm in trouble. York must be corrected for fighting the old negro and there is no one willing to do it for me. It seems that people are getting afraid of negroes."[34] A few weeks later, Emily lost her temper and beat "Old Will" with a stick, although she thought she got the worst of the encounter, indicating he perhaps struck back..."but," she protested, "the negroes are becoming so imprudent and disrespectful that I cannot bear it."[35]

These journals, a remarkable compendium of family comment, give voice to many of the ills tormenting Confederate daily life as the war effort faltered—slaves doing much as they pleased, theft rampant, taxes and inflation continuing to increase in tandem. On 1 November 1863, over a year before Emily's angry outburst at the word "Confederacy," her husband, having served several military hitches in the Charleston area, was about to leave home once more. Surveying the world about him, David Harris made these general observations.

> I am called into servise. One of my best hands is demanded by the Government. A tenth of all I make is taken by the Government. I am taxed upon all I sell, or have to sell, and still have to buy at these extravegant prices while the Government gives me only eleven dollars per month. But the money is very plenty, by far too plenty. Every man, woman, child & negro has their pocket full. It is hard upon those who have nothing to sell. Hard upon the Solildier's wive & widow who have nothing but children & they do not seem to bring much of a price at present.[36]

One can view these comments as musings tempered with slight exaggeration and bits of sarcasm, yet at least one statement was right on the mark: nearly everyone, including slaves, had money to spend. In the spring of 1864, for example, when Columbia's Bee Store was about to close its door for a time, or at least until another blockade runner reached port, the editor of the *South Carolinian* suggested on 10 March that it might be well to set a day apart for black shoppers as had been done in Charleston. The following week the management agreed to admit them for two days. This editor complained in January of the same year that Negro porters at Columbia's depots were charging travelers too much— $2-4 to carry a trunk and $5-10 for conveyance to a hotel, and in November his paper reported some merchants were bowing to the demands of black tailors who had struck for higher wages.[37]

There are also hints that wartime pressures bent racial barriers ever so slightly. In the fall of 1863, John Judge & Company, a Columbia concern producing stockings for the army, advertised for one hundred workers "without regard to color," and in March 1864 the owner of a local boarding house was looking for "a white or colored woman or man" who could make biscuits, rolls, etc.[38] To the horror of Augustine Thomas Smythe, wounded Yankee prisoners, some of them black, were being housed in the confines of his alma mater, South Carolina College. "It was a desecration to use them [the college buildings] for our own soldiers, but to put negroes, Yankee-negroes [there] is too bad."[39] By 1864, the Soldiers Rest maintained by Greenville women was welcoming blacks employed by the Confederate Army. Their records indicate that on the night of 25 September the ladies "entertained" a lone soldier and a "colored" teamster.[40] And in one of the remarkable twists of those years, early in 1864 the Confederate Surgeon General's Office offered free smallpox vaccinations to all Columbia youngsters, white and black, and any interested adults as well. There was only one proviso: "Persons will be required to return the *scabs* for the use of the army."[41]

Yet it will surprise no one to learn that racial interplay, at least as detailed by the press, continued to present a muddled, confused picture. Early in the war the *Charleston Daily Courier* suggested on 5 June 1861 that all "old black women" be put to work knitting socks for the soldiers and reported on 6 August, without explanation, that a colored fireman was assaulted and stabbed en route to a fire. In addition to complaints concerning the fancy gowns of black women, the *Courier* on 1 December 1862 told of one who spent a night in jail for placing a light mulatto child in a white school, indicating this was by no means an isolated incident. A city ordinance passed on 6 January 1863 decreed that, one year after peace was declared, it would become unlawful to bury blacks, slave or free, anywhere except in potter's field. But that same year Charleston opened a hospital for black residents.

In May 1864, Columbia's chief of police (John Burdell) published an ad seeking return of "my boy March," dead or alive; and, commenting on a dismal sale day when a $3100 mule could not find a buyer while a slave sold for $1500, the *Edgefield Advertiser* (20 March 1865) had this suggestion: "Why don't people swap off all their mules and horses for *niggers* (they swap *even* down in Barnwell) and make a crop with a hoe? A nigger eats nine-tenths less than a mule."[42]

White residents of Camden, on the other hand, heaped lavish praise upon the Lone Star Minstrels whose concert in Temperance Hall netted $215 for the relief of servicemen in the fall of 1864. According to a notice in *the Camden Daily Journal* (28 October), these individuals, undoubtedly slaves, presented a dozen lively numbers such as "Little More Cider," "Poor old Jeff," "Sugarcane Green," and "The Elephant Dick," concluding with a grand "bone" solo and a rousing sermon by "Brother Bones." A few days later, the group received this special note of appreciation: "The President and Committee for the Soldiers' Rest most gratefully return their thanks to 'The Lone Star Minstrels' for their kind remembrance of this resting place of the sick and weary soldier. Can we ever be conquered by our foe, when kind domestics so generously share their hard earnings to contribute to the comfort of those brave men who are laying their all on the shrine of their country?"[43]

But a pleasant evening of music could do little to counter mounting conviction that blacks were not "doing their part" to win southern independence...though why they should exert themselves to remain in bondage is a perplexing puzzlement indeed. Hand in hand with complaints that both slave and free were idle, profiteering, aiding the enemy, too dressy, and had too much money to spend came (as the Harris journals and several newspapers reveal) general disquiet concerning their demeanor.

Although Francis M. Tucker, writing from various army camps, often reminded his Spartanburg District wife to "tell the negroes howdy," as early as June 1862 he expressed fears concerning their behavior and that of a new overseer, a man named Wilder.

> *I want you to be certain that if the negroes are in any*
> *way saucy or insolent to you—to get Shelby Howard or*
> *some body else to punish them severely for it—* Give them
> to understand that they will have to know their places—
> Wilder is just no account— He is a perfect negro spoiler—
> any man who will pretend to be an overseer & equalize
> himself with those whom he is to govern is no better
> than they are & I rue the day I ever employed him—but
> I hope I have learned something by experience—[44]

On 13 August, now in Virginia, Tucker again commented on troubles his wife was having at home. It might be best, he suggested, to buy Wilder's share of the crop and let him go. Perhaps neighbor Isaac Evins could give "Pink" a good whipping. Then, in a sarcastic or humorous vein, Tucker added, if she could not manage their slaves without Wilder, she might as well "turn them all loose & go to boarding." His wages, he remarked facetiously, might support her.

In succeeding years, as we know, residents of various South Carolina communities, among them, Charleston, Columbia, and Sumter, expressed similar misgivings, and, as war dragged on, comment concerning unruly blacks increased. In September 1863, James H. Hammond wrote to Governor Bonham endorsing with some vehemence a petition for a magistrate to be named for the Silverton community in Barnwell District. In this instance, the criticism turned sexual: "The country around there is without exaggeration in a *desperate* condition. Negroes are uppermost, openly keeping white, & some very pretty, girls, & getting children by them. They do not conceal that they steal corn, meat &

every thing they [need] to support the fathers & mothers of their Sweet heart. There is not a Magistrate any [where] in reach."[45]

A few months later, a Laurens District slave named Arter asked Clarissa A. Shockley if she had any cloth to sell. When she said no, he came at her with a knife "and Said that he had come to sleep with her that night & he would be Damned if he did not, to do so, then he [went] out at the door and Said that it would not be long Before he would be as free as She was and then he Swore that he would have her for his wife and Said that she mite tell it as Soon as She damed please for he would kill her before any person could git him."[46]

Despite this seemingly outrageous boast, Arter, slave of James Milner, only was charged with a misdemeanor. Isaac, the property of a Clarendon District resident named Hoyle, fared less well. In March 1865, he walked into the home of Mrs. Agnes Tuckbery and demanded a ticket to go home. This blunt request was not, however, what got Isaac into trouble; it was the fact that he *sat down*! Faced with the seriousness of his indiscretion, Isaac pled guilty and received thirty lashes.[47]

But the subtle stirrings of independent spirit evident among blacks throughout South Carolina in 1864-1865 usually did not lead to judicial proceedings; instead, whites such as Emily Harris lashed out at the offending slave or merely complained bitterly to each other and wrung their hands in despair. Typical are the comments of Sarah Jane Sams in letters to her husband shortly after Sherman's cavalry left Barnwell Court House. Sick at heart, she remarked that her servants were "perfectly unmanageable." Six days later, as the last foot soldier departed, she added, "Negroes are slow to obey and hold their heads somewhat higher than they should, [and] are behaving worse on the plantations than in town."[48]

There was, at least until Sherman appeared early in 1865, a simple solution to many aspects of this general malaise: convert slaves into

---

ALL TRADING FORBIDDEN.

Notice. The subscriber has discovered that an improper intercourse exists between some of his Negroes and people residing in or near Camden, very injurious to them; he therefore forbids all trading of any kind with either slave or freeman with any of his negroes; the law will be enforced against all offenders.

James Chesnut.
Camden Journal, 22 April 1864.

Confederate soldiers. This presumably would end idleness, curb assertiveness and theft, stem the flow of manpower to enemy lines, and greatly increase the ranks of the men in gray. But, to quote Prince Hamlet, "Ay, there's the rub!" How does one transform "boys" into free men while fighting a war to keep those same individuals in bondage?

Following Gettysburg and Vicksburg, several South Carolina editors called for a draft of free blacks to be used as teamsters. Some 20,000 troops were detailed for such duty, Sumter's *Tri-Weekly Watchman* said on 24 August 1863, men who easily could be replaced by free blacks, thus releasing white soldiers for more important tasks. On the other hand, the *Yorkville Enquirer* (19 September) attacked a Mississippi newspaper that put forth a similar suggestion. Nevertheless, in succeeding months this campaign gathered steam, and on 17 February 1864 Congress passed an act enrolling all free black males ages 18 to 50. These recruits were to receive the same pay and subsistence as soldiers while erecting fortifications and working in various war-related enterprises such as factories and hospitals, but they would not actually join in the fighting. (The title of this legislation, since it also encompassed the impressment of another 20,000 slaves, is somewhat misleading: "An act to increase the efficiency of the army by the employment of free negroes and slaves in certain capacities.")

Yet talk of slave soldiers continued; and, while addressing Congress in November 1864, Jefferson Davis hinted such a step might be necessary. The result was a violent tug-of-war lasting several months. Some argued the North was using slaves for war purposes and the South should do the same. However, many South Carolinians were wary since any who fought undoubtedly would expect freedom in return. Writing from Richmond early in 1865, James W. Wingard told his brother Simon, stationed near McPhersonville, that blacks in uniform would be an admission of defeat: "Congress is owning to the world we are whiped [sic] by wanting to put negroes in the army. What would have been done to a man had he advocated the cause of Emancipation two years ago, he would have been called disloyal and hanged without any judge or juriors." Wingard vowed the army was not disheartened and could fight on for several more years, "but our Congress and Executive head discourage me very much." They seem determined, this soldier moaned, to throw away everything the army has accomplished. It was "truly humilating" to see the government "we so much love" on the road to destruction.[49]

Meanwhile, die-hard secessionists fumed. The immediate cause of secession, R. Barnwell Rhett declared in a letter to ex-governor Aiken

Robert Barnwell Rhett (1800-1876).

published simultaneously in the *Charleston Courier* and *Mercury* (19 November 1864), was northern interference with the institution of slavery. Any proposal that the Confederate States of America purchase and emancipate slaves in order to make them soldiers was ridiculous. Edmund Rhett, his son, not surprisingly was equally adamant, although William Porcher Miles, Charleston's spokesman in the Confederate Congress, waffled on this issue, that is, until the younger Rhett whipped him into line. In October 1864, Miles advised General Robert E. Lee to consider arming "some" blacks, end promotion by seniority, and reorganize his cavalry.[50] Then, early in the new year, Edmund Rhett dispatched a blazing fusillade to Miles blasting virtually the entire military establishment. The reserves and militia were worse than useless, and the whole rotten system should be scrapped: "They use arms (or rather, they fling them away) that are much wanted—they consume commissary stores, that are needed—they will not fight, and produce panic, destroy discipline in those around them, and produce disorganization where ever they go."

Talk of Negro soldiers, in Rhett's opinion, was nothing but "the resort of semi-abolitionists, and childish weakness." The blacks may not be a very intelligent race, he conceded, so one could not expect them to lack as much sense as some of the government leaders in Richmond. All we can offer the slave who fights for us is individual liberty. "We feed him in the mean time on ½ rations and no meat, or molasses," he continued, "and we invite him to get killed for us. The enemy clothe him well, are the *winning side*, and offer him general and entire freedom and equality for his whole race. To suppose that when the alternative is force[d] upon him he will not go to the enemy, is to suppose him to be without even the common instincts of a monkey."

If slaves were turned into soldiers, Rhett was convinced South Carolina simply would hand thousands of armed recruits over to the enemy—thus losing an equal number of field hands and having that many more men to fight. Blacks would rather make corn than wage war and were willing to "leave us to settle the question among ourselves." There was no manpower shortage, he noted with emphasis, simply too many soldiers at home. Wheeler, for example, had 27,000 men on his rolls and could not muster a tenth of that number: "He is an imbecile, and his men are nothing but a herd of straggling ruffians, no order, no disciple, no responsibility." The fundamental problem with the Confederate Army, Rhett concluded, was "the want of discipline," and there was little point in trying to create it among the rank and file until officers were held accountable for their actions...perhaps some of them shot and others cashiered.[51] Reeling from this onslaught, seventy-two hours later, using many of the arguments put forth by Rhett, Miles informed General Beauregard that, upon second thought, Negro troops really were not a good idea.[52]

As one would expect, the *Mercury* (13 January) continued to breathe smoke and flame: "*We want no Confederate Government without our institutions....*The soldiers of South Carolina will not fight beside a nigger—to talk of emancipation is to disband our army. We are free men, and we choose to fight for ourselves—we want no slaves to fight for us. Skulkers, money lenders, money-makers, and blood-suckers, alone will tolerate the idea. It is the man who wont fight himself, who wants his nigger to fight for him, and to take his place in the ranks. Put that man in the ranks. And do it at once."

Yet at least one South Carolina weekly endorsed the proposal so scorned by the Rhetts and their newspaper. Tentatively at first and then with gusto, the *Edgefield Advertiser* said yes, let blacks bear arms and fight. The initial statement of 18 January was a mass of qualifications, but the editor eventually decided "the negro would, or could be made to, fight manfully in our cause." "We have arrived at a crisis," he concluded, "when it seems to us, the present and future interests of both races require that measures should be taken to bring them together shoulder to shoulder, in this war, as near as it is practicable to bring two races so different."

Then on 22 February this gentleman spoke out more forcefully. This was something the South had to do. One could not ignore the fact it would lead to freedom in return for good service, but this was the price the Confederacy must pay: "The highest and holiest and dearest of all causes, *freedom*, demands it. Which is more precious—our freedom or our slaves? Which *ought to be the* more precious?"

Finally, Confederate lawmakers agreed on 13 March that slaves ages 18 to 45 could become soldiers, a bill endorsed by both President Davis and General Lee. This measure, carefully phrased, said nothing about freedom or compelling an owner to release his slaves so they could enlist. Such matters were left to the states. Of course, the end was so near that this legislation was meaningless.

Still there were those unwilling to accept even the possibility that a slave might gain freedom in battle and equally reluctant to face reality. On 19 April—ten days after Lee and Grant met at Appomattox Court House in Virginia—"Ninety Six" published a lengthy essay in the *Edgefield Advertiser* entitled "How to Achieve Southern Independence, and perpetuate the institution of slavery." The basic arguments were not new—all Christians know slavery is sanctioned by the Bible and always will be with us in some form, South Carolinians who talk of abolition are traitors, and, in order to win, *every* man 16 to 60, with no exceptions, must shoulder a gun. This included slaves who would, the writer vowed, fight without any promise of freedom, although no proof of this strange assertion was forthcoming. "The institution of slavery," he declared, "is now passing through a fiery ordeal, but it is like good brass; the more it is scoured by Northern fanatics and Southern traitors, the brighter it shines." Following yet another warning to stand firm for principle and fight to the end, "Ninety Six" penned this religiously inspired but puzzling conclusion: "And if we are to be subjugated, wo[e] be to these Confederate States! Better for us, had it been, that the child, *Secession* had never been born."

One aspect of the wartime equation rarely mentioned by South Carolina's leaders actually is a key element in the homefront story. Remember those figures cited earlier in this chapter in Table 2? This state was nearly 60% black in 1860; and, despite glowing newspaper accounts of slave loyalty, only a fool would believe that many of those dark of skin really were cheering for the Confederacy. Add to that numerical majority a few disenchanted whites—whose ranks were growing rapidly after July 1863—and you discover that perhaps two-thirds of the population either was indifferent to the Confederate cause or rooting for the enemy. This is hardly a recipe for success. Viewed in this manner, the role of South Carolina's blacks, slave and free, takes on vital importance. Even if outwardly passive, by sheer numbers they had the potential to create turmoil and trouble. Certainly their reaction to any Union troops seen in South Carolina did little to inspire confidence.

Thus those in uniform, men such as Francis Tucker, always were mindful of the threat of unrest at home, which helps to explain why so many of them were there and not with their units as black assertiveness increased. Ironically, these same deserters heightened fears of what renegade *whites* might do. However, this anxiety concerning black behavior stands in stark contrast to widespread insistence that slaves in general were loyal and true to the Confederacy. (One can't have it both ways.) Despite the defiant post-Appomattox rhetoric of "Ninety Six," one paramount question faced by many South Carolinians during the final months of the struggle was not how to achieve independence but how to extricate themselves gracefully from a "lost cause." Yet another involved the institution of slavery. Was it really worth fighting for or had it perhaps been so transformed by four years of civil unrest as to become worthless? And, if we went to war in 1861 to preserve slavery, why was the Davis government in effect planning to abolish it? What were our goals in this struggle?

NOTES

[1]*Charleston Daily Courier*, 12 July 1861.

[2]Among slaves, 381,226 were classified as black, 21,180 as mulatto. The breakdown among free colored was 2,780 black, 7,134 mulatto. The only other state with a black majority in 1860 was Mississippi, where blacks outnumbered whites 437,404 (includes 773 free blacks) to 353,899.

[3]By comparison, the 1850 census totals were 274,563 white, 8,960 free black, and 384,984 slave. During the decade, state population grew from 668,547 to 703,708, a modest 35,201 and proof of substantial out-migration.

[4]Newberry District General Sessions Journals, South Carolina Department of Archives and History. Despite the words of this presentment, the ranks of free blacks were not increasing very rapidly in the 1850s. Jury members also thought the current method of "freeholders" hearing black criminal cases in a special court should be revised. For a description of these unique judicial bodies see Terry W. Lipscomb and Theresa Jacobs, "The Magistrates and Freeholders Court," *South Carolina Historical Magazine* (January 1976), pp. 62-65.

[5]In all, Lucy filed three appeals—#26, 13 October 1860, #15, 18 November 1861, and #11, 25 November 1862. Jackson's (#79) was filed 27 September 1861.

[6]For details of this phenomenon, see especially the introduction to Michael P. Jordan and James L. Roark (eds.), *No Chariot Let Down: Charleston's Free People of Color on the Eve of the Civil War* (Chapel Hill and London, 1984). Their *Black Masters: A Free Family of Color in the Old South* (New York and London, l984)—tale of the remarkable Ellisons of Stateburg—also includes data relative to Charleston c. 1860.

[7]Quoted in Johnson and Roark, *Black Masters*, p. 293. To convince English readers that free blacks supported the Confederacy, Elizabeth Collins reproduced the appeal to Gantt in her *Memories of the Southern States* (Taunton, 1865), pp. 88-89.

[8]Johnson and Roark stress in *Black Masters* (p. 306) that the Ellisons compiled a solid war record. They produced food, not cotton, hired out their slaves (apparently for war work), paid various taxes on time, and invested in Confederate notes.

[9]Marszalek, *Diary of Miss Emma Holmes*, p. 86. This comment was recorded on 3 September. Two days later she told of a meeting of her "shooting" club, a group of young ladies eager to learn how to handle a pistol.

[10]Reports of the General Assembly (1861), # 39, South Carolina Department of Archives and History. Nevertheless, on 28 April 1862, the state Executive Council suggested that 2% of all slaves (18-45) be ordered into service as "axe-men, spadesmen, and ditchers" drawing soldiers' rations, clothing, and pay—the latter to go to their owners or agents. See Cauthen, *Journals of the South Carolina Executive Council*, p. 160.

[11]Quoted in the *Charleston Daily Courier*, 20 April 1861.

[12]*New York Tribune*, 2 April 1861.

[13]See Petition # 28 to the General Assembly (1862) and records of Anderson District's Magistrates and Freeholders Court (1862), South Carolina Department of Archives

and History.

[14]See Petition # 104 to the General Assembly (1862). The Sumter affair, which received some publicity, was noted by Emma Holmes in her diary on 1 October 1862 (pp. 202-203). Owners usually were compensated when a slave was put to death following a trial.

[15]In non-slave states the ratio of population to jobs was even more striking. Maine, for example, had fewer people (628,279) than South Carolina but over two-and-one-half times as many individuals had occupations (206,677), and New Jersey reported similar totals—627,035 residents and 213,024 occupations.

[16]Journal of Meta Morris Grimball, 6 March 1862, Southern Historical Collection, University of North Carolina. In June of the same year, Grimball hired a railway car for $75 and transported his wife, furniture, and other belongings to St. John's College, Spartanburg, where they rented several rooms for $40 a month.

[17]J. H. Easterby, *The South Carolina Rice Plantation* (Chicago, 1945), p. 190. By these words, Mrs. Allston may mean a predisposition to flee existed, as well as knowledge of and cooperation with Yankee raiding parties, which some sources indicate often was all too obvious.

[18]Ibid., pp. 199-200.

[19]Ibid., p. 291.

[20]On 3 December 1863, Governor Bonham forwarded a Confederate Army circular to Richmond indicating it was impossible to stop Yankee raids along the coast above the Savannah River. There was, it stated, constant communication among the enemy, runaways, and plantation Negroes, the "best" guides in the world: "Not a change of picket-post is made but that they know it in a short time." See *War of the Rebellion*, First Series, LIII, p. 302.

[21]*War of the Rebellion*, First Series, XIV, p. 199.

[22]See "The Minutes of the Commission Appointed…to Provide for the Removal of Negroes…," South Carolina Department of Archives and History. At a meeting held on 16 April 1862, members agreed slaves should accompany their owners in the same railway car, plus baggage, and any free blacks would be kept separate from slaves. Since the commission met only intermittently for two years (1862-1863), the task apparently proved to be overwhelming and virtually impossible to perform.

[23]*Tri-Weekly Watchman*, 3 September 1862.

[24]*Daily Southern Guardian*, 28 September 1863.

[25]*Charleston Daily Courier*, 5 June 1862.

[26]A. J. L. Fremantle, who visited Charleston in June 1863, commented on the smartly dressed black women he saw on Sundays; mulattoes, he noted, were not permitted to wear veils. See Freemantle, *Three Months in the Southern States, April-June, 1863* (New York, 1864), p. 186.

[27]The writer apparently does not mean prostitutes but merely free black women seen strolling about town.

[28]Mary Milling to James S. Milling, 20 November 1863, 16 February 1864, James S. Milling Papers, Southern Historical Collection, University of North Carolina.

[29]Hannibal S. Johnson, *The Sword of Honor* (Worcester, 1906), p. 40.

[30]See W. H. Shelton, "A Hard Road to Travel out of Dixie," *Famous Adventures and Prison Escapes of the Civil War* (New York, 1898), pp. 243-97.

[31]John Azor Kellogg, *Capture and Escape: A Narrative of Army and Prison Life* (Madison, Wisc., 1908), p. 90. Kellogg's words first appeared in the *La Crosse Leader* (1869-1870) and then were amplified shortly before he died in 1883.

[32]Racine, *Piedmont Farmer*, p. 355.

[33]Ibid., p. 350.

[34]Ibid., pp. 357-58.

[35]Ibid., p. 365.

[36]Ibid., p. 308.

[37]*Tri-Weekly South Carolinian*, 30 January, 3 November 1864.

[38]*Tri-Weekly South Carolinian*, 29 October 1863; *Daily Southern Guardian*, 4 March 1864.

[39]Augustine T. Smythe to his aunt, Jane Ann Adger, 8 September 1863, Smythe Letters.

[40]Minutes of the Greenville Ladies Association, South Caroliniana Library.

[41]*Daily Southern Guardian*, 23 February 1864.

[42]Although the full import of this strange proposal is unclear, it probably was a slur against neighboring Barnwell coupled with frustrations engendered by outrageous prices and impending defeat.

[43]*Camden Daily Journal*, 4 November 1864.

[44]F. M. Tucker to his wife, 25 June 1862, Duncan, Kinard, Sanders, Tucker Papers. At that time Tucker was on James Island.

[45]J. H. Hammond to Milledge L. Bonham, ? September 1863, Bonham Papers, South Carolina Department of Archives and History.

[46]See records of the Magistrates and Freeholders Court, Laurens District, 19 April 1864, South Carolina Department of Archives and History. Nearly all of the cases heard by such bodies were third party affairs; that is, slaves reportedly confronted, assaulted, or stole something from someone other than their owner. This depository has scattered records of these wartime tribunals held in Anderson, Clarendon, Laurens, Spartanburg, and Union districts. Of 153 Anderson cases (1861-1865), only twenty-two ended in acquittal. In Spartanburg (1862-1864), 103 individuals were arraigned and over 75% of them punished in some fashion.

[47]This incident is described in a small collection of Magistrates and Freeholders Court records for Clarendon District found at the South Carolina Department of Archives and History.

[48]Sarah Jane Sams to Randolph Sams, 9, 15 February 1865, Sams Family Papers.

[49]James W. Wingard to Simon P. Wingard, 7 January 1865, Simon P. Wingard Papers, Special Collections Library, Duke University.

[50]William P. Miles to Lee, 24 October 1864, William P. Miles Papers, Southern Historical Collection, University of North Carolina.

[51]Ibid., Rhett to Miles, 11 January 1865.

[52]Ibid., Miles to Beauregard, 14 January 1865.

VI

WOMEN—DOWN FROM THE PEDESTAL?

Despite the thousands of pages written about the Civil War and recent interest in women's history, the role of women in the 1860s—as this chapter title indicates—may always be something of a mystery, thanks in part to cultural attitudes of that era. This is especially true in South Carolina where women were praised as saints and saviors one moment and then, in the next, told very firmly to remember their true place in the social pecking order. There is no question that wartime strains opened doors to several hundred who became treasury clerks in Columbia and others who organized relief efforts in behalf of soldiers or ministered to their needs in hospital wards. Yet their numbers were relatively small, those salaried were paid less than their male counterparts and risked social ostracism (at least malicious gossip), and the same doors that swung open wide in 1861 were slammed shut in 1865.

Although census returns for 1860 tell us the female population of South Carolina was 356,388, during the struggle that followed only a handful had an opportunity to step down from an imaginary pedestal and contribute directly to the Confederate war effort. The reasons for these limitations vary. Over two hundred thousand of these women were black or Indian (thus presumably "unpedestalized"); and, of 145,140 white females, only 78,566 were 15-60 and thus of an age to aid the "cause" in any meaningful fashion. And of this group perhaps a mere 20,000 lived in cities, towns, and villages where organizational efforts had impact. Even that total dwindles when one considers those opposed to the conflict (such as Caroline Petigru Carson, who fled to New York City) and others so burdened with day-to-day chores that, whatever their sentiments might be, often were too tired to knit, sew, and attend meetings.

Three decades later, as the United Daughters of the Confederacy took shape, scores of South Carolina women began to reflect upon their wartime experiences, although local chapters seemed to bristle at the word "UNITED" and suppressed it whenever possible, calling themselves simply "Daughters of the Confederacy." In 1897, at a meeting held in Abbeville, the state division announced plans to issue a history of South Carolina women during the war years, which eventually appeared in two volumes, the first in 1903, the second in 1907.[1] The result is an ambitious undertaking of 656 pages that largely ignores anything not calculated to bolster the image desired—that of all-out sacrifice by white, upper-class women of good lineage and preferably "Daughters" themselves. Significantly perhaps, forty of those pages are devoted to an extremely complete surname index, which includes an occasional black and a few prominent adversaries, each carefully identified, such as "Sherman (U. S. A.)."

Somewhat strangely, in view of the outcome, the first volume opens with warning that the *full* story must be told, and the second closes with an emotional plea by Mrs. Thomas Taylor, the lady who spearheaded this effort. The women of the 1860s were, she emphasized in an address delivered in 1900,

> organizers, manufacturers, moral government among hordes of negroes, overseers, lumber millers, land clearers, traders...these women transferred slave forces from plantation to plantation, quelled resistances, they ditched and drained fields, built storage barns, standing over their negro workmen, cheering, urging, and checking. Write these stories.
>
> They were in civil departments, fled with government property, abandoned private goods to aid in saving State values. In much of all this they had the aid and direction of the old men here and there, and every man was ready to assist a woman.
>
> Being domestic economists, they were also managers for the public benefits. They kept up supplies in the land, crops were planted, and by hook or crook the negroes were fed and so cheered on by the endeavours of their owners that they were willing to labor, for they saw that the field laborer was considered before the family, when the choice was forced. Sheep were raised, wool was hoarded, spinning wheels were run by ladies who had perchance never before seen a spinner dance to and from the whirling droning round. Some who for dainti-

hose and satin shoon [sic], now would mount any dromedary of a 'condemned horse' and rampage counties to gather sustenance for aggregations of dependants to enable them to work on crops and raise supplies. Old relations gave them allies in almost all cases among the reliable men on different plantations.[2]

However, no one was listening when Mrs. Taylor said "write these stories," for only those who *volunteered* to *organize* something somewhere in behalf of the soldiers are eulogized in these volumes. The result is a patchwork of newspaper clippings, snippets of organizational records, and random recollections that disclose little concerning the war years. Nothing is said about women who actually worked for the Confederate government or labored in the fields. This is, above all, selective memory with strains of "Dixie" heard now and then amid the crooning of happy darkies. Jane Carson Brunson, writing in February 1899, sums up relief work in Greenville in this fashion: "All the land devoting itself to the army! Such an inspiration of patriotic devotion to the defenders of our homes! I look back to it with admiration!"[3]

What these good women clearly demonstrate is the zeal South Carolinians displayed during the opening months of the war as 124 ladies aid societies took shape in all parts of the state, their goal being to provide food and clothing for soldiers and comfort to the wounded.[4] The records of a Fairfield District group cited by the UDC list typical contributions of that era.

Mrs. M. Jordan and Miss E. Laughlin—Three pairs slippers, one bottle turpentine, one bottle No. 6.

Mrs. Gaillard and Mrs. Dwight—One gallon blackberry wine, two bottles blackberry cordial, one bottle lime juice, one bottle rosewater, one bottle each of Hyson and black tea, loaf sugar, six pounds crushed sugar, one bottle brandy, eleven sheets, sixteen handkerchiefs, twelve pillow-cases, four shirts, four pairs flannel drawers, old cloth.

Mrs. E. J. Hall—Four pairs drawers, two shirts, two pairs socks, three packages coffee, three packages tea, candles, one bottle blackberry wine.

Mrs. G. H. McMaster—Four sheets, four pillow-cases, three pillow-cases, two comforts, two towels, eight pairs socks, four pairs drawers, three shirts, three handkerchiefs, one jar blackberry jelly, one bottle acid.

Mrs. Mobley—Six shirts, four pairs drawers, four pairs socks, old linen cloth for bandages, dressing-gowns.

Mrs. McK. Elliott—One shirt, two pairs drawers, two pairs pants, two shirts, two pairs socks, towels, pillow-slips, old cloth for bandages, loaf sugar, tea, sweet oil, and sage.

Mrs. Gamble—Two quilts, twelve yards cloth for bandages, six pillow-cases.

Mrs. E. Barber—One gallon wine, one gallon grape wine, towels, sheets, linen, sage, and catnip.[5]

But these random accounts also reveal that, within a year or so, many of these volunteer groups ran out of steam. The Fairfield ladies met for the last time in August 1862 and received their final cash donation six months later. The real problem was shortages—thread, material with which to make things soldiers needed, transportation of those items to various camps, and perhaps on occasions a shortage of spirit as well. As a result, relief efforts tended to shift focus to those housed in nearby hospitals or merely passing through a community. The latter frequently required only a meal or a place to spend the night, giving rise to numerous temporary facilities near railroad depots bearing names such as "Wayside Home" and "Soldiers' Rest."

In a few instances, especially along the South Carolina Railroad, volunteer groups carried these efforts a bit further, taking food and comfort to those on trains. In August 1862, Orangeburg women (and some men) were traveling on that line between their homes and Branchville tending to the needs of ill servicemen, and two years later seven stations established a daily dinner schedule. Midway fed passing soldiers on Monday, Bamberg on Tuesday, Graham's Wednesday, Blackville Thursday, Ninety Six Friday, Williston Saturday, and White Ponds Sunday. The *Charleston Daily Courier* (27 June 1864) characterized those who organized this program as "The Angels of the Seven Stations."

This story was repeated in the Sumter area with a slightly different twist. Five relief societies appeared in that district in the summer of 1861, but a year later the *Tri-Weekly Watchman* (10 October 1862), reduced to a single sheet, pointedly reminded readers that the local "Wayside-House" *still* was in business. Editor A. A. Gilbert said trains "now pass this place at such an early hour that no provisions are carried by the ladies to the depot...." However, he urged that contributions continue, noting those "for strictly hospital purposes" were much needed. A few days earlier on 6 October, this same newspaper aired rumors that local commissioners appointed to care for soldier families were not doing their duty, which led on 13 October to a lengthy denial by one of those gentlemen.

Alarmed by such disclosures, townspeople sprang into action and at a public meeting on 16 October formed a new group, "The Society for the Relief of the Soldiers from Sumter." Significantly, this gathering was convened and presided over by men, although they named an executive committee of six women, who would meet each week and operate the organization. The entire membership, it was agreed, would hold monthly meetings.

In succeeding weeks these ladies peppered the community with frantic appeals for help.

> Behold their gaunt and famine wasted faces, their thin and tattered garments, their bruised and bleeding feet! and see their tender bodies shivering in the wintry blasts of northern snows and tempests:—then turn to your own comfortable homes,—your carpeted floors—your damask curtains—blankets—woollen cloths—your silver plate—your golden ornaments—pianos and costly furniture, and silken dresses—and say—*shall these things be* while our soldiers, the noble defenders of all we hold dear in life are consigned to suffering, to want, disease, death, and the grave, for the want of bare necessities? Women of the South! the answer rests with you.[6]
>
> Daughters of the land! The Winter is upon us—and our brave boys who are facing death in a thousand bloody forms, turn their imploring eyes, and stretch forth their shivering hands *to you* to save them from the piercing bitter cold, and driving rain and sleet. Stay not to weave and spin, but bring what you have in your homes, to meet the pressing emergency.
>
> Brussels Carpeting makes the best soldiers overcoats, capes, coats, and loose jackets in the world—the warm nap is turned within, and it needs no lining, while the

outside is all one uniform color, and is about as impervious to water as oil cloth.

The other kinds of Carpeting make excellent pantaloons, vests, and blankets, and the worsted curtains and table covers will do for shirts.

Women of the South, will you tread upon carpeted floors while the *naked* bodies of your countrymen stand a living freezing wall between you and piteous want, and shame, dishonor, and the grave?

The Society will work night and day if you will give the materials, and by the close of this week, boxes of warm blankets and clothing will be on the way to our suffering and heroic army.[7]

Keep the soldier warm. Work for him, sew for him night and day. He is out on a blessed mission of patriotism, exposed to cold, hunger, and the bullets of the enemy. How sweet ought to seem the toil which promises him some Comfort![8]

Despite some confusion—first being told not to weave and spin but bring whatever one had at hand and then to sew "night and day"— this campaign at least moved local Presbyterians to donate all of their carpets "to the benefit of our gallant, suffering soldiery."[9] Then, early in 1863 the ladies realized $7.00 from an earring raffle and reported on 12 January that two bales of supplies had been forwarded to Columbia, followed by three more in February.

The little village of Edgefield, not on a rail line, also stirred itself in behalf of local servicemen, although in 1861 church women often funneled their contributions through organizations based in Columbia. On 11 December, the *Edgefield Advertiser* admitted the district fund to aid soldier families was exhausted, and six months later a new group appeared, "The Southern Sisters Aid Society," with the avowed goal of assisting destitute military kinfolk. By the end of 1862 there were similar organizations in Beech Island, Red Oak Grove, Antioch, Duntonville, Curryton, Hamburg, and virtually every other crossroads community throughout the district. Despite the absence of rail traffic, in June 1864 a band of local women decided Edgefield should have a hospital for transient military personnel. The following month the scheme for a "Wayside Home" apparently was abandoned, only to be revived as "The Soldiers'

Fair Grounds Hospital.

We are requested to state that sweet milk is very much needed at the hospitals at the Fair Grounds. Families having even small quantities to spare will please send the same to Mr. John McKenzie's store every morning before 8 o'clock.

There is also a considerable demand amongst our sick soldiers for small Bibles and Testaments. Persons having these to spare will do a kind service by sending them to J. Monroe Anderson.

Daily Southern Guardian (Columbia),
26 October 1861.

Heaven," which by the end of August reportedly had entertained twenty young men.

At times these relief schemes took bizarre turns. According to the *Charleston Daily Courier* (6 July 1861), forty-five members of that city's Jackson Female Juvenile Association had collected $100 to aid soldier families and were busily "employing their patriotic little fingers in making haversacks for the army." Their Saturday meetings at a Society Street home also included bow and arrow exercises, at which, the *Courier* said, they already had become "quite proficient." Students at Madame Sosnowski's Columbia school for select young ladies set up their own relief program when each student promised to complete so many garments according to an established schedule. Those who failed to fill their quotas—one pair of socks each month and gloves, drawers, or shirts every two months—had to pay the cost of the items, plus a $2.50 fine.[10]

Actually, wartime relief passed through several phases. At the outset in the spring of 1861, women met to devise ways to assist soldier families in their communities. Then, as campaigning began in earnest, they developed associations designed to supply those in the field, and in the winter of 1861-1862 it was not unusual for a prominent matron to deliver a box of food, clothing, etc. to men serving in Virginia or near Charleston. But government officials at various levels ostensibly took over the task of caring for destitute military dependents, and late in 1862 a semiofficial Central Association headquartered in Columbia began more systematic dispatch of supplies to the front. All of these programs were, of course, supervised by men, relegating womenfolk to subsidiary roles. These trends, as well as various shortages and depressing war news, may well have dampened original ardor.

In addition, ladies who organized hospitals such as the one formed at Columbia's State Fair grounds in October 1861 discovered that, when their creation expanded to the campus of South Carolina College, control passed out of their hands. Nor can one discount bickering among volunteers themselves as a distracting factor. Older women of that same community were not pleased when the Young Ladies Hospital Association composed of seventy-three unmarried girls opened a facility for soldiers at the Charlotte railroad depot. Pressured by mothers and aunts, they subsequently merged this "rest" with that of their elders near a station a few blocks away serving South Carolina Railroad trains connecting with Charleston and Greenville. The result was the Wayside Hospital, which opened on 10 March 1862.[11] But the dissension did not stop there; for, once Columbia claimed this was the first "Wayside" in the Confederacy, Charleston disagreed. And it is true that a facility in that city bore the name "Wayside" from November 1861 to February 1862 when it became the Citadel Square Hospital.

In December 1861, when Emma Holmes tried to get clothing for Navy men, Hester Drayton, superintendent of the Ladies Charleston Volunteer Aid Society, said no. Everything on hand had been promised to soldiers; and, besides, she objected to assisting non-military personnel. This reaction infuriated Emma, who subsequently learned the Rhetts had quit the society following insulting language by Miss Drayton, who apparently offered to direct clothing to her nephew's company *if* he got a commission, causing still others to abandon an organization that seemed to be run in a very arbitrary manner. Emma was even more agitated upon learning two months later that all of the clothing made by this volunteer group had been sold to the Confederate Quartermaster's Department. Thus, as a refugee in Camden in October 1862, she probably was not surprised when a public meeting called to form yet another soldiers' aid society attracted only six people.[12]

Nevertheless, some such groups obviously made solid contributions to the war effort, and facilities established for itinerant military personnel—called "homes" or "hospitals" interchangeably throughout the state—were extremely popular. On 7 January 1863, the *Yorkville Enquirer's* Columbia letter reported that the high price of powder curtailed Christmas fireworks displays, salt from Wilmington was selling for $17½ per bushel, a proposal was afoot to change the name of Union District to Gregg, and sixty-five Tennessee Unionists had passed through town en route to a Richmond prison.

> The *morale* of the city is good for the times.
> Wounded soldiers throng the streets, some to have fur-
> loughs extended, some to get transportation; but all have
> a horror of the hospitals, which seem to be common
> among soldiers. The 'wayside,' however, of the Ladies,
> which furnishes temporary relief, is an exception—it is
> so well 'patronized' as to render it eminently worthy the
> attention of the charitably disposed.

Before fighting ceased, Charleston would be home to at least eight
true hospitals caring for the sick and wounded, and Columbia could
boast of several more. The best known of these were located at the college. By March 1864, the former classrooms and dormitories, occupied
over faculty objections, could accommodate about five hundred patients.
These wards, presided over by nine surgeons, were served by 176 non-
medical staff, 60% of them black. At times, tents were erected nearby to
care for yellow fever victims, and it was at facilities such as these that
many well-mannered housewives labored in behalf of the "cause."[13]

On 2 December 1862, the sister of Wilmot G. DeSaussure said she
was sorry she had not written to him earlier, but life was very busy in
Charleston, even for a spinster.

> Two or three mornings of every week, given over to the
> Hospitals, then the various Societies, Ladies Benevolent
> Fund, Fuel, Soldiers Relief, &c., then Quarter Master's
> work to be cut out, and given to the poor to be made,
> who are in great want, and beg even for a single shirt to
> make, to help them along; I fear the sufferings of the
> poor this Winter, will be very great, and the Societies
> will not be able, I fear, to afford them as much help as
> usual, from the high price of all supplies, 'God help the
> poor,' through this hard and bitter struggle.[14]

This lady went on to say the panic of the summer months inspired
by martial law and internal passports had subsided: "I think the panic
people must have nearly all left the City." Folks were acting more ratio-
nally, she thought, and there seemed to be less sickness and fewer hospital
patients. Actually, as we shall see later, Charleston was about to embark
upon a rather gay winter season, the last before Union shells began to
burst over that beleaguered peninsula.

Records of the Greenville Ladies Aid Association—three slim volumes now at the South Caroliniana Library—detail the rise and fall of a typical volunteer group. At an organizational session held at the Baptist Female College on 19 July 1861, charter members agreed to elect officers, levy a 25¢ initiation fee, charge 10¢ in monthly dues, and launch efforts to assist local soldiers in any way possible. Within a week, committees were named and work was under way. The general membership, which soon totaled 224, was to gather on the first Saturday of each month. Sixteen "directresses" (ladies who headed committees and cut out material but did not sew) were to meet weekly. Male contributors could become honorary members and forty-one Greenville men achieved that status.

By 1 July 1862, these women had assembled, packed, and sent to the front thirty-five boxes of food and clothing, although this schedule was temporarily interrupted in November 1861 when no cloth could be found. In any case, these cartons usually went off to Virginia or the lowcountry whenever someone was willing to deliver them personally. However, during the next thirteen months (July 1862-August 1863) only half as many boxes were packed, and apparently none were shipped by the association after that time.

Meanwhile, in mid-1862 the members established a small "hospital," really only a few rented rooms used by transient servicemen, quarters subsidized in part by the town fathers. Minutes for the weeks from October 1863 to April 1864 have been lost, and throughout the remainder of 1864 there was not much to report. Officers often failed to appear at meetings, little or no business was transacted, and, on one occasion, only a lone directress was present. This pattern continued until February 1865 when the "hospital" began to do a flourishing business—sixty-one soldiers housed in one week alone, together with 150 unregistered guests. In mid-March this facility moved to larger quarters at the Goodloe House, a local hotel, and servicemen (presumably on leave) continued to flow into Greenville. As the war was dragging to a close in April, nearly five hundred men were entertained, some of whom took bedding with them when they left. This story ends with an abrupt entry dated 1 May indicating there was no general meeting of the membership that day because Yankee raiders had stripped the "hospital" of "every article it contained, leaving the Society without the means of carrying on any farther operations."

Few groups throughout the state could boast of such a dramatic demise; instead, they simply faded from view long before April 1865.

This does not mean the women praised so highly by the UDC ceased raising money or no longer contributed to the welfare of those in uniform, only that the organizational apparatus disappeared as members were overwhelmed by shortages and much of their work usurped by males.[15]

But, as Mrs. Taylor stressed, these were not the only women who helped the Confederacy; and, as she essentially conceded, the great majority of South Carolina's female population did not enjoy the luxury of "volunteering." Instead, both free and slave, they *had* to work at various tasks in order to survive; yet, regardless of their political views, if any, whatever they produced and harvested was of great benefit to the government. A handful, among them rural schoolteachers, were acutely aware they replaced men who could take up arms. In June 1863, Mary Milling, who lived near Camden, received a letter from her sister bragging of her part in the war effort. "You see," she wrote, "that is the manner in which I exhibited my patriotism, by permitting my gentleman teachers to go to the wars. And supply their place. Do I not deserve credit?"[16] However, this transition was less apparent in urban areas where women already dominated the teaching profession. In 1860, for example, of about fifty teachers in Charleston's public schools thirty-one were female, several serving as principals and five holding positions in the "male" departments of grammar schools.

The 1860 city directory indicates that community also had a sprinkling of women in the market place, perhaps a hundred or so operating various commercial enterprises in their own right. Their ranks included twenty-five milliners, eight dressmakers, eighteen boarding house keepers (about one-third of such establishments), and the proprietors of seventeen dry goods stores (one-fifth of those in the city). These undertakings present few surprises, but six groceries and three of Charleston's ten hotels were being run by women, as well as two of that community's three wig shops, a "fancy goods" outlet, "pattern emporium," restaurant, jewelry store, china shop, basket factory, junk store, tobacco and "segar" shop, and two saloons—Mrs. McClardy (7 Market Street) and Mrs. Shannon (13 Tradd). Also, as noted, women were very prominent in Charleston's classrooms.

Columbia (population 8,052), about one-fifth as large as Charleston, presents a similar picture on the eve of war. Women operated six of the state capital's eleven boarding houses and presided over half of the students in its fourteen schools (public and private). Columbia also was home to three milliners, a dress trimmer, and two female grocers.

Just how women operating boarding houses, wig shops, "segar" stores, and saloons contributed to the war effort is debatable, but one very obvious boost came from a minuscule but vitally important body of factory workers. According to the 1860 census, 6,066 males and 898 females were employed in manufacturing throughout South Carolina. Of the latter, 549—some of them slaves—worked in cotton factories located in Anderson, Chester, Edgefield, Greenville, Lexington, Spartanburg, and Union districts. By far the largest of these operations was William Gregg's Graniteville plant employing 169 male and 230 female workers, and cotton mills were the only form of manufacturing where women usually predominated. An equal number of men and women (169) cleaned rice in Georgetown District, and a few female workers could be found in various regions weaving woolen goods, distilling turpentine, making brick, pottery, and porcelain, sawing lumber, producing lime, and fashioning hats, boots, and shoes.

Although difficult to prove, it seems quite probable that, as the war progressed and the draft worked its magic, more and more of these industrial workers were women, and impromptu manufacturing enterprises in all parts of the state undoubtedly employed some members of the fair sex. One such operation was the stocking factory of John Judge & Company in Columbia, which, thanks to machinery brought through the blockade, by the spring of 1864 was turning out 1,000 needles and 2,500 socks each day. The *Charleston Daily Courier* (24 April) said this factory employed some seventy people, most of them women, and provided work for about seven hundred housewives who "finished off" stockings in their homes. However, Columbia's *Tri-Weekly South Carolinian* indicates the ranks of those involved actually may have been twice as large; for, on 16 June 1863, Judge published the names of eleven women *by number* (103 to 1,484) who had failed to complete work and return it as promised. Most of them owed him ten to twenty pairs of socks.

By August 1864, nine other machines smuggled through the Union fleet and erected in a trio of buildings on the State House grounds were producing seventy-five to ninety pairs of cotton cards each day. Yet these cards (paddles with metal teeth that were used to comb and clean cotton) were distributed in a puzzling manner. This factory was a creation of the state government, and the cards, much in demand, were supplied at cost to district relief boards, whose members then *sold* them to destitute soldier families, often charging these poor folk freight fees as well.

Records of St. George's Parish at the State Archives reveal the local board was assisting 124 families (382 individuals) in 1863, allowing $5 per quarter for each woman and $3 for each child. By mid-year board members had distributed seventy-two pairs of cards at $10 per pair, which they acknowledged would "not half supply the demand." It would be helpful, they suggested, if any fourth-quarter appropriation from the state could be sent in the form of cotton cards, not money.

Other innovative enterprises that perhaps had female employees include the wooden shoe-sole factory developed at Bivingsville, a Newberry bonnet frame plant, and Guerin, Matoue & Company, a Charleston concern producing "segars." Yet another cotton card establishment was incorporated by seven Greenwood gentlemen in December 1864; however, there is no indication "The Ladies' Card Factory" ever produced anything.[17]

Of special importance was the Quartermaster Department work mentioned earlier by Wilmot DeSaussure's sister, although this program was not without problems. A huge crowd gathered in Columbia in August 1861 to hear Mrs. L. J. McCord, president of that city's Ladies Working Association, explain how housewives could earn money by sewing. In the years that followed, this organization allegedly employed the families of sixty-four local soldiers to make 12,529 garments worth $10,557.[18]

In Charleston, this scheme seems to have functioned well enough in its initial stages. At the same time that Mrs. McCord's group was swinging into action, Confederate officials placed ads in various newspapers seeking women to sew for the Quartermaster Department. Several weeks later, an anonymous letter to the *Courier* (22 October) complained that most of the winter clothing for soldiers was being made by blacks. In one establishment, according to the writer, fifty black girls were at work while poor whites were denied employment.

> Is it right? Shall we see the poor widow and orphan suffer? No! it should be known to all, that these contractors are taking the bread away from our poor whites and giving it to the negroes. Many of these ladies have husbands and sons now on the battlefield, and the only support now left to them, is the needle. With the exception of the Quartermaster's Department, nowhere can the poor widow get work, and may the blessing of God rest on him and his clerks, is the prayer of a FRIEND OF THE POOR.

In March 1863, however, when the *Courier* praised the same department for making excellent contracts at low rates and thus assuring many indigent females of "remunerating employment," a "Poor Lady Seamstress" protested vehemently. J. Rugheimer, 50 Anson Street, she insisted, was paying local women 50¢ more for coats and 25¢ more for jackets than Confederate officials would offer.

Some sixteen months later, as he surveyed the world from his home near Aiken, botanist and agricultural writer Henry William Ravenel (1814-1887) had these comments on women and war.

> The necessities of war have given rise to many kinds of business & employment before unknown. At Richmond & at Columbia now, large numbers of females are employed to cut money, i.e. to separate the bills from the large sheets. They get at present $3000 a year. The clothing Bureaus at different places also give employment to many. A large number of females in Aiken take in govt work (clothing for the soldiers) from Augusta. A stocking factory in Columbia also gives out the work to be sewed up & fitted. Mary [Ravenel's wife] is today learning how the work is done, expecting to take some of it. The govt. work has been the means of giving a living to many persons who have lost their all during the war. Widows of Officers & soldiers, refugees without a home, & other destitute persons have thus been enabled to live.[19]

Whatever the truth concerning government contracts and their effect, the number of women sewing for the army, turning out manufactured goods, and doing volunteer work pales beside the legions of white and black females producing badly needed foodstuffs on farms and plantations throughout South Carolina. Yet it is quite possible many of these individuals were doing much the same thing in the 1840s and 1850s. In short, they were what Phillip Paludan calls "invisible" farmers—mothers, wives, and daughters who, year in and year out, ploughed, tended animals and crops, gathered hay, picked corn, and so on.[20] Paludan, who was talking about life in the North, contends a shortage of men and boys made such folk *visible*. This may have been less so in the South because agricultural mechanization was not well developed and backbreaking labor by young and old of both colors and both sexes more common.

Henry William Ravenel (1814-1887).

Two English visitors, however, saw things not seen by local eyes. Reverend William Malet, ultra pro-southern, wrote as he traveled near Conway in 1862, "In the fields the women were ploughing, for their husbands had all gone to the army...."[21] Elizabeth Collins, who was living with the Plowden J.C. Westons and refugeed with them in the same community, thought "the real ladies" in America were "more like farmers' wives in England, or perhaps a tradesman's wife. The greater

CONWAYBORO'S METHODIST CHURCH

I think the Methodist Church at Conwayboro will beat any Church I have seen for disorder and dirt.... Its height is about 50 feet, length and breadth 38 feet, and, in order to keep it dry, it is built on heavy blocks of wood about 4 feet high. I may here say, that such blocks form part of almost all buildings in South Carolina. There is a flight of five or six steps which lead to the door; these steps are in bad condition, and quite dangerous to walk up and down. The seats are open... [and] free for any one, but the women sit on one side, the men on the other. The latter are accommodated with a spitoon, one in every three or four seats; there is also one at the table, and I have no doubt the pulpit contains another, for the preacher seldom begins a sermon without disposing of the quid, or something like it. There is a little shelf attached to the pulpit, a receptacle for tumblers and books, In front of it is a round table, generally used, I suppose, when the Sacrament is administered; but when I have seen it, there has been a collection of school-books, and now and then a hat, scattered about it, much resembling a card-table. I am quite unable to say in what way the school is managed: I can only say there is not the least sign of a scholar in the Church when the service begins.

It is generally admitted that education in the South is at a low ebb; but *one* thing I see is taught here, love of country and country's cause.

Collins, *Memories of the Southern States*, pp. 62-63.

part of them assist in cooking, cutting garments, &c.; and, as far as education goes, they, like myself, are sometimes at a loss for grammar. The want of education," Collins mused, "is greatly owing to their marrying so soon...."[22] Two other aspects of life in eastern South Carolina she found equally disturbing—the tendency of white women to smoke pipes almost continuously and the rapidity with which they aged. At thirty, in her opinion, they looked as old and round-shouldered as English women at seventy...perhaps, she surmised, the intense summer heat was responsible for this phenomenon.

English-born Mrs. Weston, according to this raconteur, did not let war effect her daily routine unduly, even though her rice-rich husband, then lieutenant governor of the state, was an officer campaigning with the Confederate Army in Tennessee. On their Georgetown plantation,

Martha Ann Fewell (1830-1890).

Weston traditionally called off the roll of workers each morning; but, after the slaves moved to Conway, his wife thought this awkward and suggested they simply knock on her window at 6 a.m. and give their names.[23]

Moving down the social scale a bit, it is apparent that the Emily Harrises and Jane McLures, women with far fewer slaves and husbands away at war, deserve high praise for the manner in which they shouldered unfamiliar responsibilities. Another such lady is Martha Fewell of York County, wife of Alexander Faulkner Fewell, who, like Harris, served several hitches in uniform. Here is a sample of Fewell's advice to his wife, a detailed message dispatched from Petersburg on 27 October 1864.

> I Suppose you have put your wheat in by this time. have it well ploughed in and as Soon as you get done the wheat you had better Sew a part of your Oats. have that ploughed in So as not to have the furrows Running too Straight up and down hill and try to guard against making washes. and in the Red field you will make them open that ditch from the mulberry tree So as to keep the water from Running across the hill below it also the one above the Spring as it filled up this Summer and washed Considerable across that piece of land. You must make them be Careful of fire both about the house and in the fields. I am glad to hear that you were So fortunate as to have a part of your Shoes made before Mr. Brown Closed his Shop. you must be Saving of leather as possible for we wont have any for another year. there is 2/3 of a hide at Finleys that if you have not got it must be ready. it is a good Sized hide & would make Several pair of Shoes. it is the hide of the old black Cow & will be upper leather. let me hear from you and what you are doing and how the negroes are doing. you must make them mind you and each one attend to their respective duties.[24] I Suppose you have moved the Cow pen. dont manure that Sand hill too Strong for we want it for potatoes and then it Soon Sinks in the Sand. when you manure all that we had Sown in oats moove the pen into the Stalk land. You must have your potatoes well put up [but] not too many in a hill and either Cover with plank or boards So as to keep the water off the hills. let them eat as many as they Can Save then Sell Some if you Can get a fair price for them or feed them to the hogs, two bushel of potatoes are nearly equal to one of Corn for fattening hogs. Sam is your Calves & Sheep in good order. you must Salt & feed them as Soon as the pastures are done. I must Close

now for the present and Shall add Some in the morning perhaps if I have time.[25]

A few weeks later, Fewell urged his wife to include in any box sent to him something to sell…"as I dont never want to get under $75.00 on hand for fear Something happens & I could not get from home and I am obliged to buy Something to eat almost every day.[26] Then, early in the new year, cautioning Martha not to tell anyone, he expressed "a Rather poor opinion" of rebel currency and suggested she trade his Confederate bonds for something if possible, "not for negroes for Reasons I have before given."[27]

Despite the many things Emily, Jane, Martha, and thousands like them did in behalf of the Confederate cause, there is a "down" side to this tale as well. The same women who stepped in and took the place of loved ones in 1861-1862 frequently undercut the war effort in succeeding years by begging husbands and sons to come home to protect them, thus fomenting desertion. Nor is it clear that even their original burst of energy was prompted in every instance by a keen sense of patriotic ardor; instead, they merely may have been trying to make a living for themselves and their families. Any assistance given to the Confederate States of America—much like the labor of their slaves—perhaps was incidental to survival amid trying conditions.

Nevertheless, it is apparent that, under twin banners of patriotism and war, some women embraced behavior that would have been thought unseemly in peacetime. In the spring of 1861, for example, when several young Charleston dandies joined a cavalry unit destined never to see action, a band of females presented them with petticoats.[28] A short time later, writing from Hilton Head where he was serving in the army, Langdon Cheves, Jr., told his wife she should consider making her way to the mountains from their home near Savannah: "Ladies are moving about independently these days as a matter of ordinary necessity, and with a nominal escort such as you can always find, it would be better for you to go without waiting for me, than that you yourself or the children should suffer.…"[29]

Theodore Honour, on the other hand, in September 1863 warned his wife, an upcountry refugee, never to ride in public, horseback or otherwise, except with her father and brother. "There may be no evil in it," he wrote on the 19th, "but it lays you open to remarks, and this world you know is a censorious one." A few days later, she was cautioned to attend no more surprise parties. What would happen, he asked, if in the midst of such revelry she received word that he was seriously wounded?[30]

Proper Charlestonians such as General Thomas Sumter's grand-daughters were shocked when the *Courier* printed their names in full in May 1861. According to Emma Holmes, this breach of etiquette caused considerable "mortification and vexation."[31] In succeeding years, women of their class who refugeed in Camden clung tenaciously to established rules of social conduct, and no lady could invite anyone to a party or picnic until she first made a formal call at that person's residence and exchanged pleasantries.[32] And, even as the war was ending, Augustine Thomas Smythe expressed approval in January 1865 when his fiancée (Louisa McCord) chose not to participate in Columbia's huge charity bazaar. The affair at the State House might well be for a worthy cause, but he agreed with her mother that young ladies should not go around selling things.[33]

Yet there is the strange spectacle of "gentle" womenfolk actually working for wages. On 19 June 1862, Susan Middleton described life in Columbia to cousin Harriott in Flat Rock in this fashion: "This place fills up daily—there are six ladies supporting themselves by clipping Con[federate] notes. The widow of Gen. [Francis S.] Bartow and several from Washington and Richmond. They work six hours a day and are paid forty dollars a month. We are going sightseeing soon to see the money made, and to the top of the new State House."[34] Perhaps it was the making of money that attracted Susan's attention, but one suspects upperclass women at work for pay was a sight equal to that of the panorama to be seen from Columbia's loftiest structure.

By August 1864 their ranks had swelled to over one hundred and fifty, and these young ladies undoubtedly were the subject of even greater comment, not all of it complimentary. Bettie J. Clarke, a Virginia lass transferred south from Richmond, complained in a letter to a friend of stifling heat, though she conceded it really was no worse than at home, "except that it is so constant & we become by that accustomed to it." This young lady praised Columbia's wide streets and handsome gardens, yet thought there was "too much uniformity about the place," and some people were "stiff as ramrods... you know South Carolinians pride themselves on their hautau [hauteur] of manner, these Columbians particularly." Refugees from the coast were quite different, "so effable [sic] & charming." Nevertheless, Bettie admitted she and her friends often had been entertained by prominent local families. At that time many of these treasury workers were being housed at the Methodist Female Col-

lege but would have to vacate when classes began.[35] During these same
months there were suggestions women also become printers and post-
mistresses, thus relieving men for service, and an anonymous letter
appearing in the *Mercury* on 1 November 1864 advocated even greater
female participation in the labor force. The writer, a Pendleton lady who
chose to identity herself merely as "Carolina," noted 125,000 men ages
18 to 45 were detailed to "special duty."

> Surely our strength is not yet put forth. Many of these
> men—perhaps a hundred thousand—could be replaced
> by women. Many of our ladies are capable of carrying
> on the education, both of boys and girls, up to the ages
> of seventeen and eighteen. And some men are detailed
> to teach girls. The noble, wise and virtuous of our ladies
> would come forward, if called upon, and supply these
> places.
>
> Those offices, in the quartermaster and commissary
> departments, where the occupant is stationary, could,
> many of them, be filled by ladies. I am acquainted with
> several ladies of first rate business capacity, who, I am
> sure, would fill such offices with ability, zeal and faith.
>
> It is a conventional idea with some persons that a
> lady steps out of her sphere when she becomes useful to
> any but her own family. Oh! let us remember the noble
> Polish ladies, driven in chains to labor in the mines of
> Siberia; and, now, in this crisis of our country's fate, let
> us arise and do our part. Let us, also, be held worthy to
> toil for our country, our homes, our children and our
> dead. How noble and glorious the toil which fills a man's
> place and gives a soldier more to the armies of our coun-
> try.
>
> We have seen the whole Treasury Department filled
> by ladies. Oh! let us now see the stationary quartermaster
> and commissary departments—leaving a few men to
> perform those parts which require more strength and
> exposure [—do likewise]. Have ever the women failed
> to respond when called upon? Reward us now in allow-
> ing us to be of use.

However, nothing came of proposals such as this, perhaps because the concepts were too radical or because, as many suspected, the cause already was "lost."

In an unexpected turn of events, on rare occasions some urban housewives risked scorn and even possible imprisonment by displaying overt admiration for the enemy—certainly a profound expression of independent spirit. Why is not always clear, but the impulse to do so probably was rooted in a mix of war weariness, curiosity, self-interest, and perhaps secret admiration for the Union or disenchantment with the Confederacy. Cameraderie of this sort usually developed in a rail center far from the sound of battle when prisoners (especially officers) en route to be exchanged were granted permission to roam freely while waiting for a connecting train. Lt. Col. Frank T. Bennett, a Pennsylvanian captured at Tybee Island in March 1862 and lodged for a time in a Columbia jail, wandered about Charleston, Raleigh, Weldon, and practically every other station stop on his way to Richmond in October of the same year.[36] These were, of course, unusual circumstances. Men such as Bennett, bound for freedom, are not going to escape and cause trouble, but they could carry letters to friends and relatives in the North and exchange currency with local residents eager to secure greenbacks. Also, as in all wars, some individuals were certain humane treatment could benefit "our boys" held by the enemy, that is, they would be handled in a like manner.

The following spring, conditions such as these provoked a storm of protest in Augusta. In this instance, several hundred federals, many of them officers captured at Vicksburg or near Rome by General Nathan Bedford Forrest, arrived at South Carolina's border on Tuesday, 12 May 1863, en route to Richmond and freedom. For eight hours or so they lounged about town, ate at hotels, and drank in bars, much as they had done earlier in Atlanta. The *Augusta Chronicle & Sentinel* (14 May) was horrified.

> It is possible that one may sometimes entertain an angel unawares, though he is more apt to get hold of the Cloven Hoof in the disguise of a gentleman; but we believe there is not the slightest doubt as to the identity of the uniformed gentry who perambulated our streets on

Tuesday. They are no angels, unless 'destroying angels,' and as to disguise, neither by garb nor speech, was their true character concealed. There were circumstances, too, connected with their presence in this city, which made them known to us as the murderers and plunderers of Southern citizens. Yet with all these convincing proofs before us, one could hardly determine whether they were friends or foes, judging from the treatment they received.

These enemy troops openly indulged in "insolent swagger," were given cigars and refreshment, and even shook the hand of a Confederate officer who said he was "glad" to see them.

Did the pressure of that grip leave no stain of blood upon his fingers—the flesh that murdered his kinfolk? And women presented the unfortunate prisoners—guests, we mean, with flowers.[37] Did any of our Confederate soldiers who acted as guards to these men receive such floral testimonials of good will and female favor? Not one. No wonder the captives manifested such exuberance of spirits throughout the day, and bore their term of durance so lightly, or that they left the city at evening with the manner of an excursion party returning from a picnic. A rare jaunt they have had through 'the land of cotton.' Pleasant reminiscences will they have of their tour of the South, expenses paid—pleasant recollections of Augusta. Soon again in camp they will tell the jolly story of what rare times they had in Dixie, and long for another gallop through the land of flowers where green-backs are worth three to one, and where females kiss the hand that slew their brother.

Fresh from scenes of murder, burning, and pillage, the city welcomed these men, according to the *Chronicle*, "with a display of leniency and civility, if not of sympathy, that is absolutely criminal and women are actually found who bestow their favors upon them. What humiliation!"

The *Augusta Daily Constitutionalist* (13 May) heartily agreed, distressed that "gangs of horse thieves, negro stealers and robbers recently caught desecrating our sod" were greeted as long-lost friends. "They were not waging legitimate warfare," this editor shouted. "They were

Charleston Jail Yard.

stealing and devastating a country they have not the power to conquer in a fair, manly contest, and the meanest felon that rots in our dungeons is more deserving of courtesy and respect than they." However, in succeeding days the *Constitutionalist* used this incident to advantage. Deploring "ill-timed hospitality" fostered by profiteering and love of ease, it asked the mayor to organize home-defense companies at once. A roll of those refusing to serve, the editor said, would indicate how many traitors actually were living in the Augusta area.

Two months later, it was Charleston's turn, although this display of affection—studiously ignored by the *Mercury*—occurred under quite different circumstances. Yankee prisoners lodged there presumably were under guard...or at least not on their way to be exchanged. Yet this notice in the *Courier* (18 July) hints at even more blatant approval of the invader.

> *The Yankee Sympathizers.*—We understand that the petticoat sympathizers with the Yankee prisoners were again busy, in their shameful vocation, yesterday. If husbands, brothers and fathers do not interfere, and check these offensive demonstrations of prurient interest in the wickedest and vilest of foes, they need not be surprised at an order of expulsion.
>
> We cannot avoid the suspicion that the imprudent females in question are hoping for and calculating on

the capture of Charleston; and we invoke the attention of
the Mayor and our military authorities to the subject. Let
the police, too, be on the alert, *and arrest the offenders.*

Perhaps, as this editor surmised, some of these women, thinking
Charleston doomed, were prepared to gain whatever they could by em-
bracing the victor (literally). It is noteworthy, of course, that this incident
occurred as federal forces seemed to be closing in on Charleston itself,
Vicksburg and Port Hudson had fallen, the horror of Gettysburg was
becoming apparent, and lists of dead and wounded were growing ever
longer. The same day that the *Courier* lashed out at these "petticoat
sympathizers," the rival *Mercury* began printing the names of South
Carolinians killed and wounded in Pennsylvania. In succeeding days
the sad toll mounted (two-and-one-half columns in the *Mercury* on the
21st), augmented by casualties suffered on the local scene during spirited clashes on James and Morris islands.

Ladies aid groups in virtually every community, big and small,
marshaling volunteer efforts of all kinds, plantation mistresses running
things while the master was away, hundreds of treasury clerks cutting
up bills, little girls learning to shoot bows and arrows (just why is not
clear), a handful of women lavishing attention upon enemy prisoners of
war (which is equally puzzling), housewives sewing for the Confederate Quartermaster Department, women ploughing, working in mills and
factories, teaching school for the first time, and at least one young miss
advertising for a husband (see page 193) ... it all adds up to a rather
muddled but intriguing picture.

Nevertheless, several facts emerge. In the early 1860s, South Carolina women enjoyed a brief period of exhilaration not unlike that
experienced by their slaves. Not complete freedom, true, but more independence than some of them had ever known. Ellen Elmore of
Columbia recalled four decades later the thrill of becoming business
agent for her mother's plantations in York and Lexington districts after
male relatives went off to war and overseers who replaced them proved
incompetent. Bursting with pride of accomplishment, she supplied the
Confederate government with timbers and was told by many that affairs
never had been "so satisfactorily conducted." "This was truly a feather
in my woman's cap," she wrote, "but we feminines before the war ended,

YOUNG MEN ATTENTION
Double! Double! Double!

A YOUNG LADY of twenty summers, medium size, blue eyes, auburn hair, fair complexion, and agreeable disposition desires to open a correspondence with young gentleman with a view to matrimony.

Any young man of good moral character, and fair prospects in life who thinks of assuming the duties and responsibilities of the wedded state can address me, with the permission of the editor, through the columns of the Abbeville *Press*, giving his age, description of his personal appearance, prospects in life, &c., &c.

CHARLOTTE V
Pleasant Hill Jan'y 15th, 1863.

[On 30 January 1863, the *Press* printed two responses to this ad. One young man (James R. D., age 26, of Monterey) seemed to be sincere; the other gentleman, a wounded veteran with a girth of 5½ feet, apparently was not.]

were to pick up many a one dropped from the helmets of our brave fellows who had work to do beyond our powers, and in which we could aid them only by doing what it had been theirs to do hitherto."[38]

In a social sense, for women such as Ellen the door *did* slam shut after Appomattox, and some of her friends probably were quite content to retire to the safety and security of the pedestal, that is, assuming they ever left it. But others chafed under these restrictions. If not, why did the UDC faithful go to such great lengths at the turn of the century to recapture the "glory" days of the 1860s and boast of past deeds? As we know, people tend to suppress memories of pain while treasuring experiences that bring joy into their lives, and these good women ran true to form. The two volumes of Confederate memorabilia edited by Mrs. Taylor and her associates talk not of death but, for the most part, of pleasure… "the many happy hours" spent working for "our boys" and the *excitement* of those bygone days. Sacrifice, yes, amid the tumult of cheerful cooperation and the warm satisfaction of worthwhile tasks well done.

Mrs. James Hoyt of Greenville vowed she was glad to have lived through the war because it taught her womanliness, character, and endurance.[39] Even after forty years, others remembered the most intimate

details of concerts, fairs, and bazaars held to raise money for the reli
of soldiers and their families. In their UDC world, *all* men were bra\
and away battling the hated invader, *all* slaves were loyal and trustwo
thy, *all* women valiant and dedicated to the "cause." Then Sherman can
and laid waste that perfect realm, slashing his way across the state fro.
Hardeeville to Cheraw and leaving in his wake desolation, hunger, ar
chaos.

These volumes (and others like them) are, of course, the found.
tions of the mythical "Old South" we confront today. The achievemen
cited are impressive, even though the tales told often exude both char
and venom, regional hospitality and revenge. But the reader should r
member those speaking represent, for the most part, a certain class
women whose lives were changed dramatically by the events of t
1860s, perhaps shattered beyond repair. And, since these ladies are d
scribing events nearly half a century after they occurred, often thin;
they did not see, they can indulge in the luxuries of hindsight, embe
lishment, and selective memory.

One might ask at this point why the UDC has no Yankee counte
part? Northern women took on many of the same tasks their souther
sisters assumed such as raising money, helping soldier families, nur
ing, and teaching school. Perhaps the answer lies in the fact they nev
were quite as "pedestalized" and able to move more independently bo
before and after 1865. As a result, freedom of action generated by w;
did not seem to be an aberration, at least not to the same degree as in t
South. Besides, their side won, depriving them of the emotional appe;
of a "lost cause," perhaps the UDC's most valuable asset. Irony of ir
nies, the catalog of good works assembled by South Carolina
"Daughters" would have won easy endorsement of Suffragettes an
maybe even a quiet round of applause from women "libbers" of mo
recent decades.

Out of this maelstrom of unprecedented female activity, sudde
disaster, and repression there emerged a uniquely southern creation–
the "steel magnolia"—the demure Dixie belle and her matronly moth
exuding quiet charm, smiling beguiling smiles, and speaking in ho
eyed tones yet determined of will and possessing substantial inner streng
and resilience. Some of this genus, widowed by war or consigned t
discreet spinsterhood, were left with the task of raising hordes of o
phans. Among this number were the Elliott aunts of Oak Lawn in Colleto
District who cared (very well indeed) for six Gonzales nieces and nep
ews. Others who took over household and plantation in 1861 discovere

they still had a full-time job after 1865 as well, perhaps because males in the family were killed, crippled, or unable to function as before. And, much like Ellen Elmore, they quickly concluded, if one takes on great responsibility, then that individual deserves credit for whatever successes ensue.

The seeds of this change obviously were sown during the war itself. On 18 February 1863, the editor of the *Edgefield Advertiser* tried to make sense of what was happening in his rural realm.

> ...did you ever think, boys, there was so much vim, and hope, and zeal, and energy, and ability in the women of the South as the times have shown up? Bless their good and brave and warm-beating hearts, they are (and of right ought to be) the pride of creation, and man is but the— Well, comparisons are odious and it isn't worth while to run out the antithesis just now. *Some* folks *do* say that our 'sublime women' are beginning to find out their level is several strata above that of their associates in the *genus homo*, and that troubles in the wigwam may succeed these ugly days of strife and danger. Not a word of it— not a word of it—don't believe a syllable of it. And yet there are some funny things turning up now and then.

"Several strata above that of their associates" sounds very much like a pedestal; and, placed there by worshipful southern males, in post-war decades some women shrewdly turned that elevation into a personal fortress. As Lee learned to his sorrow at Gettysburg, it is always dangerous to yield the high ground to the enemy.

NOTES

[1]See Mrs. Thomas Taylor, *et al* (eds.), *South Carolina Women in the Confederacy* (2 vols.; Columbia, 1903, 1907).

[2]Ibid., II, p. 217. Note: "Shoon" is an archaic word for shoes.

[3]Ibid., I, p. 28. Catherine Prioleau Ravenel, a Charleston refugee, still was irked four decades later because Sherman shelled Columbia in February 1865 without giving "notice of such intention" to the proper authorities (vol. II, p. 149).

[4]Ibid. One hundred such groups are listed in volume one (pp. 21-25) and another twenty-four in volume two (pp. 91-92).

[5]Ibid., I, p. 46.

[6]*Tri-Weekly Watchman*, 22 October 1862.

[7]Ibid., 29 October 1862.

[8]Ibid., 24 November 1862.

[9]Ibid., 28 November 1862.

[10]*Daily Guardian*, 21 January 1864.

[11]According to records at the South Caroliniana Library, this institution assisted some 70,000 young men during the next three years.

[12]Marazalek, *The Diary of Miss Emma Holmes*, pp. 102-103, 128, 206.

[13]See Lee McNinch, "Civil War Hospitals of the South Carolina College" (senior thesis paper, 1977) at the South Caroliniana Library. Except for a large hospital developed in Summerville during the middle years of the war, most such institutions—other than those located in Charleston and Columbia—were little more than overnight quarters for servicemen and their dependents.

[14]Henry William DeSaussure Letters, Special Collections Library, Duke University.

[15]On 4 July 1864, for example, Greenville women reported proceeds of $95.25 from a lecture delivered in their community by Paul Hamilton Hayne. When they sought permission to publish the address, which they had sponsored, Hayne said no. It was, he replied, "only written for delivery & too imperfect for printing."

[16]Margaret —— to Mary Milling, 12 June 1863, James S. Milling Papers, Southern Historical Collection, University of North Carolina.

[17]In a bid to increase industrial output, in May 1862 a Confederate general offered Union POWs who were shoemakers liberty and good pay if they would go to work. When rebuffed, according to the diary of Frank P. Bennett, he stormed out of a Charleston jail. See Bennett diary (15 May 1862), Special Collections Library, Duke University. Bennett says Charleston newspapers also suggested that Union prisoners be put to work repairing railroad lines.

[18]*Daily South Carolinian,* 13 March 1864.

[19]Arney Robinson Childs, *The Private Journal of Henry William Ravenel, 1859-1887* (Columbia, 1947), p. 199.

[20]Phillip Shaw Paludan, *"The People's Contest": The Union and the Civil War* (New York, 1988), p. 157.

[21]William Wyndam Malet, *An Errand to the South in the Summer of 1862* (London,

1863), p. 36.

[22]Collins, *Memories of the Southern States*, pp. 36-37. Malet, brother-in-law of Mrs. Weston, came to America to see her on family business.

[23]Ibid., p. 16

[24]Two years earlier, in January 1862, Martha cautioned her husband "pleas dont get excited and go near the ennym. keep out of danger and be on youir gard." Then she added this comment concerning slaves (p. 16), "I get all out of umor some times with the Negre but cousin John dont like for me to say a word but I cant help but do it when I see them walkin a bout and Idling their time a way." And a few months later in April of the same year (p. 52), she was distressed to learn her husband was existing on potatoes: "you have to work so much harder than them [your slaves] and dont live half so well."

[25]Robert Harley Mackintosh, Jr. (ed.), *"Dear Martha...," The Confederate War Letters of a South Carolina Soldier, Alexander Faulkner Fewell* (Columbia, 1976), p. 154.

[26]Ibid., p. 182.

[27]Ibid., p. 183.

[28]William Elliott to Isabella Elliott Barnwell, 29 June 1861, Elliott Family Papers. In this same letter, written in Virginia, Elliott told of an amusing exchange. When General Kershaw lamented that Bull Run was an "exceedingly ugly name" for the upcoming clash of arms, General Beauregard remarked he did not think "Cow-pens had much the advantage of Bull Run and that no South Carolinian had any objection to hearing the former mentioned."

[29]Langdon Cheves, Jr., to Charlotte McCord Cheves, 10 August 1861, Langdon Cheves West Papers.

[30]Theodore Honour to Rebecca, 19, 27 September 1863, Theodore Honour Papers.

[31]Marszalek, *The Diary of Miss Emma Holmes*, p. 43.

[32]William Elliott to Isabella Elliott Barnwell, 18 November 1863, Elliott Family Papers.

[33]Augustine Thomas Smythe to Louisa McCord, 23 January 1865, Augustine Thomas Smythe Letters.

[34]"Middleton Correspondence," *South Carolina Historical Magazine* (April 1962), p. 70.

[35]Bettie J. Clarke to "Lizzie," 27-30 August 1864, Bettie J. Clarke Papers, South Caroliniana Library.

[36]See Bennett diary. This officer, who signed a parole and promised not to take up arms again, was back in a Confederate prison once more after being captured at Drewry's Bluff in May 1864. His experiences do not seem especially unique. Six Yankee prisoners who were Masons attended a lodge meeting in Columbia early in 1862, much to the horror of some residents. Bennett and A. O. Abbott—a New York lieutenant and author of *Prison Life in the South* (New York, 1865)—both describe how "generally friendly" most civilians were in centers such as Charleston and Columbia.

[37]On 31 May 1863, just back from a delightful week "in Town" (Charleston) and now

in "horrid" Columbia, Lizzie P. Smith penned a brief note to Isabella Middleton Smith in Augusta. In a hasty postscript she added, "Give my love to Cousin Em and tell her we are curious to know whether she was one of the 'these ladies' in Augusta who presented bouquets to Yankee soldiers and received them so hospitally." See *Mason Smith Family Letters*, p. 44. The Smiths undoubtedly read of this incident in the *Mercury*, which provided full coverage on Saturday, 16 May, the same day that it published two columns of South Carolinians killed and wounded at the Wilderness and Chancellorville.

[38]Taylor, *South Carolina Women in the Confederacy*, I, p. 198.
[39]Ibid. p. 371.

VII

MOOD SWINGS & MORALE

The question of morale in South Carolina during the Civil War can be tackled in various ways. One is to look for confirmatory evidence of highs when the correspondence of both civilians and those in uniform should reflect euphoria—say, following the attack upon Fort Sumter and successes at First Manassas and Fredericksburg. Conversely, the federal invasion of South Carolina in November 1861, disheartening news from the Mississippi Valley in the months that followed, and the twin blows of Gettysburg and Vicksburg in July 1863 undoubtedly cast a pall over the populace. Yet personal letters can be deceptive. A wife or mother might paint an overly bleak picture to entice a loved one to come home or put up a brave front in the face of disaster in order to boost spirits. On 1 July 1863, for example, the *Yorkville Enquirer* cautioned readers to write only "cheerful" letters to soldiers. Also, public pressure to back the war effort was so intense at times that many undoubtedly were wary of expressing their true feelings, even to friends and relatives.

Local newspapers of those years shed some light on the public mood, but how much is uncertain since most editors backed the Confederate cause with considerable passion (at least in print) and were notoriously optimistic to the very end. Even when criticizing the policies of President Davis or struggling with momentary setbacks they usually saw ("with God's help") a silver lining somewhere, somehow. William Elliott became so frustrated that in November 1863 when he learned that Charleston's telegraph office had been destroyed by enemy shells he told his fiancée, "Pity they would not blow up all the newspaper offices in the Confederacy."[1] In addition, a paper shortage tended to strangle the words of many journalists. Nearly all standard, four-page newspapers soon were reduced to a single sheet. The *Charleston Mercury, Yorkville Enquirer,* and Columbia's *Daily Southern Guardian* made this transition in 1862; the *Charleston Courier* in April 1863. Before doing so, some publishers tried to ward off the inevitable by reducing type size, eliminating a column, or perhaps printing slimmer columns.

The *Daily Southern Guardian* even changed its name to the *Daily Guardian* as pages shrank.

But editors in some communities simply quit and closed up shop, among them weeklies published in Anderson, Camden, Darlington, Georgetown, Kingstree, Lexington, Newberry, Orangeburg, Pickens, Walterboro, and Winnsboro. One daily, the *Charleston Evening News,* also expired in 1861 as its staff donned uniforms. On the other hand, at least three new publications appeared during wartime—the *Camden Confederate*, Columbia's *Confederate Baptist*, and the *Horry Dispatch* (Conway)—and, on the eve of hostilities, Darlington could boast of a short-lived, anti-secessionist sheet, the *Confederation*.

In sum, this means perhaps half of South Carolina's newspapers disappeared during the opening stages of the conflict. Those that remained limped along, for the most part as single sheets (what printers call "half" sheets) dominated by ads, official proclamations, battlefield news, and casualty lists, which left little space for local matters.[2] In any case, editors usually stuck close to views expressed in the columns of dailies produced in Columbia, Charleston, and Richmond, rarely expressing divergent opinions.

In addition to personal letters and newspapers, interpretive studies of the Confederacy and the Civil War—works by scholars such as E. Merton Coulter, Mary Elizabeth Massey, T. Harry Williams, David Donald, Richard Current, Wilfred Buck Yearns, Emory Thomas, Frank Vandiver, and Richard Beringer—tell us something about morale in a general way, that is, what role it played in the Confederate nation as a whole. "Morale," according to Coulter, "was the most potent weapon the South had; and with all of the Confederates' unco-ordinated efforts at building it up and maintaining it, they lost this weapon, and, therefore, the war."[3] In his final pages, Coulter is even more blunt. Despite all of the problems faced, he concludes "the fact remains the Confederacy never fully utilized the human and material resources it had. It never succeeded in developing an *esprit de corps*, either in its civil or military organization, and in that sense it did not deserve to win."[4]

The views of other students of the period, though less stern, usually contain similar observations concerning morale. Yearns thinks things went rather well until the spring of 1862. Then, as the pace of war quickened, the central government passed emergency measures to get more men, money, and supplies. This led to conscription, impressment, higher taxes, inflation, crop limitations, and occasional suspension of *habeas corpus*, all of which dampened public ardor. Areas invaded by federal forces had to be treated differently (exemption from some laws, for example), thus increasing the burden on other regions. These factors, plus a deteriorating military situation, led, he believes, to a natural conclusion that the war was being conducted improperly.[5] Nevertheless, Current considers morale only a secondary cause of defeat. The prime reason, in his opinion, was economic—shortages of all kinds. As he stresses with analytical precision, the North only had to draw upon its vast resources an amount *equal* to whatever the South somehow could assemble.[6]

These "over-all" views are revealing, but how do they relate to the local scene? Each state within the Confederacy was different and faced special and unique problems as fighting progressed. South Carolina was a relatively small expanse of territory compared to Georgia and Texas, lacked the mountain kingdoms of several of its neighbors, certainly was more unified on the question of secession than any other state, and, as a result of migration in the 1840s and 1850s, probably had a more homogeneous white population than most. At least at the outset, it harbored no communities (such as could be found in Alabama, Tennessee, North Carolina, and Virginia) that were outwardly hostile to severing federal ties. In fact, files of the Southern Claims Commission of the 1870s indicate South Carolinians who opposed the war often were "loners," people living in isolation in coastal swamps or wooded recesses—middle-aged or elderly folk with no ties to the outside, no sons in uniform, etc.[7] Individuals of that sort obviously had little impact upon public opinion.

Several other factors set South Carolina apart from other states within a new nation. Until the final months of the war, except for raids along the coast and the shelling of Charleston, its homefront rarely heard enemy gunfire. Perhaps most important of all, South Carolinians bore a special burden: they started this whole affair or at least had to shoulder considerable responsibility for the war. As things began to unravel, just think how many men and boys must have told South Carolinians as they gathered around army camp fires—"You damned hot-heads got us into this" or "We tried to tell you this would happen, and you fools wouldn't listen!"

In time, upcountry South Carolinians undoubtedly said much the same thing to their lowcountry cousins, opening a breach bridged momentarily in 1860-1861. If human nature has not changed since then, this burden is another piece of the morale puzzle, for few individuals want to assume personal responsibility for errors committed by others. Nevertheless, when badgered, there is natural tendency to stick up for one's kin, neighbors, and community. As a result, even after July 1863, stubborn pride continued to foster an unreal, upbeat mood in some circles throughout the state.

Another puzzle fragment, and an important one, is the fact those promoting secession in 1860 "oversold" their product by promising too much. This whipped up enthusiasm for the cause and boosted morale to dizzy heights, the descent from which, once it came, could be dramatic, bitter, and painful. This is how writer William Grayson describes their campaign.

> To induce the simple people to plunge into the volcanic fires of revolution and war, they were told that the act of dissolution would produce no opposition of a serious nature; that not a drop of blood would be spilled; that no man's flocks, or herds, or negroes, or houses, or lands would be plundered or destroyed; that unbroken prosperity would follow the ordinance of secession; that cotton would control all Europe, and secure boundless commerce with the whole world for the Southern States.[8]

James McCarter, a Charleston book dealer who moved to Columbia during the war, says when he visited the state capital early in November 1860, secession fever was red hot. In his words, "Passion had usurped the throne of Reason in the minds of men."[9] He could find only four legislators (all from the upcountry) who would even listen to those opposed to precipitous action: Samuel McAliley of Chester and Gabriel Cannon of Spartanburg (senators) and two House members, Andrew Wallace Thomson of Union and Spartanburg's James Farrow.

McCarter specifically recalls a rally before the Congaree House where Robert Barnwell Rhett proclaimed that secession was nothing more than "a quiet & easy remedy for intolerable tyranny." There was, he vowed, no danger whatsoever of war because the North would not fight. Milledge L. Bonham, later governor (1863-1864), who was standing at McCarter's side, said Rhett was wrong. The Yankees did so in Mexico, he was there, and they would again. According to McCarter, James Chesnut was one of a handful who realized that northern politicians, regardless of party, generally agreed with Lincoln and warned that secession spelled trouble for South Carolina.

So, despite scattered misgivings, those bent on independence from the federal system of 1787 carried the day and achieved state-wide unity

Secessionists rally at the Mills House, November 1860.
Frank Leslie's Illustrated Weekly, 1 December 1860.

at a crucial moment in South Carolina's history. How was this temporary consensus forged? In the opinion of Steven A. Channing and others, John Brown's raid at Harper's Ferry in October 1859 was the catalyst for action. Channing, author of *Crisis of Fear: Secession in South Carolina* (1970), says that shocking event led to widespread recognition of the great gulf between the idealized master-slave relationship and the reality of insecurity and danger, especially arson (pp. 56-57). The result was the creation of vigilance committees and community associations warning all who would listen of the horrors of abolition—black crime, financial loss, political-social-sexual chaos. Amid such turbulence, one thing all white South Carolinians, upcountry and low, could agree on was *white supremacy*, which, in their view, required the perpetuation of slavery. By December 1860 the choice was simple: separation and slavery or Lincoln and abolition. "The secession of South Carolina was," Channing concludes (p. 282), "an act of passion."

James Wylie Gettys, Jr., who has analyzed antebellum life in Greenville District, agrees that John Brown's raid converted many in that region to the cause.[10] In a truly fascinating, grass-roots study, Gettys traces the slow drift toward war over three decades. In 1832 merely a quarter of the voters in Greenville District voted for nullification, and in 1851 only a third endorsed secession, but nine years later those holding such views swept to an easy victory.[11] After 1858, he emphasizes, the local weekly, *Patriot and Mountaineer*, was edited by an all-out secessionist. Those who thought as he did transformed various public gatherings such as holiday celebrations, court sessions, and sale days into political rallies, even burning confiscated literature in front of the courthouse on one occasion. (The fire allegedly was started by a black man who begged for the honor to do so.) Business leaders, wary of a commercial break with the North and uncertain market conditions, were told separation would boost southern enterprise and create new opportunities.

In the opinion of Gettys, the theory of secession was repeated so often over nearly thirty years that it became "a constitutional principle" accepted by all but the most devout Unionists.[12] By 1860, an adult generation had heard all of the arguments thrashed out many times. What was considered extreme in the 1830s seemed relatively moderate by the 1850s and even desirable in 1860. Also, he observes that technical advances such as the telegraph and railroad changed communication over those decades. Words passed almost instantaneously from one section to another. No longer was there time for passions to cool; instead, any hot salvo was answered with equal bravado and bombast.[13]

Although there are no polls to guide us, secession fever undoubtedly "went off the charts" in December 1860 when South Carolina declared its independence from the federal union. Never again would the Palmetto State be so unified on this issue or the wartime morale of its citizens so vigorous. Seven weeks later, on 12 February 1861, the *Mercury*—one of the loudest proponents of secession—printed a draft of the proposed constitution being written in Montgomery, Alabama. Twenty-four hours after that, this same daily in effect sounded the death knell of the entire movement. Page one was dominated by four-and-one-half columns of closely reasoned argument by Leonidas W. Spratt, one-time editor of the *Charleston Standard*, delegate to South Carolina's secession convention, and commissioner to Florida in an effort to promote secession there. Long an advocate of international trade in slaves, he proclaimed all was lost.[14] The South, he argued in his "philosophy on secession," was in the process of forming a *slave* republic. What followed would not be a North-South, geographical contest but a struggle between two forms of society.

Society is essentially different from government,—as different as the nut from the bur, or the nervous body of the shell fish from the bony structure that surrounds it;—and within this Government [the United States] two societies had become developed as variant in structure and distinct in form as any two beings in animated nature. The one is a society composed of one race—the other of two races. The one is bound together but by two great social relations of husband and wife, and parent and child, the other by the three relations of husband and wife, and parent and child, and master and slave. The one embodies in its political structure the principle that equality is the right of man—the other that it is the right of equals only.

Spratt compared the North and South to two lobsters in a single shell, each striving to make government express its "social nature." And he agreed that, in theory, Seward and Lincoln were right: "The natural expression of one [society] must become encroachment on the other, and so the contest is inevitable." The special target of this gentleman's wrath, as one would expect, was an impending ban on the African slave trade. South Carolina, he argued, needed *more* slaves to till the land and build up its economy. Any constitutional prohibition was, in his opinion, "a great calamity." Yet he maintained with great vigor that South Carolina did not actually wish to re-open that foreign commerce, merely to have the matter left to the several states.

A week later, on 20 February, the *Mercury* published these bitter words forwarded by "Reviewer" from Montgomery.

Let your people prepare their minds for a failure in the future Permanent Southern Constitution. For South Carolina is about to be saddled with almost every grievance except Abolition, for which she has long struggled, and just withdrawn from the late United States Government. Surely McDUFFIE lived in vain, and CALHOUN taught for nought, if we are again to be plundered, and our commerce crippled, destroyed, by tariffs. Yet this is the almost inevitable prospect. The fruit of the labor of thirty odd long years, in strife and bitterness, is about to slip through our fingers.

"Reviewer" (who may have been Robert Barnwell Rhett) took special aim at the old "3/5ths rule" concerning representation, which he thought grossly unfair since South Carolina had so many black residents, prohibition of the foreign slave trade, and tariffs.

For what have we cast off the North as a rotten incubus, if we are thus to re-enact all of their swindles, outrages, and insolences upon our selves? To be plundered and manacled with discriminating tariffs—to stultify ourselves with half-way representation—and endorse all the [unreadable type] and insolence of the Northern States?

In the weeks that followed, the *Mercury* continued to grumble and on 14 March published the "provisional" constitution. Twenty-four hours later, it had qualified praise for the document's emphasis upon state power. Yet the editor still was distressed by prohibition of the slave trade and the "3/5ths rule." For good measure he also aired a new gripe: why not return to the original scheme of presidential election by state legislatures?

The *Mercury* was delighted with the attack on Fort Sumter ("Splendid Pyrotechnic Exhibition"), but less than happy with First Manassas. It believed the Confederates should have pressed forward into Washington, was irked by comments Virginians made concerning South Carolina troops, and continued to complain about tariffs. Soon this list of grievances grew longer—erratic mail delivery, the scarcity of small change, and especially the Confederate government's "defensive" military policy. Early in November this powerful daily became openly critical of President Jefferson Davis and, after the federal assault on Port Royal, vowed on 18 November that operations against the North following Manassas would have thwarted any invasion of South Carolina soil and also raised the Union blockade.

The rival *Courier* and other South Carolina newspapers were far less strident during the first year of the war, nor do personal letters reflect such a wide range of emotions. William Elliott, the young law student who was certain in November 1860 that there would be no war, still was looking for peace seven months later. On 20 June he wrote to his fiancée from Virginia, "I hope very much, and always believe that, when the two Congresses meet in July in such close proximity, a peace will be established—which of course must be honorable to us." [15] The following month William sent her an eye-witness account of First Manassas and in October, perhaps in reply to a query, said any advance into Washington was utterly impossible. The South simply did not have enough men to mount such an attack. The only way he would get there in 1861 was, he added, with his hands tied behind his back.

There is no question that the Manassas victory boosted spirits in hundreds of South Carolina households and created scores of sewing circles and relief societies eager to aid both wounded soldiers and the destitute families of servicemen. The invasion of Port Royal, on the other hand, sent a chill throughout the entire state. "I think," Meta Morris Grimball observed in November 1861, "we are in dark & trying times, and I am afraid. The people of the Sea board so loud in their expressions of determination while the war was in Virginia feel very faint now that it has come to us." [16] However, on 5 December she thought the panic over, noting those who rushed "in great haste" to the interior now seemed less apprehensive.

Thus, on balance, South Carolinians had no reason to fear the new year or to weigh seriously the *Mercury's* cries of doom. Nevertheless, throughout the remainder of the war they were taken on an emotional roller coaster with more low points than high. If Coulter is correct, in part this was due to failure of the central government to develop any *"esprit de corps."* Yet two other factors on the local scene should be considered: the outrageous predictions of men such as Robert Barnwell Rhett that created unreal expectations among thousands of South Carolinians (no war, no bloodshed, prosperity, and peace) and Union strategy. The blockade, an invasion of this state's soil, raids along the coast, and eventually the shelling of Charleston stirred up socio-economic turmoil that had disastrous effects on morale.

Not counting 1865 as hostilities were dragging to a close, there were three periods when despondency was most apparent—the winter and spring of 1862 as a result of bad news from the Mississippi Valley (especially the fall of New Orleans), the weeks immediately after Gettysburg and Vicksburg in the late summer of 1863, and the opening months of 1864. The best explanation for gloom early in 1864 is slow realization in many quarters that the *Mercury* had spoken the truth three years earlier: the Confederacy indeed was doomed to failure. But these dark days were relieved by the successful defense of Richmond in June

1862, victory at Fredericksburg six months later, and occasional bright spots on local fronts such as Secessionville, Fort Wagner, and Honey Hill, as well as the derring-do of blockade runners and the gallant work of those fending off Union attacks upon Charleston.

It is easy enough to find reflections of this fluctuating mood, and examples already have been presented in previous chapters. All too often, it should be noted, editors took readers to the heights of ecstasy only to puncture their rapture a few days later, which merely deepened the aura of despair and cast suspicion upon all news reports. Virtually every major battle—Antietam and Gettysburg among them—first was hailed as a resounding victory by dailies such as the *Mercury* and *Courier*. William Elliott, as we know, by November 1863 thought every newspaper office in the entire Confederacy should be blown up, and David Ballenger vowed ten months later that no longer could any editor "dupe" him.

Two years earlier, in May 1862, one such gentleman, Richard Yeadon, who edited the *Courier* for a decade or so in the 1830s and 1840s, went to Richmond at the request of a nephew (whom he recently had adopted as his son) to witness the Battle of Chickahominy, subsequently known as "Seven Pines." Tragically, the young man was killed only hours after Yeadon arrived. Nevertheless, he furnished Charlestonians with a detailed account of his journey and, back home once more, in mid-June expressed great shock that "despondency and discontent were rife" among this fellow citizens. Yeadon thought the decision to abandon Cole's Island was to blame, while cautioning readers of the *Courier* (20 June) that a shorter defense line around Charleston actually was preferable.[17] This was no time to sow distrust and dissension by out-guessing the military, he warned. As for himself, Yeadon said he would rely upon those experienced in such matters.

In August 1863, as the true impact of Gettysburg began to be appreciated, the *Due West Telescope* published a rambling essay concerning "croakers" that roamed far afield and took pot shots at numerous targets on the homefront. After conceding this was a "rich man's war and a poor man's fight" in both South and North, the *Telescope* asked, who then are the *southern* "croakers"?

> No doubt most of them are the men who were rampant for the war, and who expected their property and families would be made secure by it, but when they find everything in jeopardy they begin to *croak*, they begin

to find fault that things are not well managed. Another class of *croakers* are the speculators, blockade runners, who, while drinking their adulterated Ohio whiskey, smoking cigars and counting their money, find fault with Davis, Lee and Beauregard, about the management of the war. To this class may be added some slick-haired, heavy bearded Editor, or able bodied patricians who have managed to shirk the war by getting in for overseers of negroes, or salt-works, or who have a mill or tanyard, and like the frogs around their ponds they *croak*— Well, just let them croak, who cares? If they murmur at the way things are managed let them shoulder their guns and face the music of the shells, and march day and night without bread, sleep, or rest, through mud and rain, as in the retreat from Pennsylvania, and they will have cause to *croak* as some bleeding hearts have in this vicinity.[18]

Seven months later, in February 1864, General Joseph B. Kershaw, speaking from the balcony of Janney's Hotel in Columbia, told a cheering throng that he had been in Virginia for three years and "I thank God in my heart of hearts that, except as an invader, I have never rested my foot on the dust of a freesoil State." He had, he said, been home only three times and thought he knew what was happening here, but he was distressed, even mortified, to discover "in South Carolina, in Columbia, the hot-bed of secession, the spirit of the people has sunk so far below that of your brave defenders in the field, as to make it almost doubtful whether you are kin to the glorious community, who, at the beginning of this war, initiated this gigantic struggle. [Profound silence in the crowd, and murmurs from the soldiers 'That's right.']"

How had this happened? This distinguished Camden native thought news from beyond the Appalachians was to blame, while quickly assuring his audience that things actually were going quite well there.

I would not care one iota about the condition of affairs at home, if it did not affect the army. But your conversations, your letters, your influences and your actions are calculated to demoralize and destroy the most patriotic army that ever took the field, and you who remain at home demoralize your brave defenders! [Tremendous cheering.] I tell you that such as lies before this people if our armies fail, cannot be depicted by human imagination, because earth has never seen a parallel.

Amid great cheering, he urged those within the sound of his voice to pull out their last dollar, lay down their last bushel of corn, their last bale of cotton, their last bit of merchandise—"yes, lay down your lives"— if needed to drive out the enemy, crush those worshipping at the shrine of Mammon, croaking in their thoroughfares, abusing President Davis, and "doing everything against and nothing for the sacred cause that involves all that makes life worth living."[19]

Here in chronological order are still more personal comments concerning the course of the war by various individuals, rank-and-file citizens, most of whom we have already met, that reflect the ups and downs of homefront life. On 9 March 1862, David Golightly Harris wrote in his journal that war no longer seemed to be "the game of fun" it once was. "But now is the time for patriots to show their vaunted patriotism. When it most needed, I fear it will be the hardest to find. Now that we have our hands to the plow, and our necks in the haulter. We must not look back, nor dispond, but strain ever more to accomplish our independence." Harris even viewed success with a wary eye, observing on 10 July, "The battle around Richmond has been a fatal one, and a dear bought victory. But I hope it will return value Received."[20]

Writing from Flat Rock on 11 May 1863, Harriott Middleton informed cousin Susan of her deep depression. "...I have never felt so dispirited about the war. It seems to stretch on interminably before us, carrying off all the youths and worth of the country, I can see nothing but desolated homes, and broken hopes. We seem to make so little impression on the North, the men we kill are foreigners, and there are hundreds of thousands more to take their places...."

However, six weeks later, with Lee advancing into Pennsylvania and heady with the prospect of dead Yankees, not foreign-born recruits, Harriott was exultant. Her spirits revived, she told Susan on 24 June:

> Your letter was most particularly welcome for we got hardly any papers, and now must wait until next Wednesday. We sent to cousin Izard however for the Carolinian, and learnt all the good news to which I allude. How delightful all this fluttering is in the northern cities. Oh! Susan I feel so bloodthirsty. I want our veterans to come

Bacon in the smoke house—meat in the hopper,
If Grant roosts in Vicksburg we don't care a copper;
Lee in Pennsylvania makes the Dutchmen fly about,
And spoil their calculations and crops and sour kraut.
So three cheers for the Southern cross, and three
                          cheers for the men,
Who have whipped the Yankees often, and will
                          whip them well again.

Published in Sumter's *Tri-Weekly Watchman* (10 July 1863), the same day readers learned of the fall of Vicksburg.

in contact with the northern militia—what a slaughter there would be, but will our men burn and ravage as they ought to do. Cousin Izard declares that our men never can do such things. 'Oh' said Isabella 'Gen. Lee must set them the example.' 'But' said cousin Izard 'Lee's heart will never allow him to do such things.' 'Then' said Isabella 'let them carry a company of women along. We will do it for them with delight.' I long to hear of burning and destruction and wading in militia blood!!! for that will be Yankee and not foreign blood....[21]

But by late summer the scope of the disaster at Gettysburg was apparent. "So far as our country is concerned," Theodore Honour told his wife on 16 August, "every thing looks dark and gloomy, particularly out in the west and even I am beginning to despond of our immediate success and I fear the war will be protracted to an indefinite time though our final success is undoubted—"[22] Seven days later, viewing the struggle from Aiken, Henry William Ravenel recorded these thoughtful comments in his journal.

Still, calm & quiet here, but in other portions of our poor distracted country, how unlike the Sabbath stillness which blessed us in the days of peace. God is passing us through great tribulations for some wise purposes of his own. When I survey the field of conflict, & the causes which have produced this state of things, I never fail to be cheered with the conviction of having right & justice with us. But at the same time I must not forget that we

are poor erring creatures, whose reasonings or judge-
ment cannot be trusted;—that we are prone to think that
right, which we wish to be, that the judgements of an
omniscient being may be unlike ours, & in deep humil-
ity of spirit & entire submission to His will, we should
bow ourselves not questioning His wise decision. The
prime cause of this conflict, is African slavery in this
country. On the issue of the contest rests its triumph or
its complete over throw. In good time we will know
God's will—

The following year, on 12 September, Ravenel was distressed to
learn that his teenage son soon would be in uniform.

Received a letter from Harry yesterday. He says all the
boys of the school over 16 are ordered out in the militia.
They are to rendevouz [sic] at 'Ninety six' today for organization in obedience to the Governors call. When boys
are taken from school for defence of the country, the
need is great. We have met with reverses of late, & again
the war clouds look darker & more threatening. We will
trust in the same Strong Arm that has hitherto guided
and supported us through our fiery trials. [23]

The will of God is, of course, a prominent theme in Civil War lore;
however, this gentleman scientist was more honest than most Americans, North and South, as they sought the assistance of the Almighty. He
conceded "...we are prone to think that right, which we wish to be,"
while acknowledging God may see things differently. The dilemma
Ravenel and other Southerners faced near war's end is clearly delin-
eated by Beringer, Hattaway, Jones, and Still in *Why the South Lost the
Civil War* (pp. 351-67). Since God apparently was not on the side of the
Confederacy, what had it done to incur His displeasure? How had those
who believed in both an omnipotent being and the institution of slavery
sinned? Grudgingly, some concluded the problem was the institution
itself, about which these authors believe many Confederates always were
a bit anxious. To some, proclaiming liberty in a loud voice while fighting to keep part of a population in bondage did not seem a valid war cry.
If this sense of anxiety (or even guilt) was widespread, then abandoning

slavery and accepting defeat was made somewhat more palatable since this seemingly was "God's will."

Yet the bold assertion of these same authors (p. 391) that "the Confederate leadership changed southern war goals from slavery to independence in late 1864 and early 1865" certainly would have puzzled many South Carolinians of those days…or perhaps convinced them that die-hard secessionists had been right all along: Davis and his crowd were nothing but "reconstructionist" opportunists, always ready to bargain their way back into the Union. This confusion rose not only because slavery apparently was being jettisoned (bad enough, some would have said), but that independence was considered to be a "new" goal at that late date. Most South Carolinians thought they had been fighting for just that for some three years, plus slavery, of course.

Even at the outset of hostilities, South Carolina's relationship with the Lord was taking bizarre turns. Just before Manassas on 1 July 1861, the *Mercury* published this strange comment from an Aiken correspondent: "We are preparing for the worse [sic], with the full assurance that God will fight our battles for us." He did not go quite that far; nevertheless, after victory in Virginia, a Fairfield District gentleman told the *Mercury* (28 August), "It does seem indeed that the Great Giver of all good has smiled upon us in our harvests, as well as upon our cause in the field of battle." This brief comment is quite typical of the war years. When things were going well, "the Great Giver of all good" received a cursory "thank you." But as disaster loomed, He usually was the object of much eloquent importuning.

Word of Lincoln's two-fold plan to free slaves in all parts of the nation was such an occasion, although the proclamation of September 1862 was received relatively calmly in some quarters. The *Mercury* summed up the news in a single sentence on 27 September: "ABRAHAM LINCOLN has issued a proclamation declaring the slaves of rebel masters free, from and after the 1st of January next." Two days later it published the document in full and on 1 October heaped scorn upon "a final and desperate resort" to alarm the South, "animate" Abolitionists, revive depressed Northerners, and pacify Abolitionist sentiment in England. This editor said he was much more disturbed by Lincoln's proposal to raise more men, something the Davis government should have done months ago.

On the other hand, the *Courier* (3 October) saw danger and lashed out at Lincoln personally.

The world now beholds the rottenness of his heart. Disastrous and humiliating defeats, unexpected and ruinous reverses have compelled him to make known the base design he formed at the beginning of the war. It is an invitation to murder, and rape, and spoilation. It is robbery on a grand scale. It is a blow at the foundations of society in the South. No scheme more atrociously wicked ever entered the mind of man.

And now that the Yankee President has launched that weapon, we are fairly warned. We know the nature of the doom that awaits us, if unsuccessful in resisting the efforts making for our enslavement or destruction. And filled with horror at the though[t] of failure, we address ourselves with firmer resolve and higher courage to the great work we have undertaken. Let us put forth our whole power, and, with God on our side, we shall be triumphant. Better die freemen than live slaves to so mean and vile a despotism.

Yet it was Lincoln's subsequent scheme of gradual, compensated emancipation among *loyal* masters over a thirty-seven-year period (all slaves would be free by 1 January 1900) that sent shivers down the backs of many South Carolinians; for, they viewed it correctly as a direct appeal to those growing restless under Confederate rule. On 5 December 1862, the *Mercury* was able to comment on "the very sorry document" the President submitted to Congress a few days earlier. "The language and ideas of his address," the editor fumed on the 8th, "are but little if any above those of a well raised negro."

The rival *Courier*, truly alarmed, went racing to God for help. For four days (9-13 December) it railed against Lincoln ("stupid, wicked, and obstinate...brainless, cruel, and stubborn"), mixing insult with prayer and exhortation. "The present war is from the Lord," it assured readers on the 9th, the same day it published the President's words. The conflict has produced substantial good, they were told. Those who believe the struggle is God's doing must submit to His will; from submission comes sufficient patience and fortitude to bear any and all ills that ensue. War is the means God has chosen for our deliverance from an injurious alliance, and for our establishment as a distinct and independent power.

The road marked for our feet is indeed long and rough and beset with dangers, but if it conducts us to independence, if by pursuing it we eventually attain a position of dignity and power among nations, that were ample compensation for our sufferings.

Shall we reach that point of glory and honor? If we believe in our hearts that God is with us, that He approves our cause and seconds our efforts, we must be certain of final success, no fear can becloud our hope, and no contingency shake our confidence.

And if this be the ground whereon we build our confidence, should we not give God the glory of all our successes, and humble ourselves under all our reverses, referring our victories to His power, manifested in our approval, and our defeats to the same power exhibited in our condemnation? In the former case we should give Him thanks, making the land ring with heartfelt praises; in the latter we should repent of our wickedness, serve Him with increased fidelity and trust Him with a stronger faith.

On the 10th, readers were told war was the agent God had devised as a means to end southern dependence upon the North. The following day the enemy was lashed for the "uncivilized manner" in which he waged war, revealing his "meanness, corruption and wickedness."

The Yankee race is not merely an enemy whom we have to fight and overcome on the field of carnage; he is the defiler of our homes, the despoiler of our lands, the incendiary who has put a torch to our dwellings, the robber who has stolen our property, the wretch who has murdered our gray-haired fathers and stalwart sons. He is a personal and bitter enemy to every one of us, and in killing him we at once destroy a relentless foe and vindicate the majesty of law.

Absolute separation from such evil could only be accomplished through hatred engendered by strife. Thus all "should accept the great calamity as necessary for the attainment of the high ends we aim at, and with submissive spirits and grateful hearts, look upon danger with undaunted countenance, and reverently adore this wisdom and goodness of Almighty God."

The *Courier* rested on the 12th but, on Saturday the 13th, did battle once more, claiming the struggle, as rigorous as it might be, was producing much good.

> ...though our duties and our sufferings absolutely demand the exercise of all our strength and fortitude, the miseries bred by this war are not unmingled with blessings. The cloud that throws its black over our sunny land has a silver lining. The scent of flowers mingle with the sulphurous smoke. Soft voices, full of melody, are heard by the tranquil heart, though the ear is deafened by the thunder of artillery. Good moves side by side with evil, and evil itself is made to produce real and lasting good....
>
> We have drawn nigh to God, and, in fulfillment of His promise, He has drawn nigh to us, sustaining our spirits, succeeding our plans and purposes, purifying and elevating our character, endowing us with wisdom and sagacity, and clothing us with resistless power and invincible courage.

Six days later, word of victory at Fredericksburg arrived in Charleston, followed by loud huzzahs and relatively perfunctory thanks to the Almighty: "Southern generalship and valor have again been gloriously illustrated, and our people are called upon to pour out their hearts in praise and thanksgiving to Almighty God for these signal manifestations of His favor toward our cause. *O sing unto the Lord a new song, for He hath done marvelous things: His right hand and His holy arm have gotten him his victory.*"[24]

Lincoln's plan for gradual emancipation never gained Congressional approval so the fulminations of the *Courier* were unnecessary; however, they reveal considerable apprehension concerning the reaction of readers to such a proposal. Freedom for slaves held by true rebels elicited a relatively mild, personal rebuke when compared with that spawned by the offer of compensation to any master thought to be loyal. Fearful of the actual state of morale, the *Courier* pulled out all the stops in a direct and prolonged appeal to the Almighty. And apparently it worked. To those who believed, Fredericksburg was proof that God wore gray...at least on that occasion, they were certain He did.

But the fighting continued; and amid the despondency of August 1863 and the early months of 1864, the same "truths" concerning God and his grand design for the Confederate nation were aired once more. From 11 to 19 February, for example, the *Courier* sought to put the best face possible on the "Duration of the War." In a series of editorials, readers were told the Lord hid the length of the struggle so as to prepare the South for the woes that ensued.

> Had there been a full revelation made to us through political leaders, concerning the nature of this war, had we clearly seen the calamities we would suffer, the desolation that would sweep like a whirlwind through immense tracts of our territory, the fierce earnestness with which the foe should assail, and the tireless energy and ceaseless perseverance with which he should pursue his bloody purposes, in all likelihood we would have been appalled at the frightful prospect. The wisdom and goodness of that God whom we serve, is shown in withholding from us that dreadful and dangerous knowledge.[25]

Once more readers were reminded (during the same days when General Kershaw was trying to stir patriotic ardor) that war created the hatred needed to effect true separation from the North and that it also helped the Confederacy develop its own resources and correct the region's traditional attitude toward "mechanical occupations."

Yet it is readily apparent that wartime morale is a two-edged sword. News that brought smiles in the South had the opposite effect in the North and vice versa. Lincoln had his problems, too. He was dealing with both national and international affairs in the midst of rebellion, while facing equally diverse views among far more people scattered over a much larger area than the Confederacy, as well as an entrenched political opposition. His fellow Republicans were, we should remember, "the new kids on the block." Also, battle reports obviously were not the only factor shaping morale in South Carolina. Shortages, speculation, extortion, inflation, conscription, erratic postal service, and the increasingly independent air of blacks—matters discussed earlier—all took their toll.

In addition, effective legal machinery, one of the basic underpinnings of a stable society, crumbled. General Sessions courts, which dealt with crimes committed by whites in each district, often ceased to exist as judges, jurors, lawyers, and those charged with various offenses simply failed to appear.[26] In York, for example, twenty-two cases were filed (Fall 1861, Spring 1862, Fall 1862). Of those, twenty-one were not prosecuted (eight of them concerned absentee jurors), and only one person actually was convicted. No court was convened in that district during the remainder of the war. Spartanburg and Greenville held criminal proceedings more or less on schedule, but not much happened. Of fifty-seven cases docketed in Spartanburg (1862-64), only one of those involved was convicted, although two other individuals pled guilty. The other fifty-four defendants were dead, not indicted by a grand jury, or the district chose not to pursue the matter further. During the same period and for similar reasons, Greenville authorities convicted four out of 114 persons charged with various offenses.

According to James McCarter, only ten criminal courts continued to operate during the war: "No business or profession was so completely suspended as the Law."[27] As one would expect amid strife, shortages, and confusion, crime prospered. The press in various communities complained of robberies, shootings, assaults, and stabbings, and the arrest record of Charleston (April-September 1863) reveals whites, not blacks, figured most prominently in statistics of that sort. Of course, many of these incidents were trivial matters settled upon payment of a small fine (630, 25%) or quickly dismissed (540, 21%). Only three murders were recorded during these months.

Whites, more often than blacks, were apprehended for being drunk, disorderly, or selling illicit liquor, and 395 of those arrested (15%) evidently were in uniform. Theft in various forms seems to have been indulged in by about an equal number of blacks and whites, although the latter were more apt to be caught dealing in stolen goods. Arrests tended to decline somewhat after mid-year as scores fled the city when the federal bombardment began in earnest. Both races were locked up for "safe-keeping," with a great increase recorded among black males in September, perhaps a sign of intent to run away to Union lines now that they were closer.

As McCarter implies, the prosecution of civil cases also came to a standstill in much of this state. On 21 December 1861, the General Assembly approved "An act to Extend Relief to Debtors, and to Prevent the Sacrifice of Property at Public Sales." Generally known as the "stay

Table 3. Charleston Arrests, 1863[28]

	White		Black		Monthly Total
	Male	Female	Male	Female	
April	179	10	117	31	337
May	296	50	126	45	517
June	258	44	120	59	481
July	229	44	84	26	383
August	227	35	98	35	395
September	238	28	163	20	449
Total	**1427**	**211**	**708**	**216**	**[2562]**

law," it was continued from year to year largely to protect the property of absent servicemen from seizure. Since there apparently were no legal challenges to this legislation until 1866, it seems to have had the desired effect. However, historian D. D. Wallace thought it sheltered many of those able to pay their debts and thus "was said to undermine commercial activity." [29] But, as McCarter observes, the courts were largely "useless" during the war years; so—regardless of special legislation—debt collection requiring legal enforcement was well nigh impossible anyway.

One could cite still other factors that influenced wartime morale, notably the "dullness" that enveloped some communities as war took sons and husbands off to battle, stifled trade, and furnished little in return but rumor, headache, heartache, and sorrow. The village of Edgefield, not on a railroad line, is a prime example. Beginning in mid-1863, the editor of the *Advertiser* described creeping decay as steps collapsed, schools shut their doors, fences leaned precariously, and broken windows went unrepaired. By October of that year, there was no town council; roads, streets, and bridges were "totally impassable"; and one could cross Beaverdam Creek only by means of a log.[30] "The old place is horrid looking, and horridly deserted, and horridly dull, and altogether a horrid bore," the editor wrote in disgust at year's end.

Following a six-month hiatus, in July 1864 the *Advertiser* complained once more of "lonely streets, closed doors, fathomless dust, and implacable heat." Stray chickens and pigs wandered about the public square as an occasional wounded veteran shuffled by. The town pump, useless for months, finally had been fixed, but roads and streets were in such bad shape that even "Choctaws" would "blush and hide their faces" in shame.[31] A few months later, Sherman and Wheeler dispelled some of this "dullness," though perhaps not in a manner most residents appreciated.

Then there were unsettling casualty lists, names of those killed, wounded, and missing, that followed both victory and defeat, as well as subtle signs of trouble few wished to acknowledge. Those reading the *Charleston Courier* during its final weeks as a four-page daily may have noticed a steady increase in auction sales as Union might gathered at the harbor entrance. On 25 February 1863, five of the *Courier's* twenty columns featured commercial activity of that sort. The total swelled to eight by 10 March, and on 31 March over half of the paper was devoted to auctions. That same day, eight of the *Mercury's* twelve columns contained similar advertisements, clear indication of intent to convert random types of property into cash as quickly as possible. On 7 April, the day federal shelling of Fort Sumter began, the *Courier* was reduced to a single sheet, ostensibly because fire destroyed its source of paper stock, the Bath Paper Mill near Aiken. Seven months later, to escape enemy shells, the *Courier* temporarily suspended operations (21-29 November) and moved from East Bay to 252 Meeting Street.

Yet despite innumerable setbacks and ominous economic trends, South Carolinians of those years were, for the most part, an optimistic lot...perhaps so much so as to be considered unrealistic at times. Where others saw sunset, they saw sunrise. When a variegated spider was found spinning a web in a jessamine vine at 31 Tradd Street in October 1863, a member of Charleston's Barbot family interpreted the discovery as a fine omen.

> I read it in this manner—
> Red and Yellow Colors of the head stands for [the] Spanish flag and that Spain will be the first Nation to Recognise our Southern Confederacy.
> The Tri Colors of the Body and the Tail shew the French Colours—France secondly will acknowledge us. And in the green color of the 8 Legs, Ireland is represented. Altho' she is not an Independent Nation. Yet she deeply sympathises with us.[32]

A few months earlier, Greenville's *Southern Enterprise* (16 April 1863) reported yet another natural wonder that promised not merely recognition but independence.

Mr. S. Day, who lives near Pickensville, informs us that a negro boy of his, caught, some day or two ago, in a corn field near his residence, a large Eagle, which measured from the extremities of its wings, six feet and two inches; the talons of one of it feet, which he exhibits us, measure from each extremity nine inches. The boy who caught it, ran it down, it having lighted in a furrow before him, whilst plowing. As the bird has for centuries been adopted as the emblem of independence, we take this as a precursor of that independence which is to follow the arms of the Confederacy.

Some might think that, since the black lad caught the eagle, it was a symbol of *his* independence and freedom, but that is not how this editor interpreted the signs. Overly optimistic in 1861, some South Carolinians obviously remained so two years later. In May 1864, young Arthur Wescoat, who lived near Monck's Corner, wrote these words in his diary: "The soldiers are constantly going by on this rail road, hurrahing all along the way. Many of them never come back. We are yet still victorious, by the help of God."[33]

And nearly a year later, angered by flames that engulfed Columbia, fires set by "the cowardly dealings of a fiendish foe," on 22 March 1865, young Annie DeVeaux breathed defiance: "In the ruins of their homes our people stand unconquered, unsubdued, no regrets made for losses sustained, nothing but cheerfulness abounds, and the spirit of Secession burns with enthusiasm—all eyes are turned upon our *brave* soldiers and their noble leaders go forth and conquer; all hearts are lifted up to Heaven in prayer for victory and a blessing upon our army and land—"[34]

As noted at the outset, the question of wartime morale can be approached in various ways, for it possesses an elusive, will-o-the-wisp quality. If things are going well, one rarely hears morale mentioned. The flow of events wraps it in obscurity. Leaders can turn their attention to more pressing matters. Reverse the trend and it becomes all-important.

And that is just what happened in the winter and spring of 1862, late summer of 1863, and the opening months of 1864 as South Carolinians were beset by dark headlines and depressing news. Random successes dispelled the gloom from time to time; but, despite Second Manassas and Fredericksburg, the war dragged on. Thus, in the final year of the struggle, if omens, multicolored spiders, dead eagles, and false hopes improved one's mental attitude and made the world look brighter, so be it. During those bleak days, many South Carolinians found such things as effective as anything else as a means of sustaining spirit and stopping Sherman.

NOTES

[1]William Elliott to Isabella Elliott Barnwell, 18 November 1863, Elliott Family Papers.

[2]Two exceptions are the *Edgefield Advertiser* and *Yorkville Enquirer*, each of which published occasional comments on the homefront. The files of both weeklies are complete (1860-1865).

[3]Coulter, *The Confederate States of America*, p. 83.

[4]Ibid., p. 567.

[5]Wilfred Buck Yearns, *The Confederate Congress* (Athens, 1960), p. 223.

[6]See Richard Current, "God and the Strongest Battalions," in David Donald (ed.), *Why the South Lost the Civil War* (Baton Rouge, 1960), pp. 3-22.

[7]See John Hammond Moore, "Getting Uncle Sam's Dollars: South Carolinians and the Southern Claims Commission, 1871-1880," *South Carolina Historical Magazine* (July 1981), pp. 248-62. William V. Harvey of Beaufort County (Case # 6797) tells of a public meeting at Barker's Mill in 1860 where the participants chose sides, pro-Union men going to one side of the room, secessionists to the other.

[8]William J. Grayson, *James Louis Petigru: A Biographical Sketch* (New York, 1866); pp. 146-47. These words probably were written after the death of Petigru in March 1863. This sketch was found among Grayson's papers after his own death seven months later.

[9]McCarter Journals, Library of Congress. These two volumes, covering the years 1860-65 and apparently assembled after the war, form the basis for an article published in *Harper's Magazine* (November 1866), pp. 642-47—"The Burning of Columbia Again."

[10]James Wylie Gettys, Jr., "Mobilization for Secession in Greenville District" (Master's thesis, University of South Carolina, 1967), p. 1.

[11]Gettys points out (p. 29) that by the spring of 1860 the community had only one party, the Democrats, whose delegates to the state convention of that year were appointed by a committee of fifteen secessionists, not elected.

[12]"Hayne," writing in the *Charleston Mercury* (26 November 1860) maintained that secession was not revolution, rebellion, treason, nor any infringement of federal laws: "It is simply the exercise of *a great and unquestionable constitutional right—* a right asserted and proclaimed in the Constitution...."

[13]Gettys, pp. 90-92. Eric H. Walther stresses the same theme of a thirty-year indoctrination process in *The Fire-Eaters* (Baton Rouge and London, 1992).

[14]See Ronald Takaki, "The Movement to Open the African Slave Trade in South Carolina," *South Carolina Historical Magazine* (January 1965), pp. 38-54. Takaki indicates the *Mercury* backed Spratt in the mid-1850s, then grew cool to this proposal before returning to it once more in 1861.

[15]William Elliott to Isabella Elliott Barnwell, Elliott Family Papers.

[16]Journal of Meta Morris Grimball. Note: This entry is dated only by month and year, not day.

[17]Cole's Island is located south of Charleston in Stono Inlet, inland from Kiawah and

Folly islands.

[18]Reprinted in the *Yorkville Enquirer* (12 August 1863) and signed simply "H." Very few wartime copies of the *Due West Telescope* exist.

[19]*Camden Journal*, 19 February 1864. This weekly, which has a long, convoluted history (1826-91), suspended operations in 1861 and then reappeared in January 1864.

[20]Racine, *Piedmont Farmer*, pp. 236, 252.

[21]"Middleton Correspondence," *South Carolina Historical Magazine* (April 1963), pp. 97-98, 101.

[22]Theodore Honour Papers.

[23]Childs, *The Private Journal of Henry William Ravenel*, pp. 181-82, 200.

[24]*Charleston Daily Courier*, 19 December 1862.

[25]Ibid., 11 February 1864. It might be instructive to compare these editorials with those published in the *Courier* (17-18 July 1861), which discuss "The War—Its Duration and Ends." In that instance, the editor said the South must learn to hate the North (if it did not "our sons will have died in vain"). It also should develop its own industry, artisans, textbooks, and periodicals. A short war, the *Courier* warned, might promote quick return to old ways of dependence upon Yankee ways and Yankee things.

[26]Scattered wartime court records can be found at the South Carolina Department of Archives and History for these districts: Anderson, Barnwell, Charleston, Chester, Fairfield, Greenville, Laurens, Marlboro, Newberry, Spartanburg, and York.

[27]McCarter Journals.

[28]*Charleston Courier*, 2 June, 16 July, 12 August, 21 September, 17 October 1863. These apparently were the only such reports published during that year.

[29]Wallace, *The History of South Carolina*, III, p. 193. On 17 January 1861, Charleston merchants issued a formal protest to the General Assembly concerning "stay" laws.

[30]This was the principal waterway in the community.

[31]*Edgefield Advertiser*, 5 August, 27 October, 16 December 1863; 13 July 1864.

[32]Barbot Family Papers, 18 October 1863, South Carolina Historical Society.

[33]Graydon, "Journal of Arthur Brailsford Wescoat," p. 96.

[34]Annie DeVeaux Diary, South Carolina Historical Society. Annie, who probably did not actually see the fire, was the twenty-two-year-old daughter of Charleston cotton factor John P. DeVeaux. According to the 1860 city directory, the family lived at the corner of Coming and Vanderhorst streets.

VIII

HAVING FUN

Pleasure can take myriad forms, especially in wartime. Many caught up in this age-old drama act as if it were their last chance to grasp ever so fleetingly the golden ring of happiness and joy; and, sadly, this often is all too true. For boys rushed headlong into manhood, men stripped from everyday surroundings, and women confronted with both boredom and strange new faces the gamble sometimes seems worth the risk. The excitement of war provides ready rationale for behavior considered unseemly in peacetime. And, caught up in this whirlpool of sorrow, exhilaration, death, disease, laughter, disappointment, and unexpected twists of fate, it is apparent that many South Carolinians of the 1860s had a hellava good time.

In addition to the ecstasy generated by momentous events and the thrill of participating in them (such as the firing on Fort Sumter, which was witnessed by thousands), for some, war brought travel far beyond the confines of their valley or village and with it came new sights and keen awareness of a world altogether different from what they had known. In January 1862, a wide-eyed, York District youth described Charleston to folks back home in this fashion: "I can go to town and see lots of the prettyest girls [.] there is great white houses full of them and they ask us to go in but we never do.... one street in Charleston is worth all york [.] we can get ginger cakes plenty from the negroes [,] apples too [,] for five cens apiece...."[1] Eighteen months later, now in Jackson, Mississippi, and a more worldly lad, J. W. Pursley revealed girls in that community distributed flowers with "tickets" bearing their names and addresses so soldiers could write to them.[2]

Two young Georgians, W. J. and J. T. Nobles, who were based in the Pocotaligo-Charleston area in the spring of 1862, had similar comments, as well as plans to make the experience as comfortable as possible. On 20 April they told the folks back home "they is some fine ladies here that fixes up little nicknacks for the sick in the Hospitle." Nine days later, they asked their father to send some potatoes, white peas, and "a Botle of Whiskey if it aint to hy." A dram now and then would be refreshing, they observed, "We aint Drinked but one drink of Whiskey Sence We left Macon When We was on our Way here."

W. J. Nobles also reminded his sister and mother to finish his uniform and send it to him as quickly as possible: "I want to get it and put it on and go to meeting, for I tel you they is a heap of South Carolina Girls here—they is a Church Clost By our Camp, and I can go there to meeting and look at them." A few weeks later, now in Charleston, one of the boys remarked, "Oh it is a very large town and a pretty town, and the yankeys want it mity Bad but I dont think they will get it for we have about 16 thousand men in it and clost around it."[3]

Speaking with Meta Morris Grimball and her husband in September 1862, Dr. Whitefoord Smith, professor of English at Spartanburg's Wofford College, saw "a great benefit" in adventures such as these and in war itself. They would, he was certain, enlarge the mind of "the very ignorant, contracted country people." The families of soldiers were "taking papers," he said; and, if unable to read, they would solicit help from neighbors. In fact, Smith knew of one local couple who had become literate so the wife could communicate with her soldier husband.[4]

Some who donned uniforms discovered untold pleasure, not in new sights, but in an entirely different way of life. Lieutenant Governor Plowden Weston, the British-educated, Georgetown rice planter whose wife dispensed with morning roll call of their slaves, was one such gentleman. In April 1862, James L. Petigru, writing to his daughter in New York City, said spirits were so high both North and South that he thought anarchy more likely than peace. "Plowden Weston is an instance of the violence of the distemper in men's minds," he added. Petigru had just seen him on the street—dirty, haggard, lean, and thoroughly enamored with hard campaigning, marching, and fighting. At age forty-two, Petigru marveled, he seems to have "turned over a new leaf."[5]

Most of those who volunteered cited as their principal motives various aspects of patriotism, state pride, and defense of certain rights. Francis Marion Tucker, when told by his wife in June 1862 that a mutual friend had "a half notion" to quit and go home, replied he would not. Tucker, a thirty-three-year-old man from rural Spartanburg District, spoke for thousands when he vowed he was fighting for freedom and liberty—"it is the love of freedom—the love of liberty from oppression, which I wish transmitted to posterity—"[6] But many of his companions actually were driven more by fear than concern for freedom—fear of being labeled a conscript and fearful they might miss out on whatever their boyhood friends were destined to see and do. For, unless one lived in Charleston or Columbia, daily life throughout the war years could be a dreadful bore. With most of the men away, community activity in villages such as Edgefield, as we know, ground to a halt and signs of decay appeared on all sides.

Some in uniform—individuals much like Plowden Weston—discovered distinct personal advantages not associated directly with either patriotism or principle. War perhaps provided welcome relief from a failed marriage, squalling babies, a troubled household, or the tyranny of relatives. It also might furnish respite from debt, a hard-scrabble, near-hopeless existence, and an endless round of farm chores. And, on occasions, the military gave a lucky few the opportunity to luxuriate in positions far preferable to their civilian status. Theodore Honour, for one, chafed mightily under conditions he thought intolerable. "Privates in the army are the most veritable slaves in the world," he told his wife in October 1863. "...the quick blood boils with rage, at the indignities heaped upon a private by men far below him in a social point of view, and vastly inferior in both intellect or education...."[7] Honour obviously was *not* having fun at this time, but several of his superiors were and at his expense.

One young officer who certainly enjoyed some aspects of wartime duty was Iredell Jones, a North Carolina native who entered South Carolina College in 1858 and, after an exciting career in Confederate uniform and experience in both state and local politics in the 1870s and 1880s, finally received his bachelor's degree at special ceremonies held in 1906. In February 1863, shortly after the federal gunboat *Isaac Smith* was captured in the Stono River, Second Lieutenant Jones, then on duty in the Charleston area, told his mother what a godsend this proved to be for him and his friends. First noting he still was trying to procure salt to send to her in Rock Hill, he then proceeded to regale her with these words.

> I believe I alluded in my last to the delightful time I spent on the Isaac Smith. I feasted for a few days on all the nice things, that Yankeedom could afford, in the shape of Turkish Coffee, Tea (black & green), nice white sugar, Solidified milk, splendid old hams, fresh beef in cans, green peas and tomatos [sic] in cans, Sardines, corned Shad, Mackerel, Goshen butter, almonds, raisins, English

James L. Petigru (1789-1863).

walnuts, preserves, splendid Sugar House Molasses, and
last but by no means least, Claret, Sherry, Madeira, Whiskey, Brandy, and all those kind of things. I commenced
with the Brandy—took one drink early, and as the day
was waning took another, and then another—then came
on the Whiskey in turn, and by that time dinner was announced, at which the Madeira, Sherry, and Claret made
their appearance in rotation, successively or any other
way you please, so you can understand that they kept

going round and round, side ways, back wards, &c. Then
to keep our heads from turning off our shoulders, the
nuts were handed [around] and *all those kind of things*;
and after all came on Splendid Coffee, the aroma from
which perfumed the room with the most delicious odor.
But enough of this—after dinner we went to sleep, &c[8]

Then there were young men who, although in uniform, treated the
whole affair as an "outing" reminiscent of summer camp. The letters of
Augustine T. Smythe indicate he subscribed to this approach, at least
during the opening years of the conflict. While stationed at Camp Eutaw
on Goat Island in April 1862, he sent his watch to his mother in Charleston to be repaired, as well as dirty clothes to be washed—"I send my
clothes for the week as I much prefer Maum Chloe's washing to
Monday's."[9] Young Smythe also complained that Monday, his body servant, was slow getting breakfast. In subsequent days he thanked his
mother for flowers and candy, sent a lard pail to be filled, and requested
a tablecloth, as well as fishing lines and hooks. At the close of the month
he indicated Monday's culinary skills were improving, citing biscuits,
rice-bread, and radishes as a typical Goat Island breakfast.

Although Smythe would experience more arduous duty, sending
clothes home to be washed and reliance upon servants continued in
some circles throughout the entire war. In February 1865, writing from
Adams Run, seventeen-year-old Andrew Crawford complained to his
mother in Columbia concerning various aspects of army life, reminding
her that "Buddy" was supposed to visit him in the near future.

You musn't forget to send Doug with him. For if I am
not very much mistakened, you promised to let me have
him. Didn't you? For it will be pretty hard to get on without him, as I am by myself. Please, Mother, try to get
Father to let me have him. He isn't such a rascal as you
think he is, and on long marches he could relieve me a
good deal by carrying something for me. To tell you the
truth I could hardly get along on those long marches. If
it had not been [for] one of the officers of the commissary slipping my knapsack on the baggage wagon I could
have been left behind on the road. And another thing [,]
the negroes charge such exorbitant prices for washing
'and such things'...that a person is either obliged to have

a boy and a pocket full of money or go dirty as a dog.
Doug will be impressed by the authorities in Columbia
and I might as well have him as they.

There is a plantation near here—about four miles
off—where the boys go and get any quantity of things to
eat, but I never go for I have no money. When you send
my shirts you can send a couple of towells [sic] & a nice
piece of soap for I have no towells.[10]

Young Crawford does not appear to be having a pleasant time, yet
the point is his letter sounds much like one any boy away at summer
camp or in school could have written, especially the veiled plea for funds.

Fourteen-year-old Arthur Wescoat, who visited his brother's com-
pany in January 1863, said every man had a servant to tend to his needs.
This unit, also stationed at Adams Run, made several forays on Edisto
Island, during which Wescoat visited his former home.

Sat down all day in the house and read, Sunday.
How strange it does seem to me. Fourteen months ago
we left this place in such haste that a great many families
had no time to bring as much as one suit of clothes besides what they had on. Our parlours were left just as
they were furnished, our crops were all left gathered in
the barns, cotton was left packed ready for market and
in a great many instances burnt together with houses and
barns as in our case.

Here we are living quietly just in sight of my home
in a part of the country quite in possession of the enemy,
living, to use a phrase, on the fat of the land as if none of
us were soldiers with a negro boy to each man to cook
for us, take care of our horses, and so forth.[11]

In succeeding days, Wescoat attended a theatrical production staged
by the Washington Artillery (with men filling female roles), watched an
impromptu horse race, and helped track down abandoned farm animals
that, in his words, had gone "perfectly wild." On 24 January he wrote in
his diary, "While riding through the woods today a jack vine took me
under the chin and pulled me flat on my back. The pleasures of wild hog
& cow hunting."[12] In the spring of 1864, Wescoat visited another army
installation, this one on John's Island. While there he participated in a

fox hunt, went swimming several times, and joined friends in a campaign to exterminate rodents. On 26 April they caught twenty-seven rats and the following day killed twenty-four more in and around the stables. "Camp is so dull that any thing like this," he observed, "causes quite an excitement."[13]

All of these individuals from Pursley to Tucker to Wescoat were in uniform or soon would be (young Wescoat ran away and joined a cavalry unit a few months later), and the pleasures described are largely those of camp life. As other men and boys reacted to the effects of war, their elders frequently shook their heads in dismay. In January 1861, while still at South Carolina College, Augustine T. Smythe said he was "really troubled" to see so many boys among the soldiers flowing in Columbia—"ruined they will be for time if not eternity."[14] A year later, Gilbert Strait's mother wrote these words to her son: "I fear the war will be the ruin of the country, and the destruction of the better part of the men that is any account."[15] John B. Patrick, mathematics instructor at Columbia's Arsenal Academy, echoed these dire predictions: "Our young men, in the army, are being ruined, for all civil and peaceful avocations. Speculators and extortioners are impoverishing the families of those who have entered the service of the country. That all this may be stopped and that speedily is my earnest prayer."[16]

Even if youngsters did not march away to war, they often became restless, assertive, and contemptuous of both discipline and authority. Patrick—a rather serious, sober individual—learned this all too well. Only a few days after bewailing the plight of those in the army, he came face to face with three inebriated cadets--two of them "perfectly drunk—as helpless as dead men."[17] After an inquiry, they were allowed to remain in school. But in succeeding months he had to deal with card playing and other violations of the rules. "I have been forced to conclude," he wrote on 14 August 1862, "that we have a set of boys here this year who do not love to study. They find great difficulty with the Binomial Theorem, more I think than any class I have ever taught." Ten days later, two students were dismissed for going into Columbia's business district without permission, followed within twenty-four hours by two more. Patrick was both shocked and puzzled by such behavior: "I must confess that I have never known in the history of the Academy, such a reckless disregard of the regulations, and that two [would do so] so soon after two others had been suspended for the same offense. Young men, some of them at least, take strange views of duty and honor."[18]

Patrick, who was acting as agent for the *Confederate Baptist*, was not favorably impressed when an unlikely student subscribed to that journal. He feared the young man's motives were "selfish," not religious. "But I do not wish to be uncharitable," he wrote on 6 October 1862. Late the following month the entire corps was ordered to remain throughout the holidays to guard against "an insurrection among the negroes."

Early in 1863, two suspended cadets—apparently drunk and armed—appeared at the Arsenal once more and eventually were arrested. And in July, Patrick and the entire student body went to Charleston for a few weeks to help in the defense of that city. While there he heard rumors of drunk officers and absent soldiers at Battery Wagner and, when the cadets returned to Columbia in September, vowed they should have done so much sooner. One cannot expect parents to pay for the education of their sons, he wrote, while classwork is forgotten and they do nothing but guard duty.[19] Hardly had the boys returned to the Arsenal when twenty-one of them (including Patrick's brother-in-law) were suspended for breaking rules and regulations. According to this distraught instructor, they tried to make their actions appear patriotic, but he was not convinced this was true.

As the months wore on, matters grew worse, and in September 1864 Patrick personally intervened when four youngsters threatened to duel. They evidently planned to fight with the muzzles of their pistols touching, but he managed to settle the disagreement without bloodshed. A few weeks later, the cadets were detailed to guard Yankee POWs held near Columbia, following which several young men appeared at evening prayers drunk. Finally, on 30 November, the entire corps was ordered into active service; and, upon the approach of Sherman three months later, Patrick joined them in flight.

But it was not only Arsenal cadets who were demonstrating independent spirit. As Emma Holmes observed in her diary, young ladies of Columbia were aiding and abetting their teenage escapades and also "*rouging*" and ignoring the dictates of elders. And, as we know, young blacks were displaying similar tendencies—filling up the benches near the telegraph office, whistling, talking loudly, and even chatting with Yankee POWs.

This sort of turbulence was especially evident at railroad depots and post offices. In February 1862, the Columbia city council decreed that two policemen wearing badges should be present whenever trains or mail arrived so as to "preserve quiet and good order." Great confusion reportedly was evident among travelers as "rude and insolent persons" forced their way into cars and took seats before ladies entered. "On some of the roads, of this State," the *Charleston Courier* said on 21 February, while commenting on the action taken in Columbia, "we have also seen cars which ladies were compelled to use almost flooded with villainous expectorations of tobacco. A thoughtful gentleman will as readily smoke a segar in a lady's face as spurt tobacco juice around the floor near ladies." Several months later, the *Mercury* (3 September) said guards were needed on trains to protect the fair sex. "Turbulent" soldiers, it said, were intruding into cars set aside for women, behaving "in a style that would scarcely be tolerated in a bar room," and sometimes banding together and refusing to pay their fares. Two years later, the *Confederate Baptist* (12 October 1864) complained of "profane" servicemen on the railroad to Charlotte.

In November 1864, the town fathers of Anderson passed a resolution targeting the activities of young people in that community: "*Resolved* that the Assemblage of idle white boys and negroes on the platform at the Rail Road Depot on the arrival of the Cars of evening, and the disorderly conduct of which they are guilty in obtruding themselves into the Cars, and crowding upon wounded Soldiers, ladies and other well disposed persons, and also their Conduct on the streets from the Depot to the Post Office, and in and around the Post Office of evenings has become a public nuisance...." If such disruptions did not cease, they said, both white and black would be jailed for up to twelve hours, the latter also receiving up to twenty stripes on their bare backs.[20]

Yet the most obvious expression of homefront fun was found not in army camps or among unruly youngsters and over-exuberant soldiers but in public events organized in behalf of the war effort. These often constituted, admittedly, what one might classify as a "feel good" campaign. Women of all ages (and some men) staged concerts, bazaars, fairs, plays, raffles, and tableaux vivants (living pictures) ostensibly to raise money for servicemen and their families. However, the ladies themselves perhaps gained the most from such goings-on since these affairs boosted local morale and fostered the warm sensation that the community really was doing its part for "the cause."

Of such undertakings, concerts were the easiest to organize, something even tiny villages could do. To aid the men in Virginia, for example, in August 1861 the Philharmonic Society of Claremont gave a concert at "Needlewood," the home of Mrs. J. S. Bradford near Statesburg.[21] Two months later, Edgefield residents used $58 raised in a similar fashion to buy three hundred yards of cotton flannel that was quickly transformed into 124 pairs of drawers to be sent to the troops. Bursting with pride, the editor of the *Edgefield Advertiser* (25 September) boasted "the entire lot was made up in admirable style and without sewing machines." However, another affair held six months later in the same community netted only half as much, $27.50.

During April 1863, Charleston's Hibernian Hall was host to at least two concerts. On the 13th, the Palmetto Band rendered the music of Donizetti, Meyerbeer, and Bellini; two weeks later, the Quartet Club of Atlanta Amateurs performed a mixed program for the benefit of the Free Market. Their recitations and songs included Poe's "Raven," "Widow Macree," "Rock Me to Sleep," and the still-popular "Lorena." Admission to such events usually cost $1, although by May 1864 tickets to a benefit performance of Rossini's "Stabat Mater" to be held in Charleston's Second Presbyterian Church were being sold at area drug stores for $5.[22] And six months after that—undoubtedly a reflection of inflation—an evening of Handel, Rossini, and Hayden at Columbia's Christ Church cost twice as much.[23] During that same year, the state capital (said to be one of the Confederacy's liveliest cities) was the setting for minstrel shows, programs rendered by the Columbia Glee Club, and twice-weekly band concerts in Sidney Park.

In contrast to other fund-raising activities, musical concerts had the distinct advantage of being, for the most part, noncontroversial. Some individuals objected to plays and tableaux because they smacked too much of the theater and the evils of the "wicked stage." Raffles, bazaars, and fairs, on the other hand, featured games of chance (gambling) and required "nice" women to sell things much as a common shop girl might do. In theory at least, tableaux were a series of sedate, motionless scenes and thus not actually "acting," and on the evening of 24 August 1863 a crowd packed "like dried figs in a box" watched enthralled as marvelous visions took shape on the tiny stage of Edgefield's Masonic Hall.[24] Once more, however, obstreperous youngsters were a problem. In a glowing, one-and-one-half column review, the *Advertiser* stated the deportment of little boys, "of whom about a million were present…became so utterly frantic that [it] would have shocked a Cuffie or a Hottentot." Among the sights to be seen were, according to this weekly, bearded Turks, wild Albanians, pale Franks, Parisian belles, wounded Confederate veterans, dark-eyed houris, and queens and princesses of both present and past glories, "all mingled in gorgeous and many-hued array."

These various scenes, about a dozen in all, included Empress Eugenie and the ladies of her court, a Turkish harem, Cinderella and Prince Charming, Napoleon's Josephine signing her divorce papers, Ben Franklin being crowned with laurel leaves in Paris, and literary figures from the pages of Shakespeare, Scott, and other well-known writers. Most popular, however, were contemporary images contrasting an existence on $15,000 and $500 per year and life before and during "The War." The latter, to the delight of the audience, featured local soldiers. All of the participants (except for Dr. Franklin Griffin, who served as master of ceremonies or "announcer") were identified only by their initials and an occasional reference to an individual's place of residence. Scott's brilliant and crazy Madge Wildfire (*The Heart of Midlothian*) was portrayed, for example, by "the lovely, creole-looking Miss L——e S——r of Charleston, now a guest of Edgefield"; and, during the wartime skits, "Miss S——h and Miss C——e" sang "The Volunteer," accompanied by the soft tones of a piano...singers and player discreetly hidden from the audience.[25] (See page 238.)

A performance such as this, aside from entertainment and morale value, is somewhat puzzling. These stationary "portraits" often were staged, as was true in Edgefield, in a musical setting that verged upon the theatrical and as "charades" required movement. In fact, the *Advertiser* (19 August) billed the full program as "tableaux, charades, music, feasting, &c.," which indicates not everyone was satisfied with mere beauty and silence. Secondly, these opulent displays with their elaborate costumes are difficult to explain because, at virtually the same moment, other communities were ripping up carpets and raiding attics to find material that could be transformed into uniforms and bandages. Cloth of all kind, we are told, was very scarce and much in demand. Nevertheless, these tableaux, extremely popular, became evermore lavish as fighting dragged on.

Why? Who can say? Perhaps this was more escapism. Yet another explanation is that, after 1863, some South Carolinians no longer cared much about the war. As Atlanta was falling in September 1864, Mary Johnstone wrote these words to her sister, Emmie Elliott: "...it is wrong and very selfish but I cannot feel an interest now—as I did three months ago—and when people are longing for peace I am surprised at my indifference to the subject."[26] This attitude undoubtedly was influenced by the fact that her husband was killed by "Tories" near Flat Rock, N.C., on 10 June 1864. But only a few days after Mary disclosed her innermost feelings, a young lady in Sumter District said much the same thing.

GRAND

Scriptural Tableaux!

AT

PROF. J. ST. MAUR BINGHAM'S,

CAPT. STANLEY'S HALL,

Next door to Branch Bank.

THIS EVENING, DECEMBER 30, 1864

PROGRAMME.

1. Moses and the Ten Commandments.
2. The Altar of Incense.
3. Abraham offering up his son Isaac.
4. Worship of the Golden Calf.
5. Prodigal Son.
6. Can a Maid forget her Ornaments?

INTERMISSION.

7. Beheading of John the Baptist.
8. Head of John the Baptist in a Charger.
9. Pharisee and the Publican.
10. Blasphemer brought before Moses.
11. Ruth.
12. Death of the First-born.

P. S.—A full explanation will be given of each Tableau.

ADMISSION.—Ladies and Gentlemen, $5 each; Children, accompanied by parents, $2.50 each—none others admitted. Tickets can be procured at Dr. P. Melvin Cohen's Drug Store, Central House and at the Hall.

Doors open at 7 o'clock; curtain rises at 8 o'clock. Dec 30 1

Daily South Carolinian (Columbia), 30 December 1864.

Writing to Moultrie Reid Wilson, Sue Montgomery described a recent visit to Chester, which she thought much livelier than their hometown of Mineral Springs. "The young people seem to leave the *war* entirely for the *old folks* to think & talk about—while *riding* & *parties*, picnics & other gay amusements make you forgetful some time of so mighty and terrible a blood shed going on around you."[27] In a sense, Mary spoke for those who had suffered great loss and Sue for teenagers eager to put the struggle out of their minds and have fun.

Three months later, while petitions to the General Assembly were complaining that ill-trained boys had been sent into action without proper food, clothing, and equipment,[28] even larger tableaux were being seen in Columbia. During December 1864, Professor J. St. Maur Bingham's

Dancing Academy (next door to the Branch Bank on Main Street) unveiled a "grand revolving tableaux" that encompassed statuary, classic, and domestic themes.[29] For good measure, Bingham added an intermission reading entitled "The Maniac" and just before Christmas expanded to yet another medium—"an improved PHANTASMAGORIA APPARATUS or MAGIC LANTERN." This program, which he vowed was "most interesting and instructive entertainment," included a "beautiful & chaste" collection of scriptural scenes, fireworks, "astronomically revolving diagrams," the eruption of Mount Vesuvius, and forty comical moving figures.[30]

In addition to concerts, plays, and tableaux, larger communities sometimes held fairs and bazaars to raise money for patriotic purposes. The first wave of fairs occurred in 1862 and was part of a female scheme to buy a gunboat for the Confederate Navy, much as the women of New Orleans reportedly were doing. And the most brilliant bazaar, inspired by a similar extravaganza held in Liverpool in behalf of the Confederacy, was staged in Columbia in January 1865, only four weeks before General Sherman and his troops appeared there.

The gunboat campaign, really a series of raffles and fairs, began in March 1862. Under the skillful orchestration of Richard Yeadon, former editor of the *Courier*, it continued for over a year and still was going on long after the vessel in question apparently had been paid for. Many women throughout the state simply mailed their donation to Yeadon, while others contributed items to be raffled. In mid-March, at the first Charleston drawing, Miss C.C.M. (who held number 30) won a silver bowl, and Miss E. C. P. (number 2) received a Florentine mosaic brooch. Within a few days, other lucky participants became owners of a music box, a basket of wax fruit, and two baskets of shell work.[31]

About three weeks later, Columbia ladies held their "gunboat fair," followed by yet another in Charleston. Although the fund-raiser at the state capital was said to be a success, not everyone was happy. Louisa McCord complained to Augustine T. Smythe that no men of the "right" age were present. She and her friends, she added, wished South Carolina College would re-open. Fairs, in her view, were "rather stupid things" with no one to talk to but old men and little boys: "It was quite amusing to see the 15 year olders playing the beau, & holding up their heads as if Mr. this & Mr. 't'other, as they peeped between the ladies' shoulders."[32] Math instructor John Patrick also attended the fair; but, since this gentleman did not approve of raffles—despite the patriotic goal—he refused to join in the fun.[33]

THE VOLUNTEER, OR IT IS MY COUNTRY'S CALL

I leave my home and thee, dear,
        With sorrow in my heart,
It is my country's call, dear,
        To aid her I depart;
And on the blood-red battle plain
        We'll conquer or we'll die,
'Tis for our honor and our name
        We raise the battle cry.

Chorus: Then weep not, dearest, weep not,
        If in her cause I fall,
O, weep not, dearest, weep not
        It is my country's call.

And yet my heart is sore, love,
        To see thee weeping thus;
But mark me, there's no fear, love,
        For in Heaven is our trust;
And if the heavy, drooping tear
        Swells in my mournful eye,
It is that Northmen of our land
        Should cause the battle-cry.

Our rights have been usurped, dear,
        By Northmen of our land,
Fanatics raised the cry, dear,
        Politicians fired the brand.
The Southrons spurn the galling yoke,
        The tyrant's threats defy,
They'll find we've sons of sturdy oak
        To raise the battle-cry.

I knew you'd let me go, pet,
        I saw it in that tear,
To join the gallant men, pet,
        Who never yet knew fear.
With Beauregard and Davis,
        We'll gain our cause or die,
Win battles like Manassas,
        And raise our battle-cry.

Composed in 1861 for the Orleans Cadets by Harry Macarthy, author of "Bonnie Blue Flag," and published by Blackmar & Bro., New Orleans and Augusta. A copy can be found in the South Carolina Historical Society's Peery Collection of Confederate Imprints.

The Charleston version, which opened at Hibernian Hall on 6 May, continued for four days, aided by glowing publicity in both the *Courier* and the *Mercury*. There were fortune tellers, grab bags, raffles (of course), and things such as jewelry, silverplate, paintings, embroidery, fancy work, and baby clothes for sale. In all, the *Courier* said some two hundred and fifty prizes were being offered. Among those attending were Governor Pickens and the youngsters enrolled at South Carolina's Marine School. This is how the editor of the *Mercury* described the scene on 7 May.

> And so we lingered on, hour after hour, watching the glowing faces, and vainly trying to withstand the pleading of the lovely tempters to take a chance in their golden lotteries for the iron gunboat. Who would not be willing to exchange such metals in such a bargain? Who will refuse his contributions in aid of a cause which our wives and daughters and sisters and sweethearts determine shall succeed, and which carries with it, in no small measure, the fate of our dear old city.

Emma Holmes, who was about to depart for Camden, attended the "grand raffle," but came away empty handed: "The pearl set was won by Miss Broadie, a Baptist, a respectable woman of the lower ranks of life [but] one certainly who will never make use of it except to sell it. I don't know who got the other handsomest prizes."[34]

Some five months later, on Saturday, 11 October, the gunboat *Palmetto State* was "baptised" at Marsh's Wharf. Yeadon, the featured speaker, was joined by General Beauregard, his staff, and hundreds of spectators. The *Palmetto State*, according to the *Mercury* (11 October), cost $30,000 and took its place alongside the *Chicora*, a similar craft built at the same shipyard for the Confederate government.[35] By December, both vessels were outfitted and ready for action; however, when they remained tied up to their docks week after week, anonymous protests began to appear in the *Courier*. This outcry finally led on 30 January to a spectacular but unsuccessful attempt to lift the federal blockade.[36]

In May 1863 the "gunboat raffle" still was going on, indicating either an avalanche of prizes to be won or lack of interest in the proceedings. On 11 May the *Mercury* said these items had not yet been claimed: a sofa cushion, two patchwork quilts, assorted bits of jewelry, several elegant vases, silverware, books, paintings, three cutlasses, a

TABLEAUX VIVANTS

FOR THE

GUNBOAT FUND,

AT

MILITARY HALL.

THIS EVENING, THE 22d INSTANT.

PROGRAMME.

1. Harem Scene, Sultana and Odalisks.
2. Nourjahad receiving the Elixer of Life.
3. Gipsey Encampment, or the Stolen Child, by Finden.
4. Elizabeth of England, or Sir Walter Raleigh.
5. The Martyrs under Diocletian.
6. Titania, by Landseer.
7. Gipsey Fortune Telling.
8. Harvest Home, by Finden.
9. Conelia, the Mother of the Gracchi, and the Roman Lady.
10. Richard, Cœur de Lion and Beurengnia.
11. Cindrella.
12. Confederate States.

Admittance, 50 cents; Children, 25 cents.

Tickets for sale at the Music and Book Stores, and at the door.

Doors open at 7½, Curtain rises at 8 o'clock, P. M.

The Fort Sunter Band will be in attendance.

April 22

Charleston Daily Courier, 22 April 1862.

double-barreled gun, floral waxworks in a frame, and "crystalized grass in a glass shade."

The call for the great bazaar first was sounded in May 1864 by a small group of socially prominent women, among them, Mrs. F. H. Elmore, Mrs. John Fisher, and Mrs. A. W. Leland, all residents of Columbia, and these Charlestonians: Mrs. M. A. Snowden, Miss Eliza P. Hayne, Mrs. D.E. Huger, Mrs. A. M. Manigault, and Miss L. S. Porter. Their goal, they told friends overseas as they solicited their help, was to expand facilities for servicemen in various communities and provide clothing for Navy personnel. Then, in November, these ladies directed their appeal to the local scene, emphasizing whatever the hospitals, "rests," and the Navy did not want would be sold to the public at moderate prices. All classes could help, they said, stressing almost anything produced by farmers could be used in the hospitals.

> We would especially invite attention to the numberless articles of a useful and fancy kind which the taste and ingenuity of the ladies have developed during the war; as for instance, straw and palmetto bonnets and hats, cloth hats, knitting of every description, crochet, and tatting, camp bags, tobacco pouches, pin and needle cases. And, in a word, to the handiwork of the busy fingers which have plied so industriously in obedience to the promptings of earnest hearts in the cause of our country.[37]

By the time these words were published, many South Carolina households were "bazaar" mad. Grace Elmore, daughter of one of the organizers, said she and her friends talked of little else during the final weeks of 1864. (Early in December, she took part in a concert and, while singing, imagined she had the power "to decapitate Lincoln and enjoyed the thought greatly.") On 4 January 1865, she wrote in her diary that nearly every home in Columbia was in a state of frenzy concerning the affair.

> How strangely is the serious and the gay intermingled in our life, one moment gloomily considering the many chances of Yankee rule and the next looking with equally anxious earnestness after the pleasures and interests of the Bazaar. For with the Yankees almost at our doors, we still think of, work for and cheer our soldiers, sick and wounded in the hospitals. Money is scarce, so we will

> have a Fair to which the whole State is contributing. Each house has its corner to which tobacco bags, cloth babies, cushions, all odds and ends that can be raked or scraped from our needs, is consigned, there to rest until the great day when they will appear at the State House to tempt the fancy of every true Confederate. Since early November we've been ransacking the house for scraps, and bemoaning our extravagance in the first years of the war, in using up most of our material in foolishness for the soldiers. I remember cutting up two pretty dresses, and spending a lot of money on tassels, to make a lot of smoking caps for Captain Hoke's company. I presented them myself and was immensely pleased when the men whirled them around their heads and gave three cheers for 'the ladies.'

Now, she sighed, she wished she had the material in those dresses to help sick, brave men really in need.

Finally, on 17 January, the old State House, most of the furniture removed from both halls and the interior transformed into a fairyland of color, opened its doors to an eager throng.[38] Garlands of vines and flowers encircled columns, and banners proclaiming "Don't Give Up the Ship," "God Save Our State," and "Contribute to the Comfort of our Sick and Wounded Soldiers" floated over tables laden with food, toys, pictures, embroidered cushions, trinkets, Confederate flag handkerchiefs (made in Scotland from James Island cotton), and other odds and ends, some brought to town by railroads free of charge.

The building was open each afternoon and evening (admission one dollar), and the *Daily South Carolinian* reported 3,800 tickets were "taken up" the first day. The only discordant note, this paper said, was "a hundred or so rude boys" who, in packs of a dozen or so, dashed about tearing dresses and causing panic. *Real* coffee was drunk by the gallon, and all eyes were on a handsome wax doll from England that had the place of honor atop the speaker's desk, which was draped with gray moss. In the words of Grace Elmore, "We were a gay crowd, every body left his bad spirits and anxiety at the door, and if Sherman was mentioned 'twas in a most casual way, nobody had time for blues, we jostled each other, laughed, quarreled, made fun and forgot for a time that the battle for home and fireside was soon to commence again."[39]

A table bore the name of each Confederate state and perhaps was manned, at least in part, by individuals associated with that region. The Adams and Goodwyn families of lower Richland, whose relatives migrated to Mississippi in the early 1850s, presided over that state's table. Mississippi, South Carolina, and six other states held forth in the House of Representatives (Kentucky and Missouri sharing quarters) and five more were in the Senate chamber. Several offered restaurant meals, Texas serving up wild turkey, venison, and alligator steaks. And, although South Carolina had the largest and most lavish display, Louisiana may have stolen the show with this bill of fare: "Mock Turtle Soup, Oyster Soup, Gumbo, Roast Turkey, Boned Turkey, Daubed Tongue, Daubed Beef, Roast Ham, Partridges Stuffed with Artichokes, Vol-au-vent of Chicken, Pork Pie, Chicken Pie, Oysters, Chicken Salad, Giblet Patties, Mayonnaise, Stuffed Eggs à la Creole, French Rolls, Crackers, Coffee, Tea, Black Cake, Jelly Cake, Sponge Cake, Pound Cake, Ginger Cake, Doughnuts, Ground-nut Cake, Trifle, Jelly, Blancmange, Charlotte Russe, Custard, Syllabub, Meringue."[40] After three days and four nights, the remaining food and assorted goodies were taken to city hall, together with items that arrived late from various parts of the state, and the fun continued. Just how much money was made and how it was disbursed is unclear. The *Daily South Carolinian* (20 January) estimated each table took in $10,000-$20,000; however, the records of Columbia's Wayside Hospital indicate it received only $24,936.50 from this elaborate benefit. The editor of the *Edgefield Advertiser*, who was among those in attendance, said the lady managers told him they expected to realize $150,000.

This gentleman, who, for the most part, had high praise for the affair, described the pushing and shoving and charming sales ladies in crisp white aprons and jaunty white caps. But he thought the managers committed "a grossly utilitarian indiscretion" when they failed to provide music. He seemed even more dazed by "the fearful whirlpool of human beings" to be seen throughout all of Columbia, "the great city of the South Carolina Legislature."

Prices were "ruthlessly high," speculation rampant, scores involved in the liquor traffic, and each house, hut, and hovel "crammed." It stood, he conceded, in stark contrast to "our forlorn old den in this forlorn old town."

> Every imaginable specimen of humanity can be seen
> on the streets—and in any number. Governors of sover-

eign States, Adjutant and Inspector Generals, State officials of every grade. Generals, Lieut-Generals,
Major-Generals, Brigadiers, Colonels, Majors, Captains,
Lieutenants, Sergeants, Corporals, Privates, of the Provisional Army—and Staff officers and myrmidons
generally. Quartermasters, Commissioners, Enrolling
Officers, and their myrmidons. City Fathers, highly re-
spected old gentlemen beyond the conscript age.
Auctioneers, who sell niggers, furniture and old clothes.
Eager-eyed, hook-nosed, money-adoring Jews, sumptuous in studs, chains and haberdashery. Striplings from
the Military Academy, striplings from schools, striplings
from the alleys. Ladies of all styles, sizes and com-
plexions—fair and unfair, built in the style of Daniel
Lambert,[41] and after the fashion of a wrought-iron skel-
eton. Some of them paint their faces shamelessly; carmine
blushes flame on very many cheeks. Ministers of the
gospel, old and shuffling, young and spruce. Lawyers
and Judges, whose occupation is well nigh gone. Editors, Printers, Newsboys, free from war's wild alarm.
Innumerable gamblers, flashy, fierce, and flagrant.[42]

One strange byproduct of the bazaar was a hastily written poem
composed by three disgruntled "sibyls." The Misses W, F, and G presided over a fortune-telling booth called the "Bower of Fate" and
cautioned a reporter to be certain the final "e" appeared in whatever he
wrote. It did on 18 January, but the *Daily South Carolinian* inadvert-
ently called their operation the "Bowl of Fate." The young ladies then
put their heads together, composed these lines, and *ordered* the editor to
print them, which he did two days later.

The Doom of the Yankees on Carolina's Soil.

The Yankees came down, like the wolf on the fold,
And their cohorts were gleaming in purple and gold;
And the sheen on their spears was like stars in the sea,
When the blue wave rolls nightly on deep Galilee.

Like the leaves of the forest, when Summer is green,
That host, with its banners, at sun rise was seen;
Like the leaves of the forest, when Autumn hath blown,
That host, in the evening, was withered and strown.

For the angel of death spread his wing on the blast,
And breathed in the face of the foe as he passed;
And the eyes of the sleepers waxed deadly and chill,
And their hearts but once heaved, and forever grew still.

And there lay the rider, distorted and pale,
With the dew on his brow, and the rust on his mail;
For Lee, in his anger, had drawn his bright sword,
And struck down the foe in the name of the Lord.

For the views of a young lady who took part in the bazaar and, like the *Edgefield* editor, was impressed with the horde of military officers to be seen in Columbia, see the letter on p. 246. As spectacular as this event may have been, it was only part of a madcap fall and winter season on the banks of the Congaree. From September to February, Columbia's city hall was the setting for almost weekly concerts of various kinds, as well as the viewing of a two-headed girl in October, display of a large painting in November ("The Burial of Latane"), and minstrel shows in December. Meanwhile, Professor Bingham was staging dancing classes, balls, tableaux, etc. nearby in Captain Stanley's Hall.[43] Most of these affairs, but not all, ostensibly benefited soldiers and their families.

Ads in the *South Carolinian* indicate luxuries of all sorts were for sale in local stores—pianos, new sheet music, English toilet soap, London tooth brushes, champagne, brandy, sherry, madeira, imported whiskey, tea, coffee, sugar, and various spices such as nutmeg and cloves. In fact, that newspaper boasted on 6 December that the shelves of one Main Street emporium (Messrs. Silcox, Bro. & Co.) were dramatic proof that the Union blockade was a failure. The following day, one storekeeper offered *rouge* to those daring enough to use it.

Edward McCrady, Sr., was disgusted with the carefree attitude evident in both chambers of the State House during "these momentous times." "It seems to me," he told his wife late in December, "like the restlessness of sailors when shipwreck seems inevitable."[47] General Joseph E. Johnston, who tarried briefly in Columbia a month later, was equally distressed by the atmosphere he found, though for somewhat different reasons. Johnston, who had just toured Charleston and Florence, said he heard "either despondence or discontent" everywhere he went. The engineer responsible for the defense of Columbia told him he was not impressed with "the public spirit of the slave owners in the

---

THE GREAT BAZAAR

Bazaar—Columbia
Jan 1865

My dear friend—

Why did you not come down to attend the wonderful 'Bazaar in Columbia'—the next wonder to the eighth—after the affair at Liverpool:—but…that was a mere circumstance compared to this Southern achievement of genius! Why the feminines here nearly worked their fingers off—and everybody everywhere contributed to it you know—but alas! few could reap the benefits—for broken railroads and broken *banks* prevented [it].[44] Yet withal—it seemed that 'the world and his wife' were there, and such a quantity of *'gold lace'* never flourished before:—if all had been coined—we would have helped many a *poor private* to their necessary apparel—of which they are now deficient.

We managed to collect several *bushels* of shinplasters[45] and Confed. bills—which we hope will be of some avail in forwarding the 'good work'—

Oh you ought to have seen how the 'Angels' flourished and flaunted—in 'before the war' finery:—and seen the quantity of fancy tricks and eadibles [sic] collected by the several states—enough to tempt all to sin in the *indulgence*!

Why didn't you leave the 'dark corner of the world'—and come down to bask in the effulgence of *light* in our Capital! But enough nonsense—I haven't time for more—au revoir—

Most affectionately,
Molly Gossip.[46]

---

neighborhood." "I am regretting that we left Ga." he added in a letter to a fellow officer, "the expense of living here is much more than double my pay."[48]

Not all fun, of course, was of a public nature, nor was there always an admission charge. Men on leave frequently were honored at massive barbecues. On 31 July 1861, the Edgefield Riflemen were feted at a "barbecue and pic-nic" at Moore's Campground. *"Everyone had ribs,"* the *Edgefield Advertiser* proclaimed on 7 August. They enjoyed, the editor boasted, "barbecued meats and hash, and onion and tomato sauce, and superb wheat bread—not to mention corn-pone, irish [sic] potatoes, and the like." "There was," he continued, "indeed a glorious abundance of mutton, all rife with the most piquant seasonings and smoking from the pit."

Three years later, the *Tri-Weekly South Carolinian* (22 April 1864), while setting the stage for a report of a huge barbecue held for Wade Hampton and his men, described the state capital in this manner.

> Columbia is just now one of the liveliest places in the Confederacy. The ladies are all agog with excitement over the soldiers; private evening parties, soirees and sociables are the rage; occasionally a public concert is an episode; the barbecue has not been unlike a carnival; the streets are thronged with the fair sex; more are coming from Richmond;[49] everyone is hunting homes that cannot be found, including the writer; and things generally have taken on a new dress and a new habit, which betokens 'something in the wind.'

A special supplement published the following day told how 3500 pounds of meat were served up at long tables on the grounds of the Lunatic Asylum. Amid stained battle flags, there were jaunty banners proclaiming "Welcome Home," "Go Forth to Honor & Victory," "Trust in God & Keep Your Powder Dry," and "None But the Brave Deserve the *Fare*." And around the tables were some fifteen booths where ladies dispensed salads, pickles, pies, cakes, custards, and coffee. However, before eating, Dr. Benjamin M. Palmer, Martin W. Gary, and General Hampton addressed the throng.[50] Palmer, the principal speaker, referred to Lincoln as "the court jester from the West" and predicted that soon the map of North America might look much like that of Europe and contain perhaps as many as five "grand" republics. But first the Confederacy must protect the Republican principles of "our fathers" from "the wild Democracy of the North." "I believe, as I believe the fact of my being," Palmer said to great applause, "that the only hope of Republican institutions on this continent is to be found in the perpetuation of that institution which has been made the occasion for war."[51]

Not every festivity was so carefully orchestrated as these barbecues and various fairs, concerts, raffles, and bazaars. As Sue Montgomery of Mineral Springs indicated, despite war, young people continued to go riding and gather for picnics and parties, what one might call "private" fun. Charleston's gay winter season of 1862-1863, months when Confederate forces presumably were in desperate need of clothing and supplies, was crowded with activity of this sort. Somewhat strangely, however, public gatherings held there during those months were largely ignored by both daily papers. At that stage of the fighting, many apparently thought it best not to broadcast merriment and frivolity amid suffering and death. Also, it is quite possible the lowcountry was sensitive to repeated charges that its inhabitants ("parlour warriors") were not bearing their fair share of the war effort, while demanding upcountry slaves be requisitioned to dig fortifications in coastal areas.

That same winter, on 5 December 1862, Benjamin F. Perry described Columbia in this fashion to his wife: "The streets are full of soldiers & a very rough set. There has been less gayety in Columbia this session than I have ever known. The country is gloomy & mourning for the friends lost in the army. This dreadful war will ruin the country. Already our national debt is over five hundred millions & South Carolina's share of this debt is over fifty million." [52]

Yet even as Perry wrote, *private* fun was on the ascendant in the Charleston area, and two years later, as we know, Columbia cast off whatever reservations it may have once had concerning any display of wartime pleasure. The result was a seemingly endless round of tableaux, raffles, concerts, balls, bazaars, and so on in communities both big and small. Although these festivities undoubtedly gave local morale a momentary boost, there is the distinct possibility they also impeded the war effort at times. This was especially true if staged at a moment when energy expended could have been used to aid the military...say, for example, as Sherman was closing in on Columbia.

Family letters and diaries detail a series of grand affairs held in Charleston (1862-1863), some in homes and others at military installations. And much of the gossip centers not on the propriety of such goings-on but scandalous new "round" dances such as the waltz, during which the male, in contrast to the arms-length format of square dancing, might clasp his partner exceedingly close. On 15 December 1862, writing from Charleston, Caroline R. Ravenel told Isabella Middleton Smith of a large party apparently held at Fort Sumter. She judged the affair a success since some two hundred and fifty people were there and yet she called it "tiresome."

> You see, Belle, the girls who don't dance the round dances
> are laid on the shelf, for although the men don't allow

their sisters to dance, they are quite willing to dance themselves, & while they can get girls to waltz & polka with
them, they are not going to attend to young ladies who
don't, no matter how pleasant they may be. Now take
Mr. [Julius] Blake & his wife (Julia Lewis). She has been
accustomed to dance them always; has only been married three or four weeks; he *disapproves*, & forbids her
dancing, but dances them himself with all of her friends.
Now I think those were downright bad manners in Capt.
Blake, & although I admire Julia for bending to her
husband's will, I think it must be very hard not to dis-
obey him.[53]

Three weeks later, Caroline told "Belle" of another party at Castle
Pinckney that included a ride in an army ambulance drawn by a mule
and a dress parade. Among those present were English officers from the
steamship *Petrel*, individuals she thought "very rough" and rude to boot:
"...in the quadrille one of them caught me by the elbow, so I very quietly took my arm out of his reach, and did not let him take my hand to
turn me. The other English, when they were asked to be introduced to
the ladies, they said they would rather not. Don't you think that was
rather *singular*?"[54]

Writing in her diary in mid-January 1863, Emma Holmes noted
that Columbians who went to Charleston for a ball described the elegant
gowns of the ladies in great detail and reported there were "only three
square dances all evening." Among those attending were many whose
relatives had been killed in recent months. "I cannot understand such
heartlessness & frivolity," she wrote, "but the storm of war, which has
swept away hundreds of our brave soldiers from our homes, seems to
have [made] many of those left callous...."[55] Then, on 2 June she gave
full vent to her displeasure.

...I feel so mortified at the disgraceful character the
Charleston girls have acquired—once considered so
modest and refined & well behaved that a Charleston
lady was recognized by her lady like manners anywhere,
& now the foreigners say they have met fast girls, but
not equal to those of Charleston. And those very ones
are the ultra fashionables, who seem to have forgotten
alike the dead & the living and the grass scarce green on

the graves of their brothers, cousins & other near relatives, have shared in all the gaiety of the past winter—such
as the Rhetts, Alstons, Middletons, Ropers, and that set
of worldly, heartless fashionables.[56]

A few months later, while recuperating in Camden from war wounds,
William Elliott had penetrating comments concerning one of these same
families. Early in October, he told his fiancée in Augusta, "I went to
another tea-fight last week at Judge Withers consisting of seven ladies
and four males not men—two of them being scrubs." Among the guests
were the Misses Ropers "who were carrying on at such a rate with
Beauregards Staff last Winter and Spring. The eldest one is certainly a
2.40 nag i.e. very fast." As she was leaving, William offered to see her to
her carriage but she objected, saying the dancing was beginning and he
should remain with the other ladies. Elliott replied it made no difference
since he could not get a partner. "Oh," she smiled, "try again. Girls like
pressing." And, he added with emphasis, "meaning everything that she
said."[57]

But it is the Middletons, both as participants and observers, who
have left us the most complete record of wartime revelry, almost all of it
relating to Charleston. The extensive "Middleton Correspondence," published in the *South Carolina Historical Magazine* (1962-64), has
numerous tidbits scattered throughout. Some young Middletons bowed
to parental pressure and abjured "round" dancing, others did not. In
January 1863, Harriott, a refugee in Flat Rock, told cousin Susan in
Columbia of a "cold water" Christmas party given by "Willy" Smith in
Charleston at which an Englishman squeezed the hands of all of his
partners (they compared notes afterwards and verified this indiscretion),
and round dancing was, she said, the rule of the day.

However, Alicia, Harriott's twenty-one-year-old sister, refused to
participate, insisting, "I *as yet* remain firm as a rock."[58] A few days later,
Susan replied that it was delightful to learn that the girls were having a
pleasant time "in town."

But it is *not* delightful to think of their giving in, as I hear
they are doing, and waltzing with all those underbred
foreigners. Mrs. Waites tells me Miss Hannah Harleston
was the only unmarried woman she observed who declined round-dancing! I am very proud that Alicia 'stands
firm as a rock,' and regret that I cannot say as much for

all the Miss Middletons! Livy, in her letter yesterday, begs that Papa will consent to Emma's dancing, as 'she is dying to do it.' She expresses no desire to 'do it' herself, and, as I have often heard her express what seemed a very sincere and hearty disgust at the idea, I trust she will not be led astray by pernicious example. That Emma should wish to set aside propriety and delicacy in this way mortifies me deeply, but I have no doubt she will do it, for she is at least as self-willed as I am, and Papa says: 'Tell her I think it very indecent, but she is of age, and if she chooses to make a fool of herself, contrary to my wish and advice, I shall no longer oppose her doing so.'[59]

When Charlestonians attending a party at the Columbia home of the Hampton family (which lasted until 3 a.m.) referred to their partners as being from "*town*," local residents were not pleased. "Where do you mean? Are you not in town now?" "The distinction between *a* town and *the* town," Susan told Harriott on 2 May 1863, "seems, however, broad enough for us Charlestonians!"[60]

On 1 June, amid talk of fighting between deserters and militia in the Flat Rock area, Harriott reported again on the Charleston scene as viewed through the eyes of Cousin Caroline, who said she "supposed" they had heard of the Roper, Alston, and Whaley parties and the "extraordinary" games played at them.

We all looked very wise, and agreed that round-dancing was the opening wedge of every enormity! and Cousin Caroline deplored your father's having allowed his daughters to dance them—and they were intensely surprised at Lizzy's daughter having joined the ranks, and at her reasoning that 'whatever is fashionable is right,' which still strikes me as one of the most fearful dogmas for a mother to propound that I have ever heard. Anna Parker writing to Alice and speaking of the present state of things says she thinks it very fortunate for a great many young women that they are obliged to stay in the country until the end of the war, in which sentiment, she is sure that *I* will agree![61]

A few weeks later, on 6 July Harriott relayed still more gossip to Susan: "A young lady with an inclination to it [round dancing] told our correspondent that the officers said they have but to open their arms and the Charleston ladies rush into them—that it is very delightful to have them in their arms but it would be much more convenient on the sofa than whirling round when they often have great weight to carry! Now don't you repeat this to the girls!"[62]

In January 1864, Susan told Harriott that the "fast" ladies of Charleston were giving what they called "Consolation parties." They would meet as usual on Sunday evenings, sing psalms until midnight "when the band begins to play and the company dances till daylight...."[63] Two months later, Susan became more specific: "We are told that nothing has ever been known before like the conduct of the young ladies on Cooper River—the Whaleys, Moultries, Miss Ferguson and Helen Alston— They meet at each other's houses almost every night to dance (partners from town) and the older inhabitants of the neighborhood are greatly scandalized at their proceedings. Papa declares he will order Emma to confine herself to the 'slow side of the river'...."[64] Late in the same month (28 March), she furnished additional details of high times in the "Holy City."

> ...the gay people of Charleston are having a very gay time, it seems. We hear of a French play at the Rhetts'— acted by amateurs—Miss Elise performing the part of a fairy! Also, that the officers from New Orleans, being strongly urged by 'a party of young ladies' to dance the 'Cancan' for their amusement, consented to do so on the condition that the '*ladies*' would assemble at their (the Officers') house to witness the performance. This was agreed to, and the entertainment came off accordingly at the Bachelor establishment in very *high* style. Perhaps you saw the Cancan at the Gardens in Paris. *I* saw it on the Stage there once, and have been trying ever since to forget that I ever did see anything so purely disgusting. Lise [Rutledge] told me yesterday that she had a letter from Dolly, who said they were going on a party to Fort Sumter—in row-boats, in the evening. But the nights have been so stormy lately, I doubt if they have been able to do so....[65]

Some of this revelry was inspired by holidays such as Christmas. Sumter's younger set (ages ten to eighteen) marked the 1862 Yuletide with a tournament, a form of recreation often duplicated in other communities.[66] The Wescoat family of Monck's Corner had twenty people at the dinner table on 26 December 1863 and "a nice dance" that evening.[67] A year later, John Jenkins sent his wife (who was refugeeing in Summerville) a turkey and orders to "make an egg nog for the little Brats for Christmas night."[68] Sue Montgomery reported that Christmas 1864 in Mineral Springs was "a much gayer time than anticipated," though dull compared to the old days.[69] On 15 February she told Moultrie Wilson that, even as the community was preparing for Sherman, "a good many" soldiers were home on furlough. Some, Sue added, had been feted at "little dinners & tea vites [sic]" and seemed reluctant to return to duty. She expressed surprise that so many were allowed to visit their homes at this time and disdain for those trying to extend furloughs. Other holidays of passing significance include St. Patrick's Day, especially in Charleston, where in 1864 at least two societies staged lavish celebrations. The Hibernian Society held its 63rd annual banquet, despite war, at the corner of Warren and Thomas streets "where a bounteous collation was spread and discussed, amid a flow of wine, wit, and sentiment worthy of the best days of the time honored Society."[70] That same day, members of the St. Patrick Benevolent Society met at the Masonic Hall. May Day parties seem to have been the special pride of mid-19th century Columbia. In 1864, David Crawford wrote wistfully from Virginia to his mother, "I suppose Columbia will be kept pretty lively now with 'May Parties.'"[71]

Then there were pleasures that had little to do with holidays, benefits, bazaars, or the dance floor. For three evenings in April 1862, scores crowded Charleston's Hibernian Hall to hear "Blind Tom," an inspired black musician billed as "the wonder of the world." Included in each program (as well as in a Wednesday matinee) was his "Battle of Manassas," which was, according to the *Courier* (24 April), both "soul-stirring and thrilling."[72] The following month, Charlestonians could view "Burton's Southern Moving Panorama" at the same site for 75¢ (children under ten, 25¢). On a moving canvas eight feet high and seventy-five feet long, Burton, a Memphis artist, had created splendid views of the Bosporus, a turtle ram fight on the Mississippi, and the Yankee stampede at Manassas.[73]

And there were still other places where an adventurous young man might seek pleasure. An exceedingly frank census taker listed two houses of "ill fame" in Columbia in 1860—a designation not found in communities such as Charleston, Greenville, and Spartanburg.[74] When Francis Tucker (the Spartanburg District man who vowed he was fighting for freedom and liberty) was stationed in Columbia in 1861, he told his wife he asked God each night to take care of their children and keep him from temptation, for "this is a very wicked place—& it requires a great effort for a man to restrain himself entirely."[75]

But, even though other census takers were more circumspect, we know Columbia had no monopoly on this state's "disorderly houses." The *Charleston Courier* (23 February 1863) noted that Helen Henderson and William McQueen had been imprisoned and fined for maintaining such, and the municipal records of Anderson reflect similar conditions during wartime. The Anderson madam, a Mrs. Rush, also was charged with selling liquor without a license and trading with slaves.[76]

Of course, for every soldier who sought out such activity, there was another who both avoided and condemned it. No one, however, expressed his scorn so vividly as David Ballenger, a Greenville District man who first served as an officer with an Alabama unit and then, in 1864, joined Hampton's Legion. In May of that year, about one-third of the men, who were heading to Virginia following the Columbia barbecue, stopped in Chester for the night to have their horses shod. The ladies of the town provided supper and still more. "In the midst of this great war," Ballenger told his mother, "there is something very remarkable about the women. I never saw them in such a way as they are now in all my life. I believe that half of them have turned out to be public harlots. They are just like taking the men, wherever they go. I do not say this because I do not respect decent women, by no means."[77] The following day, he wrote much the same thing to his wife from Charlotte: "They meet the men along the road as they pass along & they are just taking them down. It would not be prudent for me to express just how they do [it]. There are exceptions of course as there are in every thing else."[78]

So, in these pages we have moved from the wide-eyed youth from York flabbergasted with the wonders of Charleston and the round-dancing gossip of the Middletons to a Greenville man shocked by what he saw in the little village of Chester. To a degree, this progression reflects the drift of life throughout South Carolina, 1861-1865—from innocence and hope to resignation and despair. Perhaps the task was too great, the concept too grand. Writer William Grayson, a keen observer of the local scene, would say those who led the rebellion simply did not understand human nature...or did not want to.[79] In any case, it is obvious that, after 1863, the fun of South Carolina was more frantic than real. Its premise was no longer prelude to a new age but a rationale for living life to the fullest now, before the deluge.

NOTES

[1] J.W. Pursley to Jane Pursley, 19 January 1862, Mary Jane Pursley Papers, Special Collections Library, Duke University. A few months later, Pursley noted on 13 May "we stand guard every place since them negroes took that steamer"—a reference to the exploits of Robert Smalls.

[2] Ibid., "Warren" to Jane Pursley, 3 June 1863.

[3] W. J. and J. T. Nobles Papers, 20 and 29 April, 14 June 1862, South Caroliniana Library.

[4] Journal of Meta Morris Grimball, 5 September 1862.

[5] Petigru to Caroline Petigru Carson, 17 April 1862, James L. Petigru Papers. In a previous letter to Caroline (7 February 1862), Petigru remarked, "The Southern people are perfectly mad. Even the sentiment of honor, which was formerly their pride, is prostituted to the rage of party— They are not to be shamed out of any thing either mean or wicked that feeds their blind animosity—"

[6] Tucker to wife, 28 June 1862, Duncan, Kinard, Sanders, Tucker Papers.

[7] Honour to wife, 19 October 1863, Honour Papers.

[8] Jones (1842-1914) to his mother, 8 February 1863, Iredell Jones Papers, South Caroliniana Library. He boasted that his battery, not that of John Gary, who was given credit for the deed by Charleston newspapers, actually disabled the *Isaac Smith*. Jones said the Yankees attached to the ship were real gentlemen who sincerely believed their cause was just.

[9] Smythe to mother, 22 April 1862, Smythe Letters. Goat Island is located south of Charleston inland from Folly Island, not far from Secessionville.

[10] Crawford to mother, 5 February 1865, Crawford Family Papers, South Caroliniana Library. An earlier letter from brother David to their mother (23 October 1864) notes that Doug had tried to run away and join the army. David also criticizes Andrew for not getting "*half* enough" exercise.

[11] Graydon, "Journal of Arthur Brailsford Wescoat," p. 75.

[12] Ibid. Two years earlier, the Washington Light Infantry and Citadel cadets, then stationed on Morris Island, marked the anniversary of Cowpens with a parade, banquet, and all-male ball. The *Mercury* (21 January 1861) admitted it is "not considered gallant for gentlemen to dance in pairs" but conceded it was done on that occasion.

[13] Ibid., p. 93. A few weeks later, Wescoat noted on 16 May that his brother's boy (Thomas) and two other black servants "had gone to the Yankees," much to the distress of Thomas's mother.

[14] Smythe to mother, 20 January 1861, Smythe Letters.

[15] Isabella Wylie Strait to son, 5 January 1862, Gaston, Strait, Wylie, Baskin Papers.

[16] Patrick Diary, 27 February 1862.

[17] Ibid., 8 March 1862.

[18] Ibid., 25 August 1862. Student Claudius Fike told his father that the first two cadets were suspended because they were drunk: "I hear it is said, and I believe it to be so,

that this class as a whole is the most unruly, that has ever been here." See Fike Papers, 24 August 1862. Young Fike also mentioned (20 April 1862) that, when their gray uniforms with black trim arrived from the Saluda Factory, they were adorned with gold buttons bearing replicas of U S. eagles.

[19]Ibid., 5 August, 3 September 1863.

[20]Anderson Town Council Minutes, 11 November 1864, South Carolina State Department of Archives and History.

[21]*Tri-Weekly Watchman* (Sumter), 5 August 1861.

[22]*Charleston Mercury*, 11 May 1864

[23]*Daily South Carolinian*, 12 November 1864.

[24]This form of entertainment—originally the creation of well-known paintings with costumed individuals fixed in place and immobile—was popular with the French court in the 1760s and soon spread to other parts of Europe. See Kirsten Gram Holmström, *Monodrama, Attitudes, Tableaux Vivants* (Stockholm, 1967) and two articles on American aspects of this phenomenon—P. O. Sullivan, "A Chapter on Tableaux," *Scribner's* (November 1880), pp. 91-103, which is basically a "how-to-do-it" guide, and M.E.W. Sherwood, "Some Society Tableaux," *Cosmopolitan* (January 1898), pp. 235-46.

[25]The *Advertiser* (2 September) said such sights, "never before seen in Edgefield," netted $320. During the war years, tableaux also were held in centers such as Yorkville, Sumter, Greenville, Graniteville, Bamberg, Columbia, and Charleston. See an ad for "Tableaux Vivants" in the *Courier* (22 April 1862) and the description of a Greenville program early in 1864 in the "Middleton Correspondence," *South Carolina Historical Magazine* (January 1964), p. 33.

[26]Mary Johnstone to Emmie Elliott, 5 September 1864, Elliott-Gonzales Papers.

[27]Sue Montgomery to Wilson, 22 September 1864, Moultrie Reid Wilson Papers, South Caroliniana Library. In a similar vein, Sally Beard told "Cousin Jimmy" on 4 October of the "large and gay" crowd present at Glenn Springs in the summer of 1864. Now home in the Newberry-Union area, she said almost every household had lost someone in the war— "every one seems gloomy and sad." However, her family was making molasses and she planned to hold a "candy pulling" soon. See the William W. Renwick Papers, Special Collections Library, Duke University.

[28]See Petition # 6 to the General Assembly (13 December 1864), really an appeal from men stationed in Pocotaligo to the Marion delegation to the legislature. In this instance, youngsters from that district had been dispatched to Grahamville and Coosawatchie with only meager rations and no tents, blankets, and cooking utensils. If boys are to be asked to fight, the petitioners maintained they should be fed and clothed.

[29]*Daily South Carolinian*, 1 December 1864.

[30]Ibid., 20 December 1864.

[31]*Charleston Courier*, 19 March 1862.

[32]Louisa McCord to Smythe, 18 April 1862, Smythe Letters.

[33]Patrick Diary, 11 April 1862.

[34]Marszalek, *Diary of Miss Emma Holmes*, p. 160.

[35]For a summary of the gunboat campaign and a description of the christening ceremonies, see the *Mercury*, 13 October 1862.

[36]E. Milby Burton's *Siege of Charleston, 1861-1865* (Columbia, 1970) provides details concerning the subsequent careers of both vessels.

[37]*Tri-Weekly South Carolinian*, 12 November 1864.

[38]Two days later, while the bazaar was at its height, the editor of Columbia's *South Carolinian* remarked in a bitter editorial how mortified Mayor Thomas J. Goodwyn must be. His 29 December call for help in fortifying the capital city had been largely ignored. He had, the editor said, received "but few hands and fewer tools."

[39]In addition to this young lady's diary, see her description of this bazaar in volume one of *South Carolina Women in the Confederacy*, pp. 243-47.

[40]A complete description of the bazaar, which even published its own little newspaper, "The Cereus," can be found in the *Daily South Carolinian*, 18 January 1865. On 29 January, without comment, the *New York Herald* reprinted these words. Grace Elmore and some of her friends thought a stranger seen at the affair was a spy and credited him with forwarding the account to the North. There is, however, no proof of such a dramatic twist of fate. Sallie Lawton, whose family was fleeing from Allendale to safety in Limestone, was shocked by both the display of food and the prices—"you would never imagine there was a war in our land, could you have seen the delicacies…but the prices were very high, they asked five dollars for a slice of cake, or the same price, for a biscuit or a slice of ham or turkey...." Sallie to John Willingham (22 January 1865), Lawton-Willingham Family Papers, South Caroliniana Library.

[41]Daniel Lambert of Leiscester, England, weighed 739 pounds when he died during his fortieth year in 1809.

[42]*Edgefield Advertiser*, 1 February 1865. The columns of the *Daily South Carolinian* indicate that theft, assault, and petty crime were becoming evermore commonplace during these months.

[43]On 22 October, Bingham also conducted classes for all ages at Hurd's Hall in Newberry.

[44]A reference to torrential rains that pelted the state in January 1865 and made travel hazardous.

[45]A piece of privately printed paper currency, usually poorly secured and of little value.

[46]Molly McCarter (who lived in Abbeville District after the war) probably was writing to "Lizzie" Bleckley, Sylvester Bleckley Papers, South Caroliniana Library.

[47]McCrady to wife, 24 December 1864, McCrady Family Papers.

[48]Johnston to Colonel ———, 23 January 1865, Joseph E. Johnston Papers, Special Collections Library, Duke University.

[49]A reference to Confederate Treasury workers being transferred from Richmond to Columbia.

[50]Palmer (1818-1902), Charleston native and ardent secessionist, was pastor of

Columbia's First Presbyterian Church from 1843 to 1854, also serving briefly on the faculty of the Theological Seminary before moving to New Orleans in 1856. Gary (1831-1881), an Edgefield lawyer-planter, rose to the rank of brigadier-general during the war and, in the last days, organized the escort that accompanied Jefferson Davis south from Richmond.

[51]Palmer was singing a different tune five months later, all was gloom and despair. Mary Chesnut came away from a mid-week prayer meeting "shaken to the depths"— "He offered us nothing more in this world than the martyr's crown. He is not for slavery, he says. He is for freedom—and the freedom to govern our own country as we see fit. He is against foreign interference in our state matters. That is what Mr. Palmer went to war for, it appears. Every day shows that slavery is doomed the world over. For that he thanked God...and then came the cry: 'Help us, oh God. Vain is the help of man.'" See Woodward, *Mary Chesnut's War*, p. 644.

[52]Benjamin F. Perry Papers, South Caroliniana Library.

[53]Daniel E. Huger Smith, *et al*, *Mason Smith Family Letters*, pp. 21-22.

[54]Ibid., pp. 28-29.

[55]Marszalek *Diary of Miss Emma Holmes*, pp. 223-24.

[56]Ibid., p. 264.

[57]Elliott to Isabella Elliott Barnwell, 6 ? October 1863, Elliott Family Papers.

[58]"Middleton Correspondence," *South Carolina Historical Magazine* (January 1963), p. 29.

[59]Ibid., pp. 29-30. Livy (Olivia) and Emma, both in their early twenties, were Susan's younger sisters.

[60]Ibid. (April 1963), p. 97.

[61]Ibid., p. 99.

[62]Ibid. (July 1963), p. 158.

[63]Ibid. (January 1964), p. 34.

[64]Ibid., p. 41.

[65]Ibid., p. 44.

[66]*Charleston Mercury*, 30 December 1862.

[67]Graydon, "Journal of Arthur Brailsford Wescoat," p. 87.

[68]Jenkins to wife, 24 December 1864, John Jenkins Papers, South Caroliniana Library.

[69]Sue Montgomery to Wilson, 23 January 1865, Wilson Papers. In the same letter, Sue commented on the shooting of deserters: "I think it is very unjust & cruel to compel you all to witness the dreadful sight of them being shot."

[70]*Charleston Mercury*, 18 March 1864.

[71]Crawford to mother, 3 May 1864, Crawford Family Papers. Like scores of Confederates, he usually added "h'ye to the servants."

[72]Two years later, Tom's owner (James N. Bethune of Columbus, Georgia) was offering him for sale for one or more years. See the *Mercury*, 31 August 1864.

[73]*Charleston Mercury*, 19 May 1862. The Bosporus is the Turkish strait between Europe and Asia, and "turtle rams" were iron-clads used on the Mississippi, so-called because of their sloping sides. The Yankee stampede at Manassas needs no

explanation.

[74]Margaret Kelly (20), house #115, lived with two other women and a collection of youngsters. Rosa Le Grand (or La Grand), age 40, house #691, resided with six young ladies at the corner of Gates and Lady streets. Rosa starred in a sensational murder in the summer of 1863, done in by a former Confederate scout, Warsaw Thaddeus Saunders.

[75]Tucker to wife, 19 April 1861, Duncan, Kinard, Sanders, Tucker Papers.

[76]Anderson Town Council Minutes, 9 March 1865.

[77]Ballenger to mother, 20 May 1864, David Ballenger Papers.

[78]Ibid., Ballenger to wife, 21 May 1864.

[79]See Grayson's *James Louis Petigru*, pp. 145-46.

IX

RUMMAGING THROUGH THE RUBBLE

T he war affected to some degree the life of everyone residing on South Carolina soil, and the roles most individuals played in that drama are well-known. These include men and boys who donned uniforms and marched off to Virginia and Tennessee or served in and around Charleston, relatives and friends who sacrificed and labored in their behalf, and the most numerous of all South Carolinians (slaves) who did their part, though perhaps largely out of habit and because they had to. Diaries, letters, and the research of historians such as Mary Elizabeth Massey disclose much concerning the plight of refugees, those who, for whatever reason, packed their belongings and moved to new abodes. The activities of some businessmen, speculators, and servicemen who charted an independent course as they tired of military routine or perhaps became "Tories" are less clear and intentionally so.

Then there are bit players about whom we know all too little. Their ranks were small, their influence minimal...local officials who became "triple-threat" individuals as they assumed ever-greater responsibility (serving on this board and that when co-workers left for the front), enemy POWs, "foreign legions" that took shape just as the war was winding down, Confederates who "came home" during the conflict (as well as those who didn't), and Unionists who, clutching proper documents, ventured through the lines to visit relatives held in rebel stockades. Also, certain themes ever-present in civilian life continued to sputter along war or no war. Among these were real estate development, investment, and—sadly—latent anti-Jewish sentiment undoubtedly fueled by market-place pressure in a time of shortage and speculation.[1]

We have already met some lowcountry refugees such as the Elliotts, Middletons, Grimballs, Emma Holmes, Theodore Honour's wife and children, the parents of Augustine Thomas Smythe, and various members of the Mason Smith family. Like these individuals, most were relatively well-to-do (it cost money to travel and move about), and they generally sought temporary quarters in centers that had hotels and were thought to be safe from enemy incursions. Thus throughout much of the war, almost every inland community with a railroad depot was host to refugees, as well as some mountain resorts such as Flat Rock in nearby North Carolina. According to Mary Elizabeth Massey, Orangeburg, Barnwell, Camden, Cheraw, Sumter, Anderson, Greenville, and Spartanburg were popular havens. Columbia absorbed the greatest number of refugees, but no more in proportion to its size than those communities. And even Charleston at times was crowded with displaced persons, especially people from other parts of the Confederacy. Massey emphasizes that, during the first eighteen months of the war, most refugees within the state were South Carolinians; but, after that date, reacting to enemy pressure, the flow from the outside increased.[2]

At the outset, Spartanburg was the choice of many lowcountry folk. By April 1862, the *Spartanburg Express* was boasting of Charleston families in residence, giving a house-by-house accounting of who had found accommodations and where. "We hope," the editor said, "the intercourse between our citizens and the visitors from below may have a good effect by bringing them to see the better qualities of each other, and thus remove much of the prejudice which often exists between the inhabitants of remote sections of the same State." This gentleman even saw a postwar role for his community as a summer resort.[3]

In December, "Personne" (F. G. De Fontaine) tarried in the region for several days, following which he heaped praise upon Spartanburg. In some instances, refugees had taken over entire streets as homeowners, eager for revenue, sought quarters elsewhere, perhaps in the nearby countryside. According to "Personne," considerable money was changing hands, streets were busy, churches crowded, and great benefit might accrue from close association of individuals from diverse parts of the state. Three local institutions, in his view, enhanced the obvious charms of the community—Wofford College, a school for young ladies, and the state asylum for the blind in nearby Cedar Springs.[4]

Even before these words appeared in print, the *Mercury* (8 November) launched a strong appeal for "better understanding" in the upcountry of lowcountry planters. Let the people of that region be charitable, it said. Lease property to their unfortunate fellow South Carolinians instead of insisting upon sale: "The impulse of patriotism, the teachings of duty, and the affinities of brotherhood, all plead earnestly in favor of such a course." Nine months later, the *Courier* indicated that plea may have had limited effect. A Williamston correspondent said a dozen or so lowcountry families found there "the same prejudice to Charlestonians so proverbial with the denizens of the interior." This outburst evidently was based upon a preference for barter instead of payment in Confederate currency.[5] Yet the good citizens of Williamston perhaps were, in fact, merely reflecting economic reality as inflation mounted, not any specific antipathy to Charlestonians as such.

Near the close of 1864, the *Courier* reported that some residents of the "upper districts" were refusing to sell firewood to refugees.[6] But, for the most part, since tales such as these were divisive and could harm the war effort, they seldom got into print. However, in private many refugees gave voice to frustration, discomfort, displeasure, and even bitterness.

Slaves taken inland by the Weston family early in 1862 did not like their new quarters, one of them commenting, "Conwayboro must have been the last place God made."[7] In May of that same year, Susan Middleton, writing from the home of a Richland District friend before her family found a more permanent domicile on Columbia's Boundary Street, told cousin Harriott in Flat Rock that she was indeed fortunate.

> How lucky you are in having a comfortable home in a fine climate ready for you! There is so much difficulty here, in this mean little town, in finding a place of refuge, even at an exorbitant price, the extortions which are practised upon the low-country refugees, by the so-called '*best* people of Columbia,' are enough to disgrace the place forever and I heard a lady say with the bitterest indignation: 'I do believe, if we had gone to the heart of Connecticut, we sh[ou]ld not have fallen among such a set of *screws*!'[8]

As a refugee, Emma Holmes quickly became equally distressed by treatment received. When her family planned to move to Sumter, she expressed an aversion to sand and Jews ("my great abhorrence") and was relieved when they chose Camden instead.[9] At first she liked that community, but within ninety days was homesick: "If we go out for a walk, we find a disagreeable sandy uneven road and scarcely ever meet an acquaintance to enliven the way."[10] And, when their rented home was sold in December 1862 and they were given only four days in which to find a new dwelling, she was furious. "We are by no means stray examples of the ungenerous treatment which the refugees have received," she stated indignantly on 30 December. "Dozens of others have had the same—and instead of the Upper and Low country being more closely united, I fear the feelings of both, especially the latter, will be more than ever embittered."[11]

A few who longed for Charleston expressed their unhappiness, not in personal letters or diaries, but in verse. In April 1863, "L," a temporary resident of Lexington Court House, poured out her sad thoughts in "A Refugee's Request." (See page 267.) Complaints reflecting understandable tension in crowded households also surface from time to time. William Elliott, while recuperating in Camden, told "Belle" he was living amid constant pandemonium, noise, and unruly children—six white and "forty seven others of various hues of the rainbow."[12] Writing from Summerton in October 1863, Augustine T. Smythe's mother confided she felt "utterly helpless" living among relatives, forced to use their belongings and rely upon their servants. To complicate matters, one elderly individual (perhaps her host) talked incessantly, stayed up late, wasted candles, and nothing could be done about it.[13]

Should these folks have remained at home? With some reservations, Mary Elizabeth Massey concluded the answer is yes. Most created problems for themselves, the communities to which they fled, and various levels of government as well. Their presence increased shortages and fueled both speculation and inflation. Those who stayed put might face the horrors of an invading army and the indignity of enemy rule; but, after a momentary flurry, an existence almost normal evolved, at least what could pass for "normalcy" during wartime. "Before the war ended," she writes, "most refugees had all of the problems of citizens who stayed at home and none of the advantages."[14]

Mary Milling, a resident of the Camden area and one of those who did not flee—even when Sherman came—told her husband some months later that it was an "awful" experience. "We had to sit quietly and see everything turned upside down. But," she conceded, "the soldiers spoke with civility and politeness...." They took a bit of clothing, Mary added, and most of the provisions, which (except for meat) had since been replaced. "The Yankees burned nothing here, destroyed no corn. But we lost nearly a hundred bales of cotton. We are almost certain it was burned by the slaves." Nevertheless, she noted all of the slaves, except eight taken by Sherman, remained on the place. The invaders also took sixteen mules and two horses.[15]

In mid-February of 1865, about the time Mary Milling was watching blue-clad soldiers rummage through her belongings, two upcountry sisters, who corresponded almost daily, pondered what they should do. On the 14th, Mary Dawkins, who lived in Union, assured Jane McLure (a resident of Pacolet) that everything would turn out all right: "The Yankees will soon be out of the State and all will be quiet again, I hope. We have only to dread stragglers and we have a pretty good organized force for this, to scout the whole district...." The governor, she stressed, had ordered Wheeler's men to cease impressment and seizure of goods. "When we can get rid of the outskirts of the army," Mary stated confidently, "we are safe and can settle down again."

But a week later she acknowledged that Wheeler's men still were a threat ("they are to be feared like robbers") and told how refugees, including Governor A.G. Magrath himself, were filling her home each night, adding, "I wish I had a Ham." The village of Union was "a perfect sight[.] streets swarming with Wagons, droves of Cattle, vehicles of all description, Negroes, Women with children—but the Enemy are getting out of the State very fast and then all will be right again—in two or more days they will be gone—and then we can send out men to catch deserters and stragglers—I have packed nothing, made up nothing, and don't think I shall—"[16] Of course, living where they did, these two ladies did not face Sherman's army, although their families, like many others, were experiencing trying times. Nevertheless, Massey would have approved Mary's decision to "pack nothing" and remain where she was.

Amid this tumult, two individuals with very different roles to play also were being buffeted by forces over which they had little control. One was the local officeholder struggling to maintain some semblance of order in his village or district; the other was the prisoner of war, a man temporarily shut off from both military and civilian life. As clerk of court in Pickens District, James Earle Hagood was bombarded from all sides with constant requests. Custodian of various unsettled estates, he frequently was asked to transfer funds, arrange for payment to dependents of those who died in the service, and purchase goods to be charged to certain accounts. In April 1863 a Rock Hill man demanded thread to make clothes for his children and a large, light weeding hoe suitable for ditching, the costs to be deducted from money being held by Hagood.[17] Local men and boys in Virginia and the lowcountry of South Carolina asked Hagood to help them find duty assignments closer to home. One gentleman not eager to go off to war sought advice in June 1864 on how to circulate and file a petition in his own behalf, hinting he was willing, under certain circumstances, to furnish the government with one hundred pounds of meat.[18] In July 1864, a Pumpkintown man asked Hagood, simply as "a faver," to send him eight pounds of coffee, a bushel of salt, sixteen-and-one-half pounds of bacon, and a bunch of spun yarn.[19]

This sort of scatter-shot approach seems to have been based upon an assumption that those living somewhere else must have access to things not found in local stores. In the spring of 1862, William W. Renwick of the Newberry-Union area received two requests for large amounts of sugar. Former governor William H. Gist of "Rose Hill" wanted three full barrels repacked in boxes because barrels "are not convenient" and eight barrels of molasses, even specifying price and quality desired. Two days later, another man sought 1,500 pounds of sugar.[20] Much like Hagood, Charleston businessman James Reid Pringle was flooded with orders from refugees seeking scarce items, all of them, of course, to be charged to their accounts.[21] And in December 1864, an incredulous S. M. Fewell, then in Columbia, asked his sister, who lived near Rock Hill, if she really wanted fifty pounds of coffee, pointing out it was selling for $20 a pound.[22]

As harassed as Hagood may have been, he sought re-election in 1864 and, like others, seems to have relished his multiple responsibilities. On 29 October 1864, one of his neighbors, Robert Thompson, who was a member of the local Soldiers Board of Relief, conceded in his annual report to state authorities that it might not be up to their standards—"but, if not, bear in mind beside *this* I am a member of *three* public Boards, Coms. of Equity, Depository, Assessor of tax-in-kind, Editor of a *Small* newspaper, *and have a baby to name.*"[23]

As this ad in the *Sumter Watchman* (6 January 1864) indicates, Julius J. Fleming, editor of that weekly, was yet another individual who wore many hats.

> J.J. Fleming, Magistrate, Coroner, and Deputy Clerk of Court: at the Clerk's Office, Court House Square.
>
> Attends to the collection of claims of deceased soldiers; negro labor on the Coast; negroes lost in the public service; applications for exemptions under State or Confederate law; petitions or memorials for discharge or furlough, in special cases, of persons already in service; and every form of deed, or other legal instrument of writing, drawn up with neatness and dispatch. Also prepares all the necessary papers for disabled soldiers, who wish appointments as Clerks, Wagon or Forage Masters, in the Quartermaster's Department.[24]

A REFUGEE'S REQUEST

Take me, oh take me back to my home—
　　Where the ocean runs wild and free,
And bid me, never again to roam—
　　From a place so dear to me.

Yes, dear to me from childhood's hours—
　　When I roamed near bright Ashley's shore,
And gathered along its banks sweet flowers—
　　When the sunbeams had passed them o'er.

I loved it then, and I love it now,
　　Far dearer, far dearer to me—
Is the soil where reposes fond friends of my youth,
　　Than all others, though brighter, could be.

Then why seek I refuge away from that home?
　　Is God not Omnipotent there?
And will he not save, if with faith in his throne—
　　We pray for protection and care?

Oh take me then, back to my sea-board home—
　　I sigh for its breezes once more;
Let me share in its trials, whatever they be—
　　From a vile and merciless foe.

God is our refuge, He will not forsake—
　　Though loved ones shall perish, and deep be our woe;
Through storms of affliction that over us break—
　　He may lead us in triumph, to conquer that foe.

Take me, oh take me back to my home—
　　His love can protect us forever,
And bid me, never again to roam—
　　From a place that can be forgot never.

Charleston Daily Courier, 9 April 1863.

*Personal passes often were required for travel throughout the Confederacy.
Kinkaid-Anderson Family Papers, South Caroliniana Library.*

All of this civic-legal activity was not pure patriotism. Fleming, for one, a man in his early forties, was doing his level best *not* to go to war and he succeeded.

Turning to the POW, South Carolina's relations with the enemy face-to-face were quite different from the cries for blood and revenge so frequently uttered by both politicians and womenfolk. Only twice were prisoners gathered on South Carolina soil in substantial numbers, say a thousand or more—at Columbia's Camp Sorghum late in 1864 and, at about the same time, near Florence, a contingent transferred there from Georgia's notorious Andersonville. Until then, local residents only saw them in transit, perhaps en route to be exchanged, or quartered for a time in district jails and facilities such as Charleston's Roper Hospital and the state mental asylum at Columbia. Curiosity, a common language (or nearly so), and, in some cases, sympathy tended to strain whatever barriers existed.

In January 1862, six prisoners, all of them loyal Masons, were guests at a Columbia lodge meeting. Jacob Levin, chairman of a group outraged by such hospitality, called for action against those extending "the right hand of friendship" to men bent upon destroying the Confederacy.

> They are our prisoners of war, who we desire to treat humanely and kindly, but not make their imprisonment a luxury. Our children, our fathers, brothers, connections and friends met them successfully at Bull Run, Manassas plains and Leesburg, as invaders of our soil, fighting under the false pretext of protecting the flag and the

Union, when their conduct showed a wicked and vicious purpose at heart of subjugating and enslaving us; rallying under the flag of 'booty and beauty,' destroying and burning our property, insulting and imprisoning innocent and helpless females, and utterly disregarding every principle of warfare recognized by civilized nations.[25]

This was by no means the last outcry concerning Columbia's wartime "guests." In mid-February 1862 the escape of thirteen prisoners led to a shake-up of the guard detail, followed by tunnels, more escapes, and in September 1864 charges by irate civilians that a Yankee officer, under guard, was seen in the market place bartering with blacks, exchanging sugar for food...*how* could this be? The captain of the guard replied it seemed reasonable enough since there was no sutler at the jail and, in turn, accused local editors circulating such tales of "sensationalism."

Well, the *Tri-Weekly South Carolinian* replied on 27 September, if that is what the military wants, here is some:

> 1st. Ladies, in passing by the prison, have been insulted by Yankees throwing kisses at them, and by making beastly grimaces.
>
> 2d. Some of the prisoners, in a state of semi-nudity, stand before the window making their ablutions, and insult by their very appearance the passersby.
>
> 3d. There is scarcely a family, resident on the square on which the prison is located, that has not, at some time, been annoyed by the shouts and curses of these Yankees, which invest the ear.

Confederate correspondence sheds more light on conditions at the Richland District Jail. In September 1863, the captain of the guard told superiors in Charleston that the building (50' by 70') was much too small. The third floor was occupied by the sheriff, and on the lower two floors he had 273 Union and 27 Confederate prisoners. Guards had to sleep on the ground in front of the jail; and, under such crowded conditions, he feared an outbreak of disease and suggested other facilities be found. Charleston reacted by shipping some men to Richmond, at the same time expressing disapproval of permitting any individual to gain his freedom by taking an oath of allegiance to the Confederacy.[26]

Drawing meat rations at Camp Sorghum.

A year later, the same guard captain (R. D. Senn), now responsible for the entire city, was spending only one-third of his time with Yankee prisoners. His force of 214 men—reserves and "light duty" personnel organized in a haphazard manner—was trying to man thirty-six posts, twelve of them at the jail. At that time it housed 231 POWs and 27 Confederate deserters, who were held separately. According to this report, the structure was clean, prisoners cooked their meals in three kitchens, and yes—as some critics asserted—they were allowed to purchase "eatables." Water had to be obtained outside the building, and each day four prisoners under guard ventured forth. Those inspecting the premises found records "in very bad order" (the names of eight POWs did not even appear), and they, like Senn before them, suggested the entire group should be moved elsewhere.[27]

Needless to point out, there were countless attempts to somehow ease the plight of such individuals. This was especially true during the final years of the war when exchange programs faltered. On 19 October 1864, this ad appeared in Columbia's *South Carolinian*: "An officer confined in Columbia wishes to make an arrangement with the friend of some prisoner at the North, by means of which the sufferings of both will be alleviated. Apply at this office."

This gentleman apparently was Captain J. W. Hetsler from Calvina, Ohio, a member of the 9th Ohio Cavalry, for the following month Mary Boykin Chesnut described how Alex Taylor was looking after the needs of an Ohio man held in Columbia and his brother was making John

Taylor equally "comfortable" on Johnson's Island in Lake Erie.[28] However, John B. Taylor's letters at the South Caroliniana Library reveal this largess did him little good, if any. His parents supplied Hetsler with bacon, flour, potatoes, and a turkey, while shipping northward similar foodstuffs, plus pepper vinegar, dried beans, okra, ginger cakes, and tobacco. Meanwhile, even if these goodies arrived at their destination, which is most unlikely, the Honorable T. C. Le Blond (a member of Congress from 1863 to 1867 and perhaps a relative of Hetsler) was supposed to be taking care of Taylor.[29] But by January 1865, this young man, still unaware of the Hetsler plan, was trying to set up a similar scheme with the aid of J. B. Lippincott of Philadelphia, who was a friend of a fellow prisoner. On 10 February, finally told about Hetsler, he informed his mother that such an arrangement required written permission from the prison commandant, at the same time conceding he had heard nothing from Hetsler, his family, Le Blond, or Lippincott...and apparently he never did.

Captain Hetsler was not the only one who used advertising to bridge the North-South gap created by war. The *Mercury* (13 April 1864) said copies of the *New York Daily News* received by the last flag of truce contained several "personals" from northern friends, two of them directed to Charleston residents. The editor reminded readers that "the latest Northern papers (Baltimore, Philadelphia, New York) [are] received at the Confederate Reading Room by every flag of truce."

Yet anyone who consulted those files could find it a shattering experience. The battle reports were fully as biased as those published in the Confederacy and often equally untrue, but the size and cost of northern newspapers hardly could have gone unnoticed. In 1863 both Charleston dailies were issuing a single sheet (six columns on each side) that cost $10 for six months or $5 for the country (tri-weekly) edition, *in advance*. By June 1864 prices had risen to $15 and $8 respectively. In those years, Manhattan residents were buying the *Herald* and *Times* for three cents on week days and four cents on Sunday. Each paper was producing eight to twelve pages every day (forty-eight to seventy-two columns) crammed with shipping and entertainment news, gossip, and help wanted ads.

The *Tribune*, equally voluminous, although it had no Sunday edition, also cost three cents a day...or $8 per year...and offered semi-weekly ($3) and weekly ($2) rates, plus "specials" to clubs and organizations eager to subscribe.[30] What this means is, Charlestonians were getting twelve columns of news and ads for ten cents or more a day, while residents of New York City got four to six times as much for three or four cents.

As a rule, Yankee papers were available in South Carolina within two weeks of publication, sometimes sooner. And as fighting continued, those who read them undoubtedly were impressed by their many pages and the ads for amusements, summer resorts, machinery, and investments, not what was said about the campaigns since they were certain much of it was false. Nevertheless, the effect upon those beset by shortages, speculation, extortion, battle fatigue, and worry should not be underestimated.

But for every South Carolinian who read northern newspapers or resorted to advertising to maintain contact with friends and relatives, hundreds simply wrote letters. If their words went through the Union blockade to Nassau and thence to the North, they could say whatever came to mind. Correspondence sent by flag of truce, however, had to conform to strict rules. It could consist of only one page with discussion limited to domestic matters. The writer had to sign his or her full name and enclose five cents if the message was to go via Fortress Monroe or Richmond, ten cents if some other port of entry was contemplated.[31]

There were a few Northerners who were not satisfied with mere letters and came through the lines to see loved ones, many of them held in prison compounds. Early in 1863, when three hundred Yankee women passed through Columbia on their way to visit kinfolk in the Deep South, the *Yorkville Enquirer* (21 January) questioned the wisdom of granting such passes. These individuals could cause trouble and should be closely watched.

The *Courier* (21 January), equally distressed, though for slightly different reasons, called upon the authorities to scrutinize such visitors with great care.

> We have evidence, amounting to reasonable proof, that some females, who never had husbands and never expect husbands, came South under pretext of visiting their husbands.
>
> Well known Southern ladies, who gave the best testimonials of their relationship, and the occasion of their visit through the lines, were rigidly and rudely searched by the Yankee menials, and in some cases were deprived of little baskets of medicine and refreshments intended for the children with them. In contrast with this, some of

POW HUMOR

On 22 September 1862, while a prisoner at Columbia, Frank Bennett, an officer in the Pennsylvania Volunteers, wrote these words in his diary, now in the Special Collections Library at Duke University.

> Out at elbows
> Out at toes,
> Out of money
> Out of clothes,
> Out of friends
> In midst of foes,
> What a cata
> logue of woes.

the applicants for passage were allowed to pass without examination.

The conduct and character of some of the passengers in female apparel were unblushingly disgusting, and it is with regret we learn that some of the officers on our side were acquainted with the character of some of those creatures who abused the flag of truce, and annoyed and insulted its honest and honorable subjects.

One Southerner living in the North who gave serious thought to coming through the lines but eventually did not was Caroline Petigru Carson, the lady who, late in the war, corresponded with Sherman. The problem was James Carson, her youngest son, who was seventeen years old in 1862. In September of that year she ordered him to join her in New York before he was conscripted, even vowing to sell her diamonds if necessary to pay for his passage. "Your duty is not to your state," she wrote on 21 October, "which has ruined all your prospects, together with the prosperity of the whole country."[32]

Despite these pleas, James enrolled at the University of North Carolina instead; and, following the death of his famous grandfather in March 1863, Caroline became even more concerned and secured a pass entitling she and a maid to travel via Newbern to Chapel Hill, using U.S. Army facilities wherever possible. However, illness and military action thwarted these plans; and, in August, in defiance of his mother's wishes, James (5'9") enlisted in a signal corps unit of the Confederate Army.

Caroline then turned her attention to another son, twenty-year-old William, who had been living in Germany for five years. Soon he was in Manhattan with his mother, much to the distress of his younger brother. What followed was an increasingly brisk exchange of views between the two boys. On 20 March 1864, while James thought his brother still in Europe, he wrote concerning military life on James Island. The fishing and food were good and he and his signal corps crew took turns being "boss dog of the shanty." "Charleston," he added, "is a dam mean place[,] dull as the devil[.] I'd ten times rather be here than there tho it is very sickly here in the summer."[33] But a short time later he learned that William was in New York City, and his tone shifted dramatically.

> ...I can't believe it possible that you have gone there for any other reason than to tell mamma good bye. If you intend to remain this is the last of my writing you shall ever see. After expressing yourself so strongly in your last letter, what excuse have you for so suddenly changing? To put it on the plea of filial affection is out of the question [—] you are old enough to tell black from white under all circumstances.[34]

A month later, on 17 May, William replied with equal force. Over the past few years, he retorted, letters to various friends and relatives in Charleston went unanswered. No one responded when he sought employment there, nor had he been able to get any information whatsoever concerning their grandfather's estate. Since he was a minor when ordered to New York, he had no choice but to obey...also, he then was without funds and soon after arriving became ill. Following recovery from an eye infection, William emphasized he was in debt and had to go to work ("I hope this confession does not shock your nerves"). The salary was modest, but at least he could support himself. He was treated well, rarely discussed politics, and yet did not conceal his opinions. William conceded he was drawn to the South by duty and family ties, but there were other matters to be considered.

> Even should I come to Charleston, what good can I effect, all the good places are taken and I should get perhaps *worse than nothing* for my pains; you know the people's opinion in regard to Mamma, if I should have the good fortune to distinguish myself, I would always remain the son of one whom they are pleased to call 'traitor'; that is

most probably the cause of the cold looks that you complain of, I have no desire to lick the hands of the grandees,
any more that I intend to submit to the tone of dictation
assumed in the letters I have had the advantage of receiving from the South, and beg you to understand once
and for all, that this blustering and threatening of confis-
cation is of no effect on me. I would rather lose twice the
amount than surrender my liberty of thought and action
into the keeping of ranting women who fancy themselves
Spartans (I dare say they are) and wily politicians whom
[,] however, the nation is bound in *self defence* for the
present to support. I left this continent a mere child, but
a citizen of the U.S., I return and find one section trying
to cut the other's throat, and vice versa. I do not clearly
understand the rights and wrongs of this quarrel (and
there are thousands in the same predicament, I fancy). I
only know that I am cut off from my resources, and that
those who are so loud in preaching to me about 'duty,'
&c. &c. are the very ones who have troubled *themselves*
the least about me heretofore, and the only favor I ask of
them is not commence now by troubling me. I might
have starved ere this, for all they have done for me....
You intimate that our relations care very little for you, so
busy they are providing for their own children, and feath-
ering their nests generally; why should I then go out of
my way to be shot for their benefit?[35]

Despite threats and harsh words, this correspondence did not cease,
although James continued to insist his brother should be in South Carolina, not New York City; and, as the war was ending, they were bickering
over a "calendar face" clock their mother wanted. On 20 April 1865,
William told his grandmother, "Jim seems to have fallen into the common Southern error of considering that a claim constitutes a title; the
absurdity of which proposition is self evident.... We shall expect the
clock by return of the Steamer."

A few weeks later, as James, now a lieutenant in the South Carolina
Cavalry, was about to be paroled near Greensboro, North Carolina, his
mother urged him to come to New York. However, if he chose to go to
South Carolina instead, she suggested he check on property held there,
especially family silver, paintings, and the controversial clock.[36] Finally,

in August 1865, after a lengthy sojourn in the Charleston area, James went north to join his mother and brother, perhaps accompanied by a clock.

Not every South Carolina family experienced turmoil such as this, nor were many sons (North or South) the subject of letters written by General William Tecumseh Sherman to their mothers. Nevertheless, the Petigru-Carson saga reveals how very complicated life can become amid civil strife.

Yet another bizarre twist was the organization of foreign legions or battalions during the final months of 1864. A desperate, last-ditch measure similar to turning slaves into soldiers, this scheme was based upon the questionable assumption that foreigners held in Confederate POW camps had been enticed into the U.S. Army through fraud and deceit. These individuals, it was thought, would willingly exchange prison life for a uniform and a gun. Some two hundred and sixty of them held in the Florence (S.C.) compound reportedly volunteered to do so in September 1864.[37] This plan soon won the endorsement of General Lee, and by November two hundred Irishmen once held at that site were on their way to join Hood's army.

In this instance, Yankee officials presumably refused to accept these men in exchange because their enlistments had expired. In return, they swore vengeance and claimed scores of American-born POWs "whose time was out" were eager to join them. Officially, at least, Richmond rejected such overtures and told recruiters to accept only *native* sons of Ireland and France, at the same time cautioning them to make full use of Catholic clergy while carrying out this scheme.[38]

By December 1864, Columbia—much to the discomfort of most residents—was home to the First Foreign Battalion. Over one thousand strong, these recruits were contemptuously referred to as "galvanized Yankees" and blamed for any disorder, mayhem, or thievery that occurred. When someone broke into General Hampton's home, stole jewelry, and left insulting messages ("Hang Hampton," "Damn Hampton," "Rebel," "Cattle Stealer"), they were thought to be responsible.[39] Virginia Military Institute cadets sent south to train this rabble faced countless problems, and both Grace Elmore and Mary Chesnut experienced some of the results first-hand. "As I passed the galvanized Yankee camp today," Elmore wrote on 4 December 1864, "I saw one fellow riding a rail and another bucked and gagged. I hope they were Yankees and not poor foreigners. I wonder if our authorities dream these men will fight for us."[40] Two days later, Chesnut, who lived next door to the encampment, told of seeing three men manacled and others dressed in "barrel" shirts. A few days earlier, she disclosed that many fully expected "the wretches" to burn the town and march out to greet Sherman when he appeared.[41] And it is true that at least one recruit was shot as a deserter when discovered on his way to join the general.

Why, a citizen asked the editor of the *South Carolinian* on 28 December, were these men always in trouble, intruding on private property, begging, and associating with slaves? Whenever "two or more persons meet," this gentleman said, "complaint [about the legion] forms the staple of conversation." Forty-eight hours later the editor defended the "First Foreign" from charges of stealing and produced a letter from some members pledging to leave the city if a petition to that effect was circulated and approved. Petition or not, the First Foreign Battalion departed for new quarters in mid-January, much to the relief of many Columbia residents.[42]

Meanwhile, a quite different, much smaller, but equally ineffective "foreign legion" was taking shape in both Charleston and Columbia. According to the *Mercury*, resident aliens met at the French Coffee House on 11 January to consider how they could aid in the defense of the city, and about two weeks later Columbia's foreign community gathered at the Athenaeum to ponder similar matters.

On 8 February, with Sherman near Branchville, the *Courier* published a brief table showing the distance from that vital rail junction to Kingville, Florence, Columbia, Augusta, Charlotte, and Wilmington, as well as the mileage from Charleston to Florence and from Florence to Wilmington. This stark little list (which for some strange reason did not disclose the distance from Charleston to Branchville) was preceded by a verbose statement by Governor Magrath painting the enemy in the most dastardly terms and pleading for all-out defiance and "scorched earth."

> Remove your property from the reach of the enemy, carry what you can to a place of safety; then quickly rally and return to the field. What you cannot carry, destroy. Whatever you leave will be of use to your foe, what he will not need, that he will destroy. Indulge no sickly hope that you will be spared by submission; terror will but whet his revenge. Think not your property will be respected, and afterward recovered. No such feeling prompts him. You leave it but to support and sustain him; you save it but to help him in his course. Destroy what

A.G. Magrath (1817-1902).

you cannot remove. He will make your return to your homes over a charred and blackened road; prepare you the same road for him as he advances. Let him read everywhere and in everything, that in this State, from one portion of it to the other, there is but one purpose and fixed resolve—that purpose is to meet him at every point, fight him at every road; that resolve is to undergo all suffering, submit to every sacrifice, welcome any fate, sooner than subjection by his army, or submission to his terms.

Ten days later, both Charleston and Columbia experienced a night of flames, looting, and horror (which one could interpret as a form of "scorched earth"), and for most South Carolinians the struggle was over. On Tuesday, 20 February, the *Courier* was issued by the U.S. Army with this dateline: "Charleston, S.C. United States of America." For all practical purposes, after nearly four years of tears, sweat, exultation, prayer, and disappointment, the homefront was no more. True, in a sense it staggered on until Appomattox a few weeks later. Yet in essence this story ends with Sherman's northeasterly slash across South Carolina from Hardeeville to Cheraw. Ahead lay more turmoil and a decade of quasi-peace, but at least the campaigning ceased and construction of a new social and commercial order, fashioned from the rubble of the old, could commence.

The world that vanished was, at best, an unreal creation—as are all homefronts. With peace, most of the major components simply disappear. Such matters as a draft, dissent, shortages, and morale are no longer of any consequence, although they may leave behind residual animosities. In this instance, freedom granted to blacks is, of course, a development of awesome importance and, to a lesser degree, that experienced by some women (1861-1865) also is worthy of note.

In retrospect, most white South Carolinians reacted to the pressures of those years much as one might expect they would. They sought to assist those in uniform, made do with less, and usually did what any good citizen is supposed to do in a time of crisis. There undoubtedly were heroic figures in their midst, though far fewer than the "Lost Cause" myth would have one believe, and most probably achieved that elevated status on some battlefield in Virginia or Tennessee, not on their native soil. Homefronts by their very nature are unkind to heroes. There are far too many crosscurrents to be navigated, too many opportunities for individual action to be interpreted as selfish or self-serving. Able-bodied males not in uniform are viewed with suspicion, as well as enlisted men and officers who somehow are avoiding front-line duty. In addition, those who lead a people in an unsuccessful revolt always will be haunted by both their own decisions and the taunts of their detractors.

Unlike other parts of the young Confederacy, at the outset few on the South Carolina homefront actively opposed the war effort; but, as time passed, all too often *self* came before community, state, and nation. For the Rhett Butlers it was a chance to grow rich by running the blockade or dealing in goods in short supply, while some women in Charleston, Columbia, Chester, Anderson, and so on saw an opportunity to test new freedom and perhaps make a bit of money, too. Even those who at first scorned speculation, high-minded men such as Theodore Honour, sometimes succumbed to that which they vowed they abhorred. In fact, the word "Confederacy," suggesting a rather loose league or voluntary association of some sort, may have hampered "the cause" since it implicitly encouraged local autonomy at the expense of central authority, thus stimulating individual enterprise. As many have observed, states rights can become a self-destructive philosophy, making it difficult for national leaders to implement policy.

The reckless bravado displayed in 1860-1861 by South Carolina as a state and its people as individuals—be they civilians or soldiers— evokes admiration and pride, but that same warm exuberance can wreak havoc in wartime, as the "Tories" of the upland foothills clearly demonstrated. Unless such zeal is channeled into productive and cooperative pursuits, it is an invitation to chaos. As we know, Rhett and the *Mercury* were predicting doom in February 1861, long before the first shot was fired. Soon slaves and free blacks were facing editorial criticism for not "doing their part," and similar charges were reopening divisions between upcountry and low that had been momentarily forgotten amid the euphoria of secession. Typical are slurs cast late in the struggle by Colonel E. B. C. Cash of subsequent dueling fame. Writing to Governor Magrath from Society Hill in March 1865, Cash described difficulties he faced as he tried to organize a home defense force in eastern South Carolina: "The Districts of Chesterfield, Marlboro and much of Darlington are almost without horses, and I fear not much is to be expected from the people of the lower Districts who have heretofore manifested very little interest in the defence of the State."[43] Of course, those voicing such sentiments, be they editors, colonels, or housewives, speak with firm self-assurance that *they* are the true patriots.

In theory, homefront morale should have been strong throughout the state during much of the war, more so than in areas ravaged by armies and gunfire. South Carolinians had at last achieved what they had been seeking for several decades and were widely acknowledged as the people who led the South out of the "corrupt" federal Union. Although some coastal communities experienced enemy pressure first-hand, for three years inland South Carolina did not, and those living there enjoyed peace and security envied by many.

In addition, since this state proportionally was home to more slave artisans than any other region in the new nation, their labor, largely undisturbed, should have mitigated the effects of war. Yet only the most rabid secessionist would expect these folk to expend much energy to keep themselves in bondage. Such assistance, often given begrudgingly, coupled with the half-hearted attitude of some whites as the war dragged on, created subtle problems for South Carolina's leaders. They faced not disloyalty but malingering and a waning or absence of zeal. By the close of 1863, the commitment of *two-thirds* of the *total* population to "the cause" probably was either weak or non-existent. Factors such as these cast a pall over the homefront...as did concern for the safety of loved ones in uniform, rumors of slave insurrections, the haunting fear of enemy raids, and the reality of disturbing news from various beleaguered strongholds.

Homefront support was relatively strong until mid-1863 and the twin blows of Gettysburg and Vicksburg, from which it never fully recovered. The work of women's organizations faltered at about the same time due to material shortages and a tendency of male authority to exert control over relief programs. Some dedicated females turned their attention to local projects such as "Wayside" homes; others found they simply were too busy making a living, especially with menfolk away, to spend time doing volunteer work.

Village life frequently ground to a halt during these years, while urban centers such as Columbia became, by contrast, a mad whirl of frantic activity. Although much of this frenzy (officers dashing about, men marching, couriers on important errands) presumably was calculated to help win a war, it is far from clear that such things as raffles, bazaars, balls, fairs, and tableaux actually had much effect...other, perhaps, than permitting those taking part to have fun, forget the war for a bit, and display for all to see their personal brand of patriotism.

Regardless of community size, white teenagers, somewhat like blacks and an occasional white woman, often reveled in new-found independence and embraced premature adulthood as their fathers either donned uniforms or became immersed in homefront concerns. Some, such as the Arsenal Academy cadets who so troubled John B. Patrick, disdained discipline, played cards, got drunk, and all but abandoned their studies. In similar fashion, according to Emma Holmes, young ladies were spurning the advice of their elders and even "rouging."

Blacks, as noted earlier, enjoyed a unique status indeed. A mighty war was being waged in their behalf, either to set them free or keep them enslaved, yet pressures of the moment undoubtedly improved their day-to-day existence. Not that they were eating better or wearing finer clothing, although a very few were; but, with master away and local authorities concerned with more important matters than patrol duty and surveillance, the personal freedom of both slave and free increased. If they were tillers of the soil (and most of them were), the produce they raised gave them even more leverage in a time of shortage.

The real enemy on the South Carolina homefront was not the speculator, blockade runner, deserter, nay-sayer, uncooperative black, or even the rare individual who actually aided the invader in some small way but the fire-eater whose outrageous claims raised unreal expectations. Told there would be no bloodshed and no bullets ("the Union won't fight"), South Carolinians soon found their husbands, brothers, and sons wallowing in one and dodging the other. These shocks—coupled with the invasion of Port Royal and raids along other parts of the coast—cast doubt upon whatever predictions of success ensued, which, in effect, undermined any morale-building campaign. Even victory became suspect. What was the true cost, those on the homefront asked, and might the result be, not peace, but renewed enemy vigor and a more determined adversary?

Stir in depressing news from military operations in other states, the manpower draft with all of its inequities, impressment of slaves and foodstuffs, shortages of all kinds, and the strains these factors produced in individual households and one begins to see the outlines of a recipe for disaster. In time, more and more South Carolinians (William Wylie and Ann Morris Vanderhorst among them) began to believe that placing their faith in predictions of peaceable secession and no war was merely part of a far greater miscalculation: the act of secession itself. And, as Davis and other leaders seemed to abandon basic goals proclaimed at the outset, even advocating creation of a slave army, doubt and misgiving multiplied.

Enemy pressure certainly plays a role in this sad tale, but there really are no firm answers to many questions raised by the specter of the South Carolina homefront, 1861-1865. Although the Palmetto State provided the spark for rebellion, what happened there during those years is merely one chapter in a much larger story of epic proportions. Nevertheless, scattered evidence indicates the Confederate homefront as a whole deserves more attention. Battles are important, but so are events behind the lines…perhaps even more so since they conspire to swell or diminish the ranks of a fighting force. Even before the first clash at Manassas, a radical handful predicted doom, and soon other South Carolinians became convinced they were shouldering an unfair burden, grumbled about their personal role in this unfolding drama, and expressed fears concerning what blacks in their midst might do. Factors such as these quickly resuscitated old animosities long evident in various sectors of the state and provided rationale for avoiding the battlefield, even if this meant outright desertion, which soon lost much of its sting.

This South Carolina story raises serious doubts concerning two themes much trumpeted by 20th Century chroniclers of the Civil War—a struggle, they claim, with an almost exclusive Virginia focus and one that, with a bit of luck, the Confederacy could have won at some point in 1863 and 1864. Yes, South Carolinians were interested in the Virginia front, but their hopes and fears followed loved ones to other regions as well, among them, Mississippi, Alabama, Tennessee, Georgia, and, of course, coastal outposts in their own lowcountry. In addition, whatever Grant and Lee were doing 1864-1865 faced stiff competition from the maneuvers of General Sherman, who was much closer to their homes.

As for some "long-shot" victory, giving the underdog a fighting chance is good story-telling since it arouses and maintains reader interest, but it may not be sound scholarship. From the homefront perspective, after mid-1863 all one can sense is dogged determination to fight on without any real hope of eventual success, coupled with resignation, boredom and perhaps a yearning for peace at almost any price. Mrs. Robert Smith (p. 29) certainly did not appreciate Lee's Gettysburg campaign, observing he seemed to have "marched up the hill & then marched down again" and, in the process, "betrayed our weakness to our enemies." David Ballenger, who was with Lee, told his wife of hordes of deserters (p. 30), who, believing Vicksburg had fallen, refused to follow Lee into Pennsylvania. And, had the South prevailed at Gettysburg, there is the distinct possibility the cost would have been too great or merely goaded the North into rekindling its war effort...fears similar to those expressed by David Golightly Harris (p. 210) and J. C. Hicklin (p. 105).

Could local homefront activity have been more effective...organized more efficiently by non-combatant South Carolinians of all ages? Nearly a century and a half later, we probably would say yes. But then we would be profiting from hindsight and experience gained in subsequent wars. Given the reality of the moment, the citizens of Charleston, Columbia, Greenville, and scores of towns, villages, hamlets, farms, and plantations were guilty of but one sin: wanton disregard for hard, cold facts. This very serious shortcoming, one that can prove fatal in wartime, stirred false hope and, in turn, incited a people to attempt to do too much with too little.

NOTES

[1]According to the *Courier* (3 November 1862), new lots had been laid out near the Summerville depot, and in March 1864 the Elliotts were discussing sale of a plantation near Port Royal to Charleston investors who planned to develop a new town (Elliott-Gonzales Papers). Anti-Jewish sentiment, as noted on page 263, is readily apparent in the writing of Emma Holmes.

[2]Mary Elizabeth Massey, *Refugee Life in the Confederacy* (Baton Rouge, 1964), pp. 81-83.

[3]Quoted in the *Charleston Mercury*, 14 April 1862.

[4]*Charleston Courier*, 6 December 1862.

[5]Ibid., 17 September 1863.

[6]Ibid., 9 December 1864.

[7]Collins, *Memories of the Southern States*, p. 17. This English-born raconteur also noted that, wherever slaves lived, they were reluctant to kill cats, believing it improper to do so. She, on the other hand, thought the Yankees should forget about abolition and exterminate "millions" of useless cats and dogs found throughout the South (p. 62).

[8]"Middleton Correspondence," *South Carolina Historical Magazine* (April 1962), pp. 65-66.

[9]Marszalek, *Diary of Miss Emma Holmes*, p. 162. She complained in August 1862 that Jews were taking over many Charleston shops (p. 192) and in November that they had bought up all of the silver suitable for wedding gifts (p. 209). Similar views are found in other collections. Mrs. J.T. Fouche of Ninety Six told her husband in September 1861 that too many Jews were moving into the area, and he should stop them from doing so (Fouche Family Papers). And in June 1862, Langdon Cheves commented in a general way about the prevalence of Jewish merchants in both Charleston and Savannah (Langdon Cheves West Papers).

[10]Ibid., p. 197.

[11]Ibid., pp. 219-20.

[12]Elliott to Isabella Elliott Barnwell, 27 September 1863, Elliott Family Papers. He indicates in other letters that there were eighteen whites in the house, plus servants and their offspring.

[13]Mrs. Smyth [sic] to her son, ? October 1863, Smythe Letters. On 15 October she noted that a box sent to him, clearly labeled, had been returned. The railroad agent at Gourdin's, she observed, was "not blessed, I suppose, with a college education."

[14]Massey, *Refugee Life in the Confederacy*, p. 280.

[15]Mary Milling to James S. Milling, 8 August 1865, James S. Milling Papers. Milling moved to Louisiana in 1859, spent most of the war there, and his family did not join him until 1866.

[16]Mary Dawkins to Jane McLure, 14 and 21 February 1865, McLure Family Papers.

[17]J. W. Norris to Hagood, 9 April 1863, Hagood Papers.

[18]J. W. Sanders to Hagood, 7 June 1864, Hagood Papers. In another letter to Hagood (21 November), Sanders reveals he is in Virginia, unhappy, and complaining about a medical board that accepted "myself [,] Pick Cole and many other disabled men and put upon 'light duty' such men as Alex Bryce and Thos Adair—little weakly fellows—Alex's Barrels of whiskey done up the business for them—"

[19]William Merrell to Hagood, 16 July 1864, Hagood Papers.

[20]Gist to Renwick, 13 April 1862; G. L. Sims to Renwick, 15 April 1862, Renwick Papers.

[21]See James Reid Pringle Papers, Special Collections Library, Duke University.

[22]Mackintosh, *"Dear Martha....,"* p. 165.

[23]Reports of Soldiers Boards of Relief, South Carolina Department of Archives and History. Actually, Hagood almost became a member of this local agency as well. On 15 February 1863, a friend named Grimshaw commented, "Did we not escape well from Soldiers Board of Relief? I would not be on [it] for any thing" (Hagood Papers).

[24]John Hammond Moore (ed.), *The Juhl Letters to the "Charleston Courier": A View of the South, 1865-1871* (Athens, 1974), p. 9.

[25]*Charleston Courier*, 28 January 1862. Masonic ties are a common theme in Civil War lore. On 15 February 1865, fearing what Sherman's troops might do, Eliza Pelot of Laurensville wrote to a friend named Sally, "I hope when the emergency comes you will be able to remember the masonic sign & you probably in that way [will] receive protection" (Lala Pelot Papers).

[26]*War of the Rebellion*, Second Series, VI, pp. 296, 305.

[27]Ibid., Second Series, VII, pp. 611-12. A few weeks later, in a letter to President Davis, Columbia's mayor suggested that sutler service to POWs be abolished since citizens, Confederate soldiers, and Confederates held as POWs in the North did not enjoy similar advantages.

[28]Woodward, *Mary Chesnut's Civil War*, p. 667.

[29]Chesnut says the would-be benefactor in Ohio was Hetsler's brother, but the Taylor letters indicate Le Blond was the Northerner involved in this matter.

[30]The *New York Times* also had a reduced-rate plan for clubs and clergymen.

[31]*Charleston Mercury*, 9 November 1863. Other sources indicate the envelope was to be left open but enclosed in yet another containing both it and the money.

[32]Vanderhorst Family Papers, South Carolina Historical Society. Note: Carson material is filed separately in this large collection.

[33]Ibid.

[34]Ibid., 13 April 1864.

[35]Ibid. William closed with these words: "I do not sign my name to this letter, as in case the 'Yanks' get hold of it, I may get into trouble.... Compliments to all my friends, tell them I am with them in spirit, as far as defending their liberties goes, and shall come unless my own kith & kin fail me. Pay your money & take your choice, two months will determine whether I am to be 'reb' or 'Yank' [—] do your duty and all will be well. Love to Adele and [a] kiss to all the pretty girls you can get at, 'only that and nothing more,' mind!"

[36]Ibid., 8 May 1865.

[37]*War of the Rebellion*, Fourth Series, III, p. 694.

[38]*Tri-Weekly South Carolinian*, 12 November 1864. This report concerning Florence, quoted from the *Augusta Chronicle*, says a Catholic priest administered the Confederate oath of allegiance to these former prisoners.

[39]Woodward, *Mary Chesnut's Civil War*, p. 678.

[40]Elmore diary.

[41]Woodward, *Mary Chesnut's Civil War*, pp. 679, 686.

[42]1t is unclear whether these men ever fought for the Confederacy during the closing months of the war.

[43]E. B. C. Cash to A. G. Magrath, 31 March 1865, Magrath Papers, Southern Historical Collection, University of North Carolina.

SOURCES

This study is based largely upon printed materials and manuscripts found in six depositories: Library of Congress, Washington, D.C.; Southern Historical Collection, University of North Carolina, Chapel Hill, N. C.; Rare Book, Manuscript, and Special Collections Library, Duke University, Durham, N. C.; South Carolina Historical Society, Charleston, S. C.; and the South Caroliniana Library, University of South Carolina, and South Carolina Department of Archives and History, both in Columbia, S.C. I would like to thank each for permission to quote from its holdings. In addition, I would like to thank Robert Harley Mackintosh, Jr., for permission to quote from *"Dear Martha...," The Confederate War Letters of a South Carolina Soldier, Alexander Faulkner Fewell* and Orville Vernon Burton for access to his unpublished research on the Civil War homefront in Edgefield District. I also am indebted to still others for assistance and guidance, among them, Alex Moore, John R. Oldfield, Thomas Price, Robert Valentine, and Steve West, who made helpful comments concerning various chapters...and especially to publisher Robin Sumner Asbury and her assistant, Christel Weaver, for careful and conscientious attention to detail.

BOOKS AND ARTICLES

Abbott, A. O. *Prison Life in the South.* New York, 1865.

Acts of the General Assembly of the State of South Carolina. Columbia, 1861-66.

Ambrose, Stephen E. "Yeomen Discontent in the Confederacy." *Civil War History* (September 1962): 259-68.

Baker, Gary R. *Cadets in Gray.* Columbia, 1989.

Bennett, C. A. "Roswell Sabine Ripley: 'Charleston's Gallant Defender.'" *South Carolina Historical Magazine* (July 1994): 225-42.

Beringer, Richard E., *et al. The Elements of Confederate Defeat: Nationalism, War Aims, and Religion.* Athens and London, 1988.

——————————————. *Why the South Lost the Civil War.* Athens and London, 1986.

Burton, E. Milby. *The Siege of Charleston, 1861-1865.* Columbia, 1970.

Calhoun, Richard J., ed. *Witness to Sorrow: The Antebellum Autobiography of William J. Grayson.* Columbia, 1990.

Carroll, Sarah Porter, ed. *Lifeline to Home for John William McLure, CSA—Union County, S. C.* Greenville, 1990.

Catton, Bruce. *The Centennial History of the Civil War.* 3 vols. New York, 1961-65.

Cauthen, Charles E., ed. *Journals of the South Carolina Executive Councils of 1861 and 1862.* Columbia, 1956.

Cauthen, Charles E. *South Carolina Goes to War, 1860-1865.* Chapel Hill, 1950.

Channing, Steven A. *Crisis of Fear: Secession in South Carolina.* New York, 1970.

Childs, Arney Robinson. *The Private Journal of Henry William Ravenel, 1859-1887.* Columbia, 1947.

Clinton, Catherine, and Nina Silber, eds. *Divided Houses: Gender and the Civil War.* New York and Oxford, 1992. Part IV (pp. 167-242) explores "Southern Homefront." No index.

Collins, Elizabeth. *Memories of the Southern States.* Taunton, 1865.

Connelly, Thomas L. *The Marble Man: Robert E. Lee and His Image in American Society.* Baton Rouge, 1977.

Coulter, E. Merton. *The Confederate States of America, 1861-1865.* Baton Rouge, 1950.

——————————. *Travels in the Confederacy: A Bibliography.* Norman, Okla., 1948.

Donald, David, *et al. Why the North Won the Civil War.* Baton Rouge, 1960.

Dowdey, Clifford, ed. *The Wartime Papers of R. E. Lee.* Boston, 1961.

Drake, J. Madison. *Fast and Loose in Dixie.* New York, 1880.

Dyer, Frederick H. *A Compendium of the War of the Rebellion.* 3 vols. New York and London, 1959.

Easterby, J. H. *The South Carolina Rice Plantation.* Chicago, 1945.

Escott, Paul D. *After Secession: Jefferson Davis and the Failure of Confederate Nationalism.* Baton Rouge and London, 1978.

——————————. "'The Cry of the Sufferers': The Problem of Welfare in the Confederacy." *Civil War History* (September 1977): 228-40.

Famous Adventures and Prison Escapes of the Civil War. New York, 1898.

Faust, Drew Gilpin. *The Creation of Confederate Nationalism.* Baton Rouge and London, 1988.

Fleharty, S. F. *Our Regiment: A History of the 102d Illinois Infantry Volunteers....* Chicago, 1865.

Foote, Shelby. *The Civil War: A Narrative.* 3 vols. New York, 1958-74.

Freemantle, A. J. L. *Three Months in the Southern States: April-June 1863.* New York, 1864.

Freeman, Douglas Southall. *R.E. Lee, a Biography.* 4 vols. New York, 1934-35.

Glazier, Willard W. *The Capture, the Prison Pen, and the Escape.* New York, 1868.

Graydon, Nell S., ed. "Journal of Arthur Brailsford Wescoat, 1863, 1864." *South Carolina Historical Magazine* (April 1954): 73-102.

Grayson, William J. *James Louis Petigru: A Biographical Sketch.* New York, 1866.

Gregorie, Anne King. "John Witherspoon Ervin." *South Carolina Historical Magazine* (July 1945): 166-70.

Holleman, Joseph T. "The Carson Through the Lines and Blockade Run Correspondence." *Confederate Philatelist* (July-October 1981): 95-103, 131-38.

Hollis, Daniel Walker. *University of South Carolina.* 2 vols. Columbia, 1951, 1956.

Holmes, Charlotte, ed. *The Burckmeyer Letters. March 1863-June 1865.* Columbia, 1926.

Hölmstrom, Kirsten Gram. *Monodrama, Attitudes, Tableaux Vivants.* Stockholm, 1967.

Hudson, Leonne M. "A Confederate Victory at Grahamville: Fighting at Honey Hill." *South Carolina Historical Magazine* (January 1993): 19-33.

Isham, Asa B., *et al. Prisoners of War and Military Prisons.* Cincinnati, 1890.

Jervey, Susan R., and Charlotte St. J. Ravenel. *Two Diaries from the Middle St. John's Berkeley, South Carolina, February-May, 1865.* Charleston ? 1921.

Johnson, Hannibal A. *The Sword of Honor.* Worcester, Mass., 1906.

Johnson, Michael P., and James L. Roark. *Black Masters: A Free Family of Color in the Old South.* New York and London, 1984.

Johnson, Michael P., and James L. Roark, eds. *No Chariot Let Down: Charleston's Free People of Color on the Eve of the Civil War.* Chapel Hill and London, 1984.

Kellogg, John Azor. *Capture and Escape: A Narrative of Army and Prison Life.* Madison, 1908.

Kibler, Lillian Adele. *Benjamin F. Perry: South Carolina Unionist.* Durham, 1946.

Krick, Robert K. "Maxcy Gregg: Political Extremist and Confederate General." *Civil War History* (December 1973): 3-23.

Lander, Ernest M., Jr., and Charles M. McGee, Jr., eds. *A Rebel Came Home: The Diary and Letters of Floride Clemson, 1863-1866.* Columbia, 1989.

Leland, Isabella Middleton, ed. "Middleton Correspondence, 1861-1865." *South Carolina Historical Magazine* (January 1962-April 1964): published in ten parts.

Link Arthur S., and Rembert W. Patrick. *Writing Southern History.* Baton Rouge, 1965.

Lipscomb, Terry W., and Theresa Jacobs. "The Magistrates and Freeholders Court." *South Carolina Historical Magazine* (January 1976): 62-65.

Long, E. B. *The Civil War Day by Day.* New York, 1971.

Lonn, Ella. *Salt as a Factor in the Confederacy.* University, Ala., 1965.

Lucas, Marion Brunson. *Sherman and the Burning of Columbia.* College Station, Texas, 1976.

Mackintosh, Robert Harley, Jr., ed. *"Dear Martha...," The Confederate War Letters of a South Carolina Soldier, Alexander Faulkner Fewell.* Columbia, 1976.

McArthur, Judith N., and Orville Vernon Burton. *An Officer and a Gentleman: A Military and Social History of James B. Griffin's Civil War.* New York and Oxford, 1996.

McDaniel, Ruth Barr, compiler. *Confederate War Correspondence of James Michael Barr and Rebecca Ann Dowling Barr.* Taylors, S. C., 1963.

McMillan, Malcolm C. *The Disintegration of a Confederate State: Three Governors and Alabama's Home Front, 1861-1865.* Macon, 1986.

Malet, William Wyndham. *An Errand to the South in the Summer of 1862.* London, 1863.

Marszalek, John F., ed. *The Diary of Miss Emma Holmes.* Baton Rouge and London, 1979.

Massey, Mary Elizabeth. *Ersatz in the Confederacy.* Columbia, 1952.

——————————. *Refugee Life in the Confederacy.* Baton Rouge, 1964.

May, John Amasa, and Joan Reynolds Faunt. *South Carolina Secedes.* Columbia, 1960.

Moore, Albert Burton. *Conscription and Conflict in the Confederacy.* New York,

1924.

Moore, John Hammond. *Columbia & Richland County: A South Carolina Community, 1740-1990.* Columbia, 1993.

————————. "Getting Uncle Sam's Dollars: South Carolinians and the Southern Claims Commission." *South Carolina Historical Magazine* (July 1981): 248-62.

Moore, John Hammond, ed. *The Juhl Letters to the "Charleston Courier": A View of the South, 1865-1871.* Athens, 1974.

Newsome, Edmund. *Experiences in the War of the Great Rebellion.* Carbondale, Ill., 1879.

Oswley, Frank L. "Defeatism in the Confederacy." *North Carolina Historical Review* (July 1926): 446-58.

Paludan, Phillip Shaw. *"The People's Contest": The Union and the Civil War, 1861-1865.* New York, 1988.

Patton, James Welch. "The Work of Soldiers' Aid Societies in South Carolina During the Civil War." *Proceedings,* South Carolina Historical Association (1937): 3-12.

Puryear, Elmer L. "The Confederate Diary of William John Grayson." *South Carolina Historical Magazine* (July-October 1962): 137-49, 214-26.

Quint, Alonzo H. *The Record of the Second Massachusetts Infantry 1861-65.* Boston, 1867.

Rable, George C. *Civil Wars: Women and the Crisis of Southern Nationalism.* Urbanna and Chicago, 1989.

Racine, Philip N., ed. "Emily Lyles Harris: A Piedmont Farmer During the Civil War." *South Atlantic Quarterly* (Autumn 1980): 386-97.

————————. *Piedmont Farmer: The Journals of David Golightly Harris, 1855-1870.* Knoxville, 1990.

Report of the Chief of the Department of the Military of South Carolina. Columbia, 1862.

Reports and Resolutions of the General Assembly of the State of South Carolina. Columbia, 1860-65.

Robertson, Ben. *Red Hills and Cotton.* Columbia, 1960.

Robinson, William M. *Justice in Grey; a History of the Judicial System of the Confederate States of America.* New York, 1941.

Rogers, George C., Jr. *The History of Georgetown County, South Carolina.* Columbia, 1970.

Rosengarten, Dale, *et al. Between the Tracks: Charleston's East Side During the Nineteenth Century.* Charleston, 1987.

Russell, William Howard. *My Diary North and South.* 2 vols. London, 1863.

Salley, A. S., Jr. *South Carolina Troops in Confederate Service.* 3 vols. Columbia, 1913-30.

Scott, Edwin J. *Random Recollections of a Long Life.* Columbia, 1884.

Sherwood, M. E. W. "Some Society Tableaux." *Cosmopolitan* (January 1898): 235-46.

Simpson, Lewis P. *Mind and the American Civil War: A Meditation on Lost Causes.* Baton Rouge and London, 1989.

Smith, Daniel E. Huger, Alice R. Huger Smith, and Arney R. Childs, eds. *Mason Smith Family Letters, 1860-1868.* Columbia, 1950.

Smith, George Winston, and Charles Judah, eds. *Life in the North During the Civil War; a Source History.* Albuquerque, 1966.

Statutes at Large of South Carolina. XII (1861-66). Columbia, 1875.

Sullivan, P. O. "A Chapter on Tableaux." *Scribner's* (November 1880): 91-103.

Sutherland, H. L. "Arms Manufacturing in Greenville County." *Proceedings and Papers of the Greenville Historical Society* (1971): 46-60.

Takaki, Ronald. "The Movement to Open the African Slave Trade in South Carolina." *South Carolina Historical Magazine* (January 1965): 38-54.

Tatum, Georgia Lee. *Disloyalty in the Confederacy.* Chapel Hill, 1934.

Taylor, Mrs. Thomas, *et al*, eds. *South Carolina Women in the Confederacy.* 2 vols. Columbia, 1903, 1907.

Thomas, Emory. *The Confederacy as a Revolutionary Experience.* Edgewood Cliffs, N. J., 1971.

——————. *The Confederate Nation, 1861-1865.* New York, 1979.

Towles, Louis P., ed. *A World Turned Upside Down: The Palmers of Santee, 1818-1881.* Columbia, 1996.

Vinovskis, Maris A. "Have Social Historians Lost the Civil War? Some Preliminary Demographic Speculations." *Journal of American History* (June 1989): 34-58.

Wallace, David Duncan. *The History of South Carolina.* 4 vols. New York, 1934.

Walther, Eric H. *The Fire-Eaters.* Baton Rouge and London, 1992.

Wannamaker, J. Skottowe, compiler. *The Wannamakers, Salley, Mackay, and Bellinger Families. ...* Charleston, 1937.

War of the Rebellion: a Compilation of the Official Records of the Union and Confederate Armies. 130 vols. Washington, 1880-1901.

Weiner, Marli F., ed. *A Heritage of Woe: The Civil War Diary of Grace Brown Elmore, 1861-1868.* Athens, 1997.

White, Laura A. *Robert Barnwell Rhett: Father of Secession.* Gloucester, Mass., 1965.

Wierenga, Theron. *Official Documents of the Post Office Department of the Confederate States of America.* 2 vols. Holland, Mich., 1979.

Wiley, Bell Irvin. *The Plain People of the Confederacy.* Gloucester, Mass., 1971.

——————. *The Road to Appomattox.* Memphis, 1956.

Wills, Charles W. *Army Life of an Illinois Soldier.* Washington, 1906.

Woodward, C. Vann. *Mary Chesnut's Civil War.* New Haven and London, 1981.

Yearns, Wilfred Buck. *The Confederate Congress.* Athens, 1960.

Zornow, William Frank. "State Aid for Indigent Families of South Carolina Soldiers, 1861-1865." *South Carolina Historical Magazine* (April 1956): 82-87.

NEWSPAPERS, 1860-1865

Abbeville Press

Augusta Chronicle & Sentinel

Augusta Daily Constitutionalist

Camden Journal, also issued as *Camden Daily Journal, Camden Weekly Journal, Weekly Journal*, and *Tri-Weekly Journal.*

Carolina Spartan (Spartanburg)

Charleston Daily Courier

Charleston Mercury

Confederate Baptist (Columbia)

Daily South Carolinian (Columbia)

Daily Southern Guardian (Columbia), also issued as the *Daily Guardian.*

Edgefield Advertiser

Horry Dispatch (Conway)

Keowee Courier (Pickens)

Lancaster Ledger

Marion Star

New York Daily Tribune

New York Herald

New York Times

Savannah Republican

Southern Enterprise (Greenville)

Sumter Watchman

Tri-Weekly South Carolinian (Columbia)

Tri-Weekly Southern Guardian (Columbia)

Tri-Weekly Watchman (Sumter)

Weekly Southern Guardian (Columbia)

Yorkville Enquirer

PERSONAL PAPERS AND MANUSCRIPTS

For information concerning South Carolina depositories, consult these publications:

David Moltke-Hansen and Sally Doscher. *South Carolina Historical Society Manu-script Guide*. Charleston, 1979.
Allen H. Stokes, Jr. *A Guide to the Manuscript Collection of the South Caroliniana Library*. Columbia, 1982.
A Guide to Local Records in the South Carolina Archives. Columbia, 1988.
Patrick J. McCawley, ed. *Guide to Civil War Records: A Guide to the Records in the South Carolina Department of Archives and History*. Columbia, 1994.

꘎꘎

South Carolina Historical Society: Allston-Pringle-Hill Families, Barbot Family, Catherine O. Barnwell, Thomas Burden, Caroline Petigru Carson, Cheves Family, Cheves-Middleton Families, Annie DeVeaux, Sophia Lovell Cheves Haskell, Charles Peery Collection, Thomas P. Ravenel, Augustine Thomas Smythe, Vanderhorst Family, Langdon Cheves West.

South Caroliniana Library: Aiken Family, Thomas Aiton, William C. Anderson, Anony-mous (slave "Eliza" to mistress), John Durant Ashmore, Lewis Malone Ayer, David Ballenger, J.T. Bleckley, Sylvester Bleckley, Milledge Luke Bonham, Bratton Family, Thomas Burden, Valentine B. Chamberlain, Bettie J. Clarke, Crawford Family, Cunningham Family, Anna Donaldson, Duncan-Kinard-Sanders-Tucker Families, Elliott Family, Grace Elmore, Claudius L. Fike, Gustavus Augustus Follin (Sr. and Jr.), Fouche Family, Gaston-Strait-Wylie-Baskin Families, Greenville Ladies Asso-ciation (Minutes of), James Earle Hagood, E. C. Henderson, Heyward Family, Emma Holmes, Theodore Honour, Mary Hort, John Jenkins, Micah Jenkins, Iredell Jones, Kinkaid-Anderson Family, Lawton-Willingham Family, Joseph LeConte, W. B. Long, McCrady Family, Allan Macfarland, MacKenzie Family, Catherine Louisa McLaurin, C. G. Memminger, Johnson N. Mundy, Neves Family, J. T. and W. J. Nobles, S. G. Owen, Palmer Family, John B. Patrick, Benjamin F. Perry, Francis W. Pickens, Henry Hunter Raymond, John Smythe Richardson, Ridgeway Relief Association, Sams Family, Sarah Jane Sams, John Rooker Shurley, James F. Sloan, William Mason Smith Family, Mary Amarinthia Snowden, Sarah Barnwell Stoney, John Forsythe Talbert, John B. Taylor, Wayside Hospital (Columbia), Moultrie Reid Wilson, Young Ladies Hospital Association (Columbia).

South Carolina Department of Archives and History:
Governors' Papers—Francis W. Pickens, Milledge L. Bonham, Andrew G. Magrath.
General Assembly—petitions to that body, committee reports, unindexed "Green" files.

State Auditor's Office—data on Greenville arms factory, lead mines, recruiting, Soldiers Boards of Relief, commissions on removal of Negroes and property, claims for lost property and slaves lost in public service, salt and saltpetre production, bonds and petitions to distill or transport liquor.

Adjutant and Inspector General's Office—letters sent, petitions for exemption from military service, overseer exemptions, draft substitutes, Wayside Hospital (Charleston).

Judicial Records—grand jury presentments, general sessions data, magistrate and freeholders courts.

Anderson—town minutes.

Anderson District—commissioners of the poor.

Fairfield District—tax-in-kind returns.

Greenville District—letters to clerk of court concerning conduct of war, writs of habeas corpus for conscription violations, discharge papers.

Unpublished federal census schedules.

Library of Congress: personal papers of Isaiah Conley, Edward Frost, John J. McCarter, James L. Petigru.

Special Collections Library, Duke University: Frank T. Bennett, John Cantey, Henry William DeSaussure. George W. Grant, Joseph E. Johnston, Louis Manigault, Lala Pelot, James Reid Pringle, Mary Frances Jane Pursley, William W. Renwick, Arthur Brailsford Wescoat, Samuel P. Wingard, Henry K. Witherspoon, Isabella Anna (Roberts) Woodruff.

Southern Historical Collection, University of North Carolina: Barkley Family, William Birnie, John Cheeseborough, David Thomas Copeland, Louis M. DeSaussure, Elliott-Gonzales Family, Meta Morris Grimball, Andrew G. Magrath, Nathaniel Russell Middleton, William Porcher Miles, James S. Milling, Benjamin F. Perry, Augustine Thomas Smythe, Spartanburg Methodist Sunday School Relief Society (Thomas Dillard Johnston Papers).

UNPUBLISHED STUDIES

Burton, Orville Vernon. "On the Confederate Homefront: The Transformation of Values from Community to Nation in Edgefield, South Carolina." Copy in possession of author.

Chapline, Carmel E. "'A Tragedy in Five Acts': The Life of Louisa S. McCord, 1810-1879." Master's thesis, Citadel and University of Charleston, 1992.

Gettys, James Wylie, Jr. "Mobilization for Secession in Greenville District." Master's thesis, University of South Carolina, 1967.

Harris, Herbert Richard. "The Confederate War Effort in Richland District, South Carolina." Master's thesis, University of South Carolina, 1976.

Honour, Katherine Lyons. "Theodore A. Honour: His Life and Letters in the Civil War Period." Master's thesis, East Tennessee State University, 1979.

McNinch, Lee. "Civil War Hospitals of the South Carolina College Campus." Senior thesis, University of South Carolina, 1977.

Moore, John Hammond. "South Carolina and the Southern Claims Commission, 1871-1880." Copies at the South Caroliniana Library and the South Carolina Department of Archives and History.

ILLUSTRATIONS

Courtesy of the South Caroliniana Library, with additional credits as follows:

Barnwell, Stephen B. *The Story of an American Family*. Marquette, 1969—pp. 18, 161.

Glazier, Willard W. *The Capture, the Prison Pen, and the Escape*. New York, 1868—pp. 155, 191, 270.

Grayson William J. *James Louis Petigru: A Biographical Sketch*. New York, 1866—p. 228.

Mackintosh, Robert Harley, Jr., ed. *"Dear Martha," The Confederate War Letters of a South Carolina Soldier, Alexander Faulkner Fewell*. Columbia, 1976—p. 184.

Martin, Isabella D., and Myra Lockett, eds. *A Diary from Dixie*. London, 1905—p. 76.

Perry, Hext McCall. *Letters of My Father to My Mother*. Philadelphia, 1889—p. 101.

Trowbridge, J. T. *A Picture of the Desolated States*. Hartford, 1868—pp. 53, 63.

INDEX

N

Neves, A. A.: on upcountry deserters, 127-28
Newspapers: in wartime, 199-200, 219-20, 271-72
Niter, 86
Nobles, J. T., 225
Nobles, W. J., 225-26

O

Overseers: exemption of, 115-17

P

Palmer, Philip, 79
Patrick, John B., 21-22, 23, 25, 33, 91-93, 231-32, 237
Perry, Benjamin F.: on speculation, 100-102; on life in Columbia, 248
Petigru, James L., 61, 226
Petigru, Mrs. James L., 84
Pickens, Francis W., 20-21, 50-52, 109
Port Royal: occupation of, 49, 51, 56-57
Prisoners of war. *See Union POWS*
Prostitution, 253-54
Pursley, J. W., 225

Q

Quint, Alonzo H., 74-75

R

Ravenel, Caroline R., 248-49
Ravenel, Henry William, 181, 211-12
Raymond, Henry Hunter, 31
Refugees, 261-64
Rhett, Edmund, 161-62
Rhett, Robert Barnwell, 160-163, 202
Ripley, Rowell Sabine, 54
Rogers, George C., Jr., 65

S

Salt, 78, 80
Sams, Sarah Jane, 100, 159
Sheldon, Lucy, 117
Sherman, William T., 61-64, 74-75
Shortages: in Chester District, 19-20; in Union District, 35; causes of, 70; examples of, 78-90

Y